Thank You For Not Losing This

You're welcome

pas de probleme

CANADIAN

CIVICS

JOHN RUYPERS
London District Catholic School Board

JOHN RYALL
Toronto Catholic District School Board

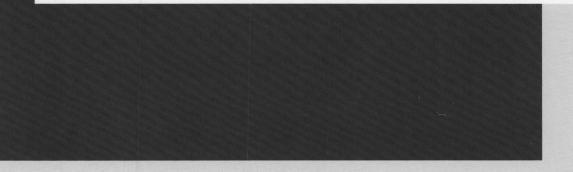

2005
EMOND MONTGOMERY PUBLICATIONS LIMITED
TORONTO, CANADA

Printed in Canada.

We acknowledge the financial support of the Government of Canada through the Book Publishing Industry Development Program (BPIDP) for our publishing activities.

To my inspiration, Jan; to two people separated by ninety years, Jeanne and Carson; to Mark, Paul, Ben, and Josh—John Ruypers

Thank you to my family, Julie, Damien, Rebecca, and Nicholas, for your contributions of faith, patience, peace, space, and time—John Ryall

Library and Archives Canada Cataloguing in Publication

Ruypers, John
    Canadian civics / John Ruypers, John Ryall.

Includes index.
For use in grade 10 in Ontario.
ISBN 1-55239-153-1

    1. Civics, Canadian—Textbooks. 2. Citizenship—Canada—Textbooks. I. Ryall, John, 1950– II. Title.

JL15.R89 2005   320.471   C2005-904577-9

Publisher
Tim Johnston

Senior developmental editor
Dayne Ogilvie

Developmental editors
Jessica Pegis   Shirley Tessier

Contributing writers
Dayne Ogilvie   Jessica Pegis

Editorial assistant
Joyce Tannassee

Production editor, copy editor, & image researcher
Francine Geraci

Image researcher & permissions editor
Lisa Brant

Cover designer, interior designer, & compositor
Tara Wells, WordsWorth Communications

Proofreader
David Handelsman, WordsWorth Communications

Indexer
Paula Pike, WordsWorth Communications

Production coordinator
Jim Lyons, WordsWorth Communications

Cover art
Greg Beettam, Time Bucket Graphics

Senior reviewers
James Delodder
London District Catholic School Board

Patrick Mason
Ottawa–Carleton District School Board

Rebekah A. Tsingos
Toronto District School Board

Reviewers
Ernest Alkenbrack
Kawartha Pine Ridge District School Board

Michelle Randall
Toronto District School Board

Lela Lilko
Peel District School Board

G. Scott Mitchell
Avon Maitland District School Board

Erene Augustyn
Montcrest School, Toronto

Bias reviewer
Rebekah A. Tsingos
Toronto District School Board

Table of Contents

Features of This Text

Civics connects you to your family, your friends, your neighbourhood, your country, and the world. Civics also challenges you to consider a number of questions. What are your beliefs and values? How do your views compare with those of other people? How are conflicts resolved? How are you involved in decision making? What does citizenship actually mean to you?

In exploring these and other questions, you will come to a better understanding of your roles in the world, locally and globally. *Canadian Civics*, through a variety of interesting features, offers you many opportunities to examine your connections and how they matter.

What You Need to Know

- What are some of the causes of civic conflicts?

What You Need to Know presents a clear statement of what you will need to learn and understand from the chapter.

Key Terms

citizenship	politics
government	power

Key Terms are the most important terms and concepts in the chapter. Key and other glossary terms are **boldfaced** the first time they're used and are also defined within the text.

Key Question

Are Canadians over-regulated?

Key Question is an overarching inquiry question that helps you to focus on the content of the chapter and on chapter sections.

CivicStar

BELINDA STRONACH
"Traitor!" "Spoiled rich girl!" "Power hungry!" These and uglier words were used to describe elected rep-

CivicStar profiles people or groups—Aboriginal people, francophones, men, women, young, old, differently abled, famous, infamous, and ordinary—who have challenged the system, created change, and made other contributions to society.

Civics Toolkit develops the critical thinking skills that you are expected to learn throughout your education.

▶ **DID YOU KNOW** ◀

The levy on CD-Rs in 2004 was 21 cents each.

☐ **DISCUSSION POINT**

Should Canadians be given the right to vote at age 16 ?

Did You Know? presents bits of information that highlight and complement the main text.

Discussion Point presents questions to spark class or small-group discussion.

FACE OFF

Face Off focuses on ideas, values, and philosophies that can come into conflict. Its scope ranges from local to global and from past to present to future.

LITERACY COACH

Whenever you read poll results, check the questions asked, the sample size, and the margin of error.

Literacy Coach offers reading and literacy tips on topics such as previewing and predicting, activating prior knowledge, reading headings, reading captions, summarizing, and note taking.

PAUSE, REFLECT, APPLY

1. How does the Aboriginal concept of justice differ from the European idea? In what way does it reflect the traditional way of life of Aboriginal peoples?

Pause, Reflect, Apply lets you check your understanding and progress at the end of each major section. Activities include summarizing, explaining ideas, organizing information into different formats, and expressing opinions with supporting evidence.

REPLAY ▪ ▪ ▪ ▪

Replay summarizes the chapter's major concepts in list form.

SOURCES

Sources offers a direct connection to important primary and original sources such as newspaper reports, legislation, editorials, cartoons, and historical photos.

STUDY HALL

Study Hall provides an extensive end-of-chapter assessment of your progress.

⌐**THE WEB** ▶▶▶──────

Learn more about levies introduced because of Internet downloading at www.emp.ca/civics

The Web points you to Web sites that offer supplementary material.

UNIT 1
Civics Basics

CHAPTER 1
Why Civics? Why Democracy?

August 1994: Rwandan children plead with soldiers to cross into Zaire. Their mothers had escaped just minutes before the border was closed. During Rwanda's civil conflict, up to 1 million people were killed in a country of 8 million.

What You Need to Know

- What are some of the causes of civil conflicts?
- How do different forms of government deal with conflicts?
- What is the difference between being a citizen and being a subject?
- How are public decisions made in a democracy such as Canada?
- What are some fundamental democratic values and beliefs?
- How can asking questions help you become an active citizen?

Key Terms

citizenship	politics
government	power
society	common good
authoritarian	rule of law
democratic	direct democracy
consensus	representative democracy

Key Question

How does a democracy work out differences among people?

Imagine that Canada's prime minister is killed in a plane crash. Police suspect terrorism. Media reports use hateful language and accuse one minority group of the "murder." In Parliament, rebels claiming to represent the majority seize control of the government. Chaos follows. Across the country, members of the minority group are hunted down. Canada is engulfed in violence. Hundreds of thousands of Canadians are killed before it ends. Nobody knows if the peace will last. Nobody knows if law and order can be restored. The countries of the world do nothing.

This scenario is extremely unlikely in Canada today. But similar events in 1994 devastated Rwanda, a small democracy in Africa.

In the past, differences, sometimes bitter ones, have divided Canadians. Our history has also seen violence. What do you know about Canadian citizenship and government systems today that help to prevent civil conflicts from spreading out of control?

Government: Why Is It Necessary?

During this course, you will explore and discuss many interrelated concepts. The first of these is **civics**. Civics can be defined as the study of the **rights** (things you are morally or legally entitled to) and duties of **citizenship**.

What is citizenship? You are a member, or citizen, of your classroom and your school. You are also a member, or citizen, of your family, neighbourhood, and so on. More formally, citizenship is defined as the condition of being vested with the rights, duties, and responsibilities as a member of a state or nation.

The study of civics raises difficult questions about decisions that involve the public. For example:

- Who defines rights, duties, and responsibilities?
- How do you balance rights with duties and responsibilities?
- Who gets to be a citizen?

If you were born in Canada, you are legally a Canadian citizen. If you were born outside Canada and wish to become a Canadian citizen, you must follow **government** procedures. This brings in another key civics concept: government. What, exactly, is it? Why is it necessary?

Government is a system by which a group of people makes the **laws** (principles and regulations) that are enforced to guide the affairs of a community.

The study of civics, then, explores citizenship, government, and public decision making. The question "Why is government necessary?" remains unanswered.

THE SHIPWRECK SCENARIO

You may already be familiar with the "shipwreck scenario." It is a good way to understand what government is and why it is necessary. A group of people are shipwrecked on a remote island. To survive, they must find food and water and create shelter and protection. Because these people form a community that shares these **basic needs and wants**, the group can be seen as a **society**.

How will the basic necessities be shared in this society? Who will perform essential tasks?

LITERACY COACH

Flip through this book and note the headings. The largest headings break the chapters into their main sections. By examining these headings, you get an idea of the chapter's scope and the main topics to be covered. Locate all the largest headings in this chapter and write them down. At any given time, this will help you understand where the chapter is going and what's coming up next.

THE WEB ▶▶▶

Check out Citizenship and Immigration Canada's online 'zine, *Citzine*, at www.emp.ca/civics

FIGURE 1.1 Earth: a society in which we are all citizens? This satellite image was released by the US space agency NASA in 1972 to celebrate Earth Day. Each April 22, people around the world celebrate the Earth and acknowledge our environmental responsibility to the planet and one another.

The group might choose a leader. Possibly the captain is chosen to make major decisions. Perhaps a smaller group is chosen to make less important decisions. Perhaps the strongest individual or group imposes its decisions. Whatever method is used, it creates a simple government: a way of making decisions.

If the group is not soon rescued, disputes will inevitably break out. The government will face the challenge of resolving problems. It will have to devise rules (laws and regulations) of conduct that it can enforce. In this way, conflict will be reduced. This will ensure the safety and survival of the whole group. Government, then, is an activity or method of making and enforcing decisions that are binding upon a society.

HOW ARE DECISIONS MADE?

Suppose a new school sports team is considering different names and logos for its uniform. Different methods could be used to make a decision:

- One person could decide for the whole team. Perhaps this is a school authority, such as the principal or coach. Team members would have little or no input. This is an example of **authoritarian** decision making.
- The team could reach a decision by giving each member a vote. This is **democratic** decision making.
- The team could discuss names and logos and make a decision only when all members agree. This is decision making through **consensus**.

☐ DISCUSSION POINT

Why do you think consensus decision making has sometimes been called the highest form of democracy?

Each decision-making method has advantages and disadvantages.

Authoritarian decision making is speedy, yes. But it takes very little account of how decisions may affect different people. Because individual members have little input, they may not support decisions.

The democratic method gives each individual equal input into decisions through a vote. The choice that gets the most votes, wins. This seems fair, but it has a downside: the other choices lose! If the issue is important or emotional, the "losers" may be resentful.

Consensus decision making respects and listens to each individual to reach a **collective** decision. This is a decision that each member of the group agrees on and supports. Reaching consensus can take a great deal of time and discussion—and may not always be possible. Group members must understand the issues and be willing to share opinions openly. Another disadvantage is that sometimes only a watered-down decision can be reached.

POLITICS: WHAT IS IT?

Back on the island, the captain is chosen to be leader by a majority vote. Some of the people, however, become upset with her. They say they have been assigned too many tasks and not enough food. They try to persuade her to make changes. She says no. They devise plans to replace her and try to win support from others. This is called **politics**: a human activity in which one individual or group opposed to another mobilizes support to obtain **power** to govern. (Power is the ability of a group or individual to get what it wants.)

The term "politics" is formally associated with governments. Informally, politics occurs whenever individuals or groups struggle for advantage. Politics can be done openly and honestly. It can also be done secretly and through manipulation, threats, and bribes.

FIGURE 1.2 This cartoon appeared in April 2005, when testimony at the Gomery inquiry was outraging Canadians. Questioning at the inquiry revealed that millions of dollars in federal money had been misspent by advertising agencies promoting Canadian unity in Quebec. It also exposed political corruption in the federal Liberal Party. How does the cartoon portray the inquiry findings? What does it say about the success of the advertising campaign?

PAUSE, REFLECT, APPLY

1. Which methods of decision making would work best in the following situations?
   - a group of friends is choosing a movie
   - a basketball team must declare its starting players
   - a class must decide on a fundraising program
   - a principal must work out a program to prevent violence on school property
   - parents are trying to work out a reasonable curfew with their children
2. What type of decision making would be best for the shipwrecked passengers
   a) immediately after the shipwreck?
   b) later, if they are not rescued?
3. Why might the captain be chosen as leader?
4. Why do you think Canada's provincial and federal governments use democratic rather than consensus decision making?
5. Describe politics, government, and citizenship in your own words. How are these terms interrelated?
6. What is the difference between formal and informal politics? Give an example for each.
7. In what sense does politics occur within a) a family, b) a school, and c) a workplace?

▶ **KEY QUESTION**
What is the relationship between you and your governments?

Types of Government

Governments are usually classified according to how they make decisions and come to power. This broadly creates two types of government: authoritarian and democratic.

FIGURE 1.3 Comic genius Charlie Chaplin played Adenoid Hynkel, of Tomania, in his 1940 film, *The Great Dictator*. What historical figure is he ridiculing?

AUTHORITARIAN GOVERNMENTS

As you learned earlier, authoritarian decision making allows little or no input from "the people" (those being governed). Often, an authoritarian government is entirely dominated by one person in what is called a **dictatorship**.

If dictators try to carry out the will of the people (what people want), they may enjoy wide public support. However, authoritarian dictatorships do not tolerate opposition. They may rely upon a large military, informers, and secret police to eliminate opposition and to stay in power.

They may also use and control the media, schools, and public events to build support for their policies.

DEMOCRATIC GOVERNMENTS

Democratic governments make decisions based on the will of the people. Usually, citizens choose individuals in elections to represent them in government. In contrast to authoritarian governments, democracies tolerate opposition. This can be expressed by individual citizens, groups, and the media. Opposition can also be expressed by other **political parties** (organizations of people who share similar political beliefs and who work to have their candidates win votes during elections).

Opposition and criticism are part of the democratic system. A true democracy, therefore, cannot rely on secret police and informers to ensure support for its decisions.

SUBJECTS VERSUS CITIZENS

How do authoritarian and democratic governments view and treat the people?

It may be tempting to believe that all authoritarian governments treat people badly, and that all democracies treat people well. But it would not be accurate. In rare instances, authoritarian governments, especially prosperous ones, provide education, health care, subsidized housing, and other social benefits. The **communist** government of the Soviet Union (which owned all land and property) provided these and other benefits to its people (from 1917 to 1989). Soviet leaders criticized many democracies—especially the United States—for ignoring the wants and needs of the poor.

In authoritarian governments, individuals are seen as **subjects**. As such, they are under the absolute control of the government and subject to its commands.

In contrast, individuals in a democracy are citizens. This means they are free to participate in politics and to act to bring about change. Citizens in a democracy can vote and hold office. In most democracies, citizens have other rights as well—to education, for example. You will learn about other rights and freedoms in later chapters. Many democratic governments today also provide social benefits such as pensions, employment insurance, and health care.

Democratic governments	Authoritarian governments
Two or more political parties	Only one political party
Free press	Government-controlled press
Free media	Censored media
Free, fair, frequent elections	Fake elections or no elections
Equal legal rights	Unequal legal rights
Courts free of political control	Courts under political control
Minorities respected	Minorities often under attack

FIGURE 1.4 Comparison of the usual features of democratic and authoritarian governments

> **FACE OFF** **Humans Are Selfish! No, Humans Are Good!**

Philosopher Thomas Hobbes (1588–1679) lived during a long period of civil war in England. He wrote that without government, human life is "nasty, brutish, and short." Because of scarcity (insufficient resources), Hobbes believed, people must be willing to surrender their freedom to a ruler. That ruler must have absolute power, backed by force. Otherwise, human selfishness would always lead to civil conflict and war.

According to Hobbes, as long as the ruler protects the people, revolt or resistance is not justified. Only if the ruler/government fails to do so is revolution justified. The people then have to find another ruler who can protect them.

French philosopher Jean-Jacques Rousseau (1712–1778) disagreed. He believed that humans' state of nature—before societies and governments came into being—was free and friendly. "Man was born free, but everywhere he is in chains," Rousseau wrote in *The Social Contract*, in 1762.

Rousseau believed that the only way people can improve morally and mentally is to come together in societies. The challenge is to preserve humankind's natural state of freedom. For Rousseau, the solution was for people to form a "social contract" with the "general will," or the **common good**, and place themselves under its direction. Majority opinion was not always the way to achieve this. One person, or a few, might realize the common good (the interests of all people in a community or society; for example, peace, justice, economic stability) more clearly than others. Government deserved to be obeyed only as long as it followed the common good in its actions.

What Do You Think?

1. a) How do Hobbes's and Rousseau's views of human nature differ?
   b) Do you agree with Hobbes or with Rousseau? Explain.
2. Which philosophy would more likely lead to democratic government and which to authoritarian government? Briefly explain your answer.
3. Compare Hobbes's and Rousseau's ideas under these headings: a) human nature, b) the purpose of government, c) the right to revolt.

PAUSE, REFLECT, APPLY

1. How is the method of decision making different in democratic and authoritarian governments?
2. How is opposition dealt with in
   a) authoritarian decision making and
   b) democratic decision making?
3. How do opposition, power, and politics connect in a democracy?
4. Is it accurate to say that authoritarian governments never enjoy public support? Explain.
5. Is it accurate to say that democratic governments, by definition, always treat people well? Explain your answer, with reference to Canada.
6. What is the difference between a citizen and a subject?

Power and Politics

Let's go back to the people shipwrecked on the island. As primary decision maker, the captain has been exercising her power. She must be able to do so for government to function. The group members have gone along with her decisions because they have seen that unity is vital to their survival.

As you can see, government, politics, and power work together. The captain's **authority** (the right to give orders or make decisions) will last only as long as she can persuade others that she is the best decision maker. If political opponents can turn the group against her, she will lose power, the ability to govern.

HOW DO GOVERNMENTS USE POWER?

The first and foremost task of any government is to preserve order within society. This means that it must find a way or ways to enforce its decisions. In other words, governments must also use power so that people obey laws.

As mentioned earlier, authoritarian governments rely heavily on the threat or use of military or police force to ensure orderly behaviour. This form of power—which uses threats and force to intimidate citizens—is called **coercion**. Democratic governments rely far more on other kinds of power to enforce decisions.

One kind of power that democracies rely on is **influence**: the ability to persuade people to do something. Governments, for example, may

> ▶ **KEY QUESTION**
> What is required of a society and its citizens for government to function democratically?

> ☐ **DISCUSSION POINT**
> If a democracy relies on coercion to maintain order, can it still be considered a true democracy?

FIGURE 1.5 Health Canada's "Be Drug Wise" campaign aims to increase young people's awareness about drug use.

try to influence people to stop smoking, speed less, and reduce family violence through advertising and public service announcements. Passing harsh laws simply might not work.

Democratic governments also rely on their authority. This form of power is based on the respect people have for the person or institution and the orders or laws they issue. Most Canadians obey laws because they respect their government and fellow citizens, not because they fear the police.

Of course, democracies do maintain police and military forces. Usually, this is done to arrest lawbreakers and to preserve public order if it is threatened.

People Power, Civil Society, and a Healthy Democracy

In a democracy, citizens also have power. To thrive, a democracy must be open and accountable to its citizens. For that to happen, citizens must use their power. Civics is the study of how to use that power effectively and responsibly.

In a democracy, citizens can do more than vote. Citizens are free—to express opinions, both for and against government. If people disagree with government, they can

- contact government representatives
- write letters to newspapers and other media
- put up a Web site
- gather support from other citizens
- form or join organizations that oppose a law or action
- organize and participate in demonstrations.

Civil society is composed of organizations and movements that citizens create outside government. People and organizations involved in civil society monitor governments. They also work for the common good by addressing social problems and needs. The focus can be as local as your schoolyard or as global as an international crisis, such as the conflict in Rwanda. You will learn more about these **non-governmental organizations** in later chapters.

CIVIL CONFLICT AND THE RULE OF LAW

Societies experience conflicts when basic needs and wants are not met. As you learned earlier, basic needs and wants include items needed for survival. Wants can also be more complex and psychological—such as the desire for recognition or achievement.

Governments, groups, and individuals use different methods to resolve conflicts. Authoritarian governments, of course, often use force to impose order. Democracies must rely on the institutions of government and the **rule of law** (the principle that government and all people must obey the law).

Different Ways to Resolve Disputes

Parties and groups involved in a conflict can also **negotiate** by discussing the issues. Sometimes this leads to an agreement. If not, the disputing parties may call in a third party (not involved in the dispute) to referee and **mediate** an agreement between them. This is known as *mediation.* If the conflict still cannot be resolved, a third party may be given the power to **arbitrate**, or impose, a solution. This process is called *arbitration.* These methods are used increasingly in schools. Students are trained as peer mediators to help other students resolve conflicts. Mediators and arbitrators are also often used in labour disputes between employees and their employers (see Chapter 8).

PAUSE, REFLECT, APPLY

1. Define authority, influence, and coercion in terms of how power is exercised.
2. Decide whether authority, influence, or coercion is being used in each of the following situations:
   a) a music star urges young people to read more
   b) a mother forbids her children to watch a television show
   c) a movie is rated "restricted"
   d) a hockey player is ejected from a game after fighting with another player
   e) police "read the riot act" to demonstrators
   f) a penalty is charged on late income tax returns
3. Do you think people are more likely to obey a law if they a) are convinced it is right or b) fear its being enforced? Support your opinion with an example of a law.
4. In what sense does "civil society" act as a check on the power of government?
5. In your own words, describe how negotiation, mediation, and arbitration can be used to resolve conflicts.

▶ **KEY QUESTION**
How and in what forms has democracy spread to countries across the world?

Becoming Democratic

No one pretends that democracy is perfect or all-wise. Indeed, it has been said that democracy is the worst form of government except for all those other forms that have been tried.

—Winston Churchill (1874–1965),
British politician and statesman

The above quotation leaves no doubt that democracy is imperfect. Nevertheless, it has become the most common form of government in the world today. Many factors account for its powerful global appeal.

THE ELEMENTS OF DEMOCRACY

1. Democratic decisions are made for the good of most people, most of the time

Citizens in democracies vote for representatives to make decisions and pass laws that they, the citizens, support. Frequent elections are an essential condition of a democracy. This means that elected representatives who defy the wishes of citizens may soon lose office.

What happens if representatives support decisions that they believe to be in the public interest, but that the voters who elected them do not support? The representatives can hope that voters come around—or forget—before the next election.

2. Democracy emphasizes legal and political equality

Ideally, all citizens in a democracy are equal before the law and in political life. All citizens, rich or poor, are equal in a court of law. All can vote. All can hold office.

Most democracies have a **constitution**. As the central law of the country, the constitution lays out the rules and principles of government power and the rights of the people. It also describes the organization of government, how it is elected, and the duties of elected representatives.

One part of Canada's written constitution is the *Canadian Charter of Rights and Freedoms*. The Charter outlines the basic rights and responsibilities of Canadians. It acts as a constant reminder to citizens, the courts, and the government to safeguard and respect individual rights.

FIGURE 1.6 Prime Minister Jean Chrétien unveils the Canadian Charter during 20th anniversary celebrations in Ottawa in 2002 as RCMP officer Jessie Rai stands guard.

3. Democracy protects minorities

The idea that minorities must be protected from the majority can be difficult for citizens to accept. This is especially true if the minority has very different values from the majority. It is often said that democracy means much more than "50 percent plus one." In other words, majority opinion must not always triumph, especially if it might crush the rights of minorities.

Because democracies favour the majority, they have not always treated minorities well. During World War II, for example, thousands of Japanese Canadians were incarcerated as "threats" to national security (see Chapter 10). Many of the families had lived and prospered in British Columbia for generations.

4. Democracy encourages peace, respect, and tolerance in citizens

How can people create and adapt to change in a democracy? The systems and methods of democratic government require people to persuade others to accept their points of view. This often means that citizens must learn to compromise. Democratic decision making can also be used in families, schools, and workplaces to reduce disagreements and eliminate serious conflicts.

OBSTACLES TO DEMOCRACY

Can any country become a democracy? This question is controversial.

It was once believed that democracy took a long time to become established. In countries in Western Europe, the process took centuries.

It was also thought that democracy did not suit some countries in Eastern Europe, Africa, Asia, and South America. However, many countries in those areas have become democracies in recent years.

Perhaps a better way to look at the question is to consider what obstacles may prevent democracy from taking root.

1. Ethnic differences and conflicts

Differences among **ethnic groups** (groups of people who share common customs and values based on language, religion, or homeland) can create disunity. In Rwanda, for example, ethnic tensions between the majority Hutu and the minority Tutsi groups led to mass murder in 1994. Iraq is also divided—between Kurdish and Arab ethnic groups, and between Sunni and Shiite religious sects. These divisions have led to extreme violence in efforts to create democracy.

Some people say that authoritarian government is better than democracy in uniting countries that are ethnically divided. Often, a military leader will head such a government. Obviously, disunity will not be tolerated when there can be no disagreement with the leader.

2. A large gap between rich and poor

It has been said that democracy requires a large middle class to work fairly. The daily struggle of the poor to survive leaves them little time for democratic involvement. Without a large middle class, the rich few dominate government and use it for their own benefit. This pattern is common in **developing countries** (countries with low average income).

3. A low literacy rate

Any country with a low literacy rate will face problems maintaining democracy. A free press is important to democracy. It allows public issues to be examined and discussed. People who cannot read cannot participate in this activity. They will also have trouble in understanding candidates' literature, voting procedures, and reading and marking ballots.

THE SPREAD OF DEMOCRACY

Regardless of imperfections and obstacles, democracy has spread quickly in the last two decades. That may be because the concept of personal freedom is a cornerstone of democracy and it has wide appeal. By 2005, it was estimated that 102 of the world's 192 countries were democracies, although they differed in the degree of freedom their citizens enjoyed. In total numbers, that is about one-half of humankind.

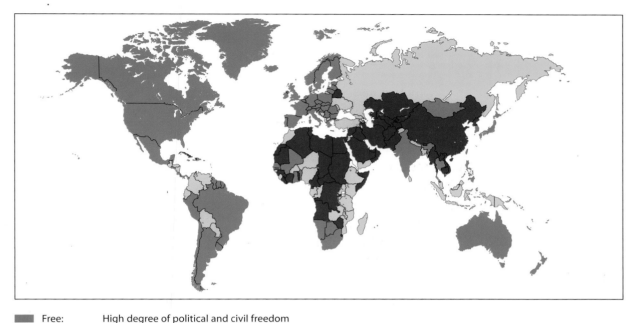

Free: High degree of political and civil freedom

Partly Free: Some restrictions on political rights and civil liberties; countries often prone to corruption, weak rule of law, ethnic strife, civil war

Not Free: Political process tightly controlled; basic freedoms denied

Free
Andorra
Argentina
Australia
Austria
Bahamas
Barbados
Belgium
Belize
Benin
Botswana
Brazil
Bulgaria
Canada
Cape Verde
Chile
Costa Rica
Croatia
Cyprus (Greek)
Czech Republic
Denmark
Dominica
Dominican Republic
El Salvador
Estonia

Finland
France
Germany
Ghana
Greece
Grenada
Guyana
Hungary
Iceland
India
Ireland
Israel
Italy
Jamaica
Japan
Kiribati
Korea, South
Latvia
Lesotho
Liechtenstein
Lithuania
Luxembourg
Mali
Malta
Marshall Islands
Mauritius

Mexico
Micronesia
Monaco
Mongolia
Namibia
Nauru
Netherlands
New Zealand
Norway
Palau
Panama
Peru
Philippines
Poland
Portugal
Romania
Samoa
San Marino
Sao Tome and Principe
Senegal
Serbia and Montenegro
Slovakia
Slovenia
South Africa
Spain

St. Kitts and Nevis
St. Lucia
St. Vincent and Grenadines
Suriname
Sweden
Switzerland
Taiwan
Thailand
Tuvalu
United Kingdom
United States
Uruguay
Vanuatu

Partly Free
Albania
Antigua and Barbuda
Armenia
Bahrain
Bangladesh
Bolivia
Bosnia-Herzegovina
Burkina Faso
Burundi

Colombia
Comoros
Congo (Brazzaville)
Djibouti
East Timor
Ecuador
Ethiopia
Fiji
Gabon
Gambia, The
Georgia
Guatemala
Guinea-Bissau
Honduras
Indonesia
Jordan
Kenya
Kuwait
Macedonia
Madagascar
Malawi
Malaysia
Moldova
Morocco
Mozambique

Nepal
Nicaragua
Niger
Nigeria
Papua New Guinea
Paraguay
Russia
Seychelles
Sierra Leone
Singapore
Solomon Islands
Sri Lanka
Tanzania
Tonga
Trinidad and Tobago
Turkey
Uganda
Ukraine
Venezuela
Yemen
Zambia

Not Free
Afghanistan
Algeria

Angola
Azerbaijan
Belarus
Bhutan
Brunei
Burma
Cambodia
Cameroon
Central African Republic
Chad
China
Congo (Kinshasa)
Côte d'Ivoire
Cuba
Egypt
Equatorial Guinea
Eritrea
Guinea
Haiti
Iran
Iraq
Kazakhstan
Korea, North
Kyrgyzstan
Laos

Lebanon
Liberia
Libya
Maldives
Mauritania
Oman
Pakistan
Qatar
Rwanda
Saudi Arabia
Somalia
Sudan
Swaziland
Syria
Tajikistan
Togo
Tunisia
Turkmenistan
United Arab Emirates
Uzbekistan
Vietnam
Zimbabwe

FIGURE 1.7 Democratic freedoms: civil and political liberties, 2004. In that year, 2.78 billion people (44 percent of the world's population) lived in Free societies; 1.32 billion (21 percent) lived in Partly Free societies; and 2.21 billion (35 percent) lived in Not Free societies. *Source: Freedom House, www.freedomhouse.org.*

PAUSE, REFLECT, APPLY

1. Why are frequent elections and legal equality essential to democracy?
2. Explain the purpose of a constitution in a democracy.
3. Which element of democracy do you think is the most important? Explain why.
4. Which obstacle to democracy do you think is the most serious? Explain why.
5. What does "50 percent plus one" refer to?
6. Explain this statement: "A democracy is defined by the way it treats its minorities."

▶ **KEY QUESTION**

How has democracy absorbed influences and adapted to change?

Democracy: Yesterday and Today

The origins of democracy go back to the mid-5th century BCE and the **polises** of ancient Greece. "Polis" means "city" or "city-state" in Greek. By today's standards, polises were actually small towns. Each polis, which included the surrounding countryside, governed itself. Athens was the most famous. Only free-born males over a certain age were citizens— women and slaves were excluded from political participation.

Democracy emerged slowly in Athens. At first, when it was considered a very radical idea, democracy was supported by the philosopher Pericles (c. 495–429 BCE), among others. Because polises were small, all citizens knew one another. This was considered essential for democracy to work. All citizens could speak out and vote on issues, which were discussed in central assemblies in each polis. Because citizens directly made the laws themselves, this system was called **direct democracy**.

As states grew in size, and it became impossible for all citizens to know one another, direct democracy no longer worked. Citizens began to vote for representatives to hold political office and voice their interests in law-making assemblies. The term **representative democracy** applies to this kind of indirect democracy.

Today, most democracies are representative. Voters have no control over elected representatives after the election. Some democracies have experimented with the **recall election**. This gives electors the chance to vote to recall a representative before his or her term is up.

As you can see in Figure 1.8, democracy emerged in other places and changed over time.

FIGURE 1.8 Important events in the development of democracy

▪ c. 500 BCE: Greek polises

origins of democratic ideas; direct democracy used to decide public policy

▪ 1st–5th centuries CE: Roman Empire

citizenship concept develops; non-Romans in Empire can become citizens

▪ c. 1150–1450: Iroquois Confederacy

(date in dispute) five First Nations (North American Aboriginal groups) unite politically; a democratic form of government based on consensus decision making; eventually became the Six Nations Confederacy and influenced drafting of the US constitution

▪ 1215: England, Magna Carta

under threat of civil war, King John signs the "Great Charter"; the once absolute (unlimited) power of the monarch is now limited by law

▪ 1775–1783: American Revolution

Declaration of Independence (1776) states that "all men are created equal"; government of the people, by the people, for the people

▪ 1789–1794: French Revolution

the people overthrow absolute monarch, establish a **republic** (a country with an elected president as head of state) based on equality; demands for civil rights spread across Europe

▪ 19th–early 20th centuries

political rights (the right to vote, run for office, participate in elections) steadily extended to more citizens in Britain, United States, Canada, and western European democracies

▪ 1918–1989

spread of democracy to non-European states; setbacks caused by rise of authoritarian governments in 1930s, World War II (1939–1945), the Cold War (1945–1989)

▪ 1989–present

democratic movements topple communist governments in the Soviet Union and countries under its influence in Eastern Europe (such as Poland); democracy spreads further into Asia and Africa

FIGURE 1.9 A Tuscarora (one of the Six Nations Confederacy) Indian burns an injunction (a court document) during a demonstration in Niagara Falls, New York, in 1971. The injunction forbade Confederacy members from demonstrating against construction of a highway through their reservation. The demonstrations continued and construction was stopped.

DEMOCRACY IN CANADA

Democracy in Canada now is very different from what it was at Confederation, when Canada became a country. In 1867, only property-owning men who were British subjects could vote and hold public office. Women, the Aboriginal peoples of Canada, and most minorities could do neither. All these groups would struggle for decades to gain basic democratic rights. Japanese and Chinese Canadians, for example, did not receive voting rights until 1948. It would be 1960 before Aboriginal peoples in Canada could vote in federal elections without restrictions. (You will learn more about the history of the vote and elections in Canada in Chapter 5.)

CivicStar

BELINDA STRONACH

"Traitor!" "Spoiled rich girl!" "Power hungry!"

These and uglier words were used to describe elected representative Belinda Stronach (1966–) after she left the Conservative Party to join the Liberal Party in Ottawa in May 2005. As a result of her move, the Liberals held on to power, and Stronach gained a powerful government position. Stronach said her reasons for "crossing the floor" were pure: for Canadian unity.

Women politicians in Canada have often been subjected to extreme scrutiny, even sexist treatment, in the media. But few have ever grabbed headlines as Stronach has. Why?

Was it because Stronach is rich, powerful, and glamorous? In 2001, she became head of Magna International, the auto-parts business founded by her father, Frank Stronach. As one of the most powerful executives in the world, Belinda Stronach was also no stranger to politics. Her father ran for the Liberal Party (and lost) in the 1988 federal election.

In 2004, Belinda Stronach launched her own political career. She ran not only for election, but also for leadership of the federal Conservative Party—a party she helped form in 2003. Stronach was elected to Parliament, but she lost her leadership bid to winner Stephen Harper.

Politics is competitive. At times, politicians do the unexpected and change parties. Yet Stronach's every move was pulled apart in the media spotlight—even her personal relationship with another member of the Conservative Party.

Stronach explained her action in a newspaper article, saying she acted on principle: "My critics say that I am ambitious. And I am—to serve the country. I entered public life in the spirit of public service to try to make a contribution to the country's future."

Your Play

1. Using Belinda Stronach as an example, what do you think are the benefits and drawbacks of being a woman in politics?
2. Find out about other women in Canadian politics who have made headlines: Agnes Macphail, Cairine Wilson, Ellen Fairclough, and Kim Campbell.

PAUSE, REFLECT, APPLY

1. What conditions allowed the Greeks to have direct democracy?
2. Why would electors want to use a recall?
3. What forms of technology could be used today to allow all citizens to vote on issues rather than just elect representatives? What form of democracy would this be?
4. Perhaps the last group in Canada yet to be given the political rights to vote and to hold public office is you, the 15- to 16-year-old age group. Make a case for or against the idea.
5. Is direct democracy desirable today in your opinion?

REPLAY ▪ ▪ ▪ ▪ ▪ ▪ ▪ ▪ ▪

This chapter has informed you of these civics concepts:

1. Government is a system of making and enforcing decisions to guide the affairs of a community.
2. Authoritarian governments use coercion to enforce decisions.
3. Democracies rely on authority and influence to persuade citizens to accept decisions.
4. Citizens in a democracy can use their power to achieve change.
5. Democracies strive to guarantee equality, protect minorities, and encourage tolerance and compromise.
6. Democracy has evolved from a direct form to a representative form.
7. Ethnic conflict, economic inequalities, and low literacy levels are obstacles to democracy.

CIVICS ▶ How to Form Inquiry Questions
TOOLKIT

As a citizen in a democracy, you will have the right to vote, run for office, contact your representatives, protest, and assemble to bring about change. The aim of this course is both to inform you about government systems and to equip you to become an active citizen. An active citizen works to bring about positive change in the community. To do that, you need to be able to identify and explore issues that concern you. You need to be able to think critically.

To inquire is to question. What are you curious about? What do you ask questions about? From early childhood, this is how we learn naturally. Listen to a two-year-old's endless stream of questions. The child asks one question and gets an answer, which leads to another question, and another. This is the inquiry method at work, and it is fuelled by questions.

An inquiry question must meet several criteria (standards or guidelines). In order to be effective, it should

- matter to you
- be specific and focused
- be answerable
- be reasonable
- lead to other questions.

Inquiring can have monumental results. In the 16th century, the Polish monk Nicolaus Copernicus questioned the relationship among the Earth, the other planets in our solar system, and the sun. Eventually, his investigations proved that the Earth and planets revolve around the sun. Powerful, educated people at the time believed that the universe revolved around the Earth. Copernicus's inquiry got him into trouble. It also opened up the science of cosmology (the study of the universe).

Some successful businesses also use an inquiry method. Using company resources, employee groups formulate inquiry questions, for example, "Are we serving customers as efficiently as possible?" The employees then gather information:

1. a question is asked
2. information is gathered
3. new ideas lead to new questions
4. the original question is refined
5. the process is repeated.

Employees in these kinds of businesses go beyond following orders. They define and solve problems, work as a group, and influence the company. They become agents of change.

You can use inquiry questions to achieve similar results. Effective citizenship requires you to learn about issues that you care about. The inquiry method is ideal for that. It has two added benefits—it helps you learn what matters to you, and it leads to action.

Skill Practice

1. a) Develop inquiry questions on the following topics: i) your school's rules, ii) school video surveillance, iii) the grade 10 literacy test, iv) your student council.
   b) Compare your questions with those of other students. Does short discussion lead you to change your questions?
   c) Decide what information sources to use to answer one of your questions.
2. Use the inquiry method to determine three issues that matter to you. Record your questions and responses and return to them during your study of civics.

STUDY HALL

Informed Citizenship

1. Consider your student council.
   a) In what sense is it a government?
   b) What characteristics of a democratic government does it have?
   c) What type of power does it use the most? Give an example of a successful use of that power.
   d) What type of power does it *not* use, and why?
   e) Can you think of any restraints or limits to its decision-making power?

2. Rank order authoritarian, consensus, and democratic methods as to a) speed of decision making and b) acceptance by those affected.

3. Why do most democracies and their citizens regard a constitution as necessary to protect individual freedom? (Consider what could happen if a nation does not have one.)

4. Draw up a chart comparing authoritarian, consensus, and democratic decision making. The chart should have three columns: advantages, disadvantages, and an example of a good use of the method. Add any advantages or disadvantages that you can think of.

Purposeful Citizenship

5. a) How can politics occur within i) a family? ii) a group of friends? iii) a sports team? Do you think such informal politics is bad, good, or neither good nor bad?
   b) Politicians are sometimes viewed unfavourably. From the way that politics is defined, do you think this view is justified?

6. a) Do you think that i) families, ii) classrooms, iii) workplaces can be run on a democratic basis? Should they be? Explain.
   b) "Authoritarian parents create authoritarian children; democratic parents create democratic citizens." Do you agree? Explain.

7. Increasingly, parents are urged not to use corporal punishment (inflict physical pain) on their children.
   a) What kinds of power are parents then forced to rely on?
   b) Do you agree with this idea?
   c) Does it "fit" with democracy?

8. When is a democratic government justified in using authoritarian decision making? Defend your answer and use examples.

9. Explain why each of the following is essential to a democracy:
   a) equality of all before the law
   b) free media
   c) minimal use of force to maintain order
   d) free and frequent elections
   e) multiple political parties
   f) minority rights
   g) judicial independence from government
   h) common good

Active Citizenship

10. Study your school's student conduct policy. Find out
    a) who drew it up
    b) how it was drawn up and decided
    c) whether it allows for frequent change and review
    d) whether it includes rights as well as responsibilities.

11. Contrast the idea of an individual as a subject with that of an individual as a citizen. What do citizens today expect of a democratic government, such as Canada's, that was not expected in the past? Are citizens asking too much or too little of their governments today? Support your answer with examples.

CHAPTER 2

What Is Government?

Dufferin Caledon
Pg 27   3-5
Pg 31   2-4
Pg 37   3-5
Pg 39   1-3

Who's in charge here?

What You Need to Know

- Why does Canada have levels of government?
- What are the responsibilities of each level?
- Why does Canada have branches of government?
- What are the responsibilities of each branch?
- Who carries out the responsibilities of each branch?
- What is Aboriginal self-government, and what forms does it take?
- How can you locate information?

Key Terms

self-government	members of Parliament
executive	House of Commons
legislative	Question Period
judicial	Senate
governor general	mayor
cabinet	councillors

Key Question

How does the organization of government facilitate democracy?

At Maple Leaf High School, the student council and the principal are discussing the spring dance. The student council wants no dress code to be enforced. Students should be allowed to come to the dance in formal, semi-formal, and informal attire. The principal says that the event has always been a formal one and that a strict dress code will be enforced at the door.

The principal knows that she has the power to override the student council on this issue. However, she does not want to create bad feelings at the end of the school year. What advice would you give her? Should the principal have this much power? What should be the ideal division of powers between the student council and the principal?

Why Does Canada Have Different Levels of Government?

Canada has three levels of government:

- federal government (for all of Canada)
- provincial or territorial government (for a province or territory)
- municipal or local government (for local communities).

At the time of Confederation (1867), Canada's constitution dealt with two levels of government—the federal and the provincial. Territorial governments were not mentioned in the constitution because that land was then owned by the Hudson's Bay Company. The territories were created through later acts of Parliament. Canada's territories are the Northwest Territories (1870), Yukon (1898), and Nunavut (1999).

Local or municipal governments are created by provinces or territories to govern local communities, including cities, towns, villages, and Aboriginal bands, or settlements. Local governments can also be changed by provincial or territorial governments.

ABORIGINAL SELF-GOVERNMENT

In Canada, Aboriginal **self-government** occurs at different levels. This refers to the right of **First Nations**, **Inuit**, and **Métis** peoples to govern their own communities. Aboriginal self-government can occur at the local or territorial level. It depends on the concentration of Aboriginal people living in the area. In the territory of Nunavut, 85 percent of the citizens are Inuit. Thus, the whole territory is self-governed. Eight Métis settlements in Alberta achieved self-government in 1989. This is an example of Aboriginal local government.

FIGURE 2.1 Levels of government in Canada

Responsibilities of Different Levels of Government

Each level of government in Canada has different responsibilities and provides different services. The responsibilities of the federal and provincial governments are the only responsibilities outlined in the original part of Canada's constitution found in the *Constitution Act, 1867* (formerly called the *British North America Act*).

RESPONSIBILITIES OF THE FEDERAL GOVERNMENT

The federal government makes decisions related to matters of nation-wide importance, such as

- foreign trade and relations
- currency (money)
- defence
- postal service
- immigration
- communications
- unemployment
- criminal law (*Criminal Code*)
- Aboriginal peoples

FEDERAL REVENUE

To pay for all the services it provides, the federal government collects income taxes, the goods and services tax (GST), and excise taxes (taxes on certain domestic and foreign goods which are hidden from the consumer).

WHERE DO PROVINCIAL AND FEDERAL RESPONSIBILITIES OVERLAP?

Federal and provincial governments share responsibilities in areas such as agriculture and environmental protection. For example, the definition of marriage, and the privileges and rights of marriage, are a federal responsibility. Individual provinces issue marriage licences, authorize individuals to perform marriages, and register marriages. The grounds for divorce are set by federal law, but the rules governing the division of property after divorce are set by provincial law.

RESPONSIBILITIES OF PROVINCIAL AND TERRITORIAL GOVERNMENTS

The responsibilities of the provinces and territories are not identical, but they all make decisions relating to

- property and civil rights
- marriage licences
- health and welfare
- education

- alcohol consumption
- natural resources and environment
- hospitals
- driver education and licensing
- motor vehicle operation and licensing
- provincial or territorial highways

PROVINCIAL AND TERRITORIAL REVENUE

To pay for the services they provide, provincial and territorial governments can collect income tax, sales tax, and "sin taxes" on alcohol and tobacco products.

Although territorial governments can raise money in all the ways that provinces do, most of their money comes from the federal government. This is because territories have much smaller populations than most provinces.

▶ DID YOU KNOW ◀
Alberta is the only province without a sales tax.

67%	69%	85%
Yukon	Northwest Territories	Nunavut

FIGURE 2.2 Territorial governments, percentage of revenue in the form of grants from the federal government, 2003–2004. *Source: Department of Finance Canada, www.fin.gc.ca/FEDPROV/tffe.html.*

RESPONSIBILITIES OF LOCAL GOVERNMENTS

Local governments are responsible for services that affect the daily lives of people living in communities, such as

- police and fire departments
- streets and roads
- water and sewage
- transit
- garbage and recycling
- libraries
- recreation
- local programs

Aboriginal local governments often have more wide-ranging responsibilities than typical local governments. For example, they may be responsible for housing, oil and gas development, and education, in addition to providing the services listed above.

LOCAL REVENUE

Local governments receive grants from the provincial government and also raise revenue through property taxes, which are paid by home-owners and businesses. In the average Ontario city, the property tax due on a home valued at $160,000 is about $2,000 a year. Money is also raised through fees charged for parking and for various licences.

Aboriginal councils receive funding from the federal government. The amount of funding is influenced by geographic location, distance from major population centres, and local climate.

FACE OFF Should Governments Sponsor Gambling?

"You can't win if you don't play." "Winning means a life of luxury and happiness." These are just some of the slogans that governments in Canada use to get people to gamble.

In 1969, the provinces and territories legalized gambling to raise revenues. Soon they started running casinos, lotteries, video lottery terminals (VLTs), and slot machines. By 2002, government-sponsored gambling in Canada was bringing in $11 billion a year.

Some people say that adults should be able to make their own decisions about entertainment. For many Canadians, buying lottery tickets or playing the "slots" is harmless fun. Statistics indicate that the average household spends about $300 a year on gaming. Government-supervised gambling creates many jobs for Canadians and revenue for public organizations.

By creating jobs, stimulating tourism and sup-porting hospitals, charity groups and cultural and recreational services, OLGC is fulfilling its mandate to maximize economic benefits for the people of Ontario.

— The Ontario Lottery and Gaming Corporation (OLGC)

Other people claim that government should not encourage an activity that can be addictive. Gambling addiction can destroy marriages and families, and lead to theft and suicide. Although casinos and slots are adult-only entertainment, teens are introduced to gambling when their fam-ilies gamble. Online gambling is growing and becoming another troubling issue. Governments should protect citizens, not exploit or harm them.

Ontario appears to derive a substantial portion of its gaming revenue from problem gamblers. Government-sponsored gambling is therefore contrary to the interest of the general popu-lace, and therefore contrary to the purpose of government.

— Robert Williams, University of Lethbridge, Alberta, November 2004

Another opinion tries to reconcile both views. It says that people will gamble, whether it is legal or illegal. Government should continue to supervise the activity but limit its advertising and ill effects.

What Do You Think?

1. For each viewpoint of government-sponsored gambling, identify the greatest good achieved and the greatest harm con-ceded (accepted as a given).
2. After answering question 1, which view of government-sponsored gambling do you agree with? Why?

PAUSE, REFLECT, APPLY

1. Find out about two decisions made by your school's student council or school council. In your opinion, were these good decisions? Why?
2. Briefly describe the three levels of government as outlined in this section.
3. List what you consider to be the three most important responsibilities of your provincial government.
4. List what you consider to be the three most important responsibilities of the federal government.
5. Create a chart to compare how governments at different levels raise money to provide services.

Branches of Government in Canada

In Canada, government powers are separated into branches. This idea comes from the French political thinker Montesquieu (1689–1755). Montesquieu thought that by separating government powers into branches, each would be checked and balanced by the others. Most democratic governments have this three-branch structure, including Canada, the United States, and Britain.

The branches of Canadian government are the **executive** (to carry out the business of government), the **legislative** (to make laws), and the **judicial** (to interpret and enforce law).

> **KEY QUESTION**
> Why does Canada have different branches of government?

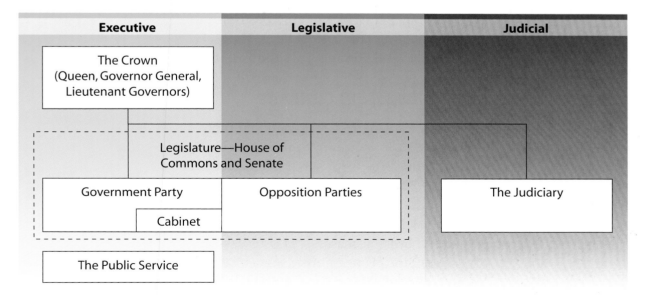

FIGURE 2.3 Branches of the Canadian government

LITERACY COACH

This chapter includes a number of tables and diagrams. These elements often summarize key information, so don't ignore them when you are studying. Diagrams can show you the "big picture," as well as relationships of parts to the whole. For example, in Figure 2.3 on the previous page, it's easy to see how all the branches of government work together.

How each branch functions at the federal and provincial/territorial level is shown in Figure 2.4. Usually, the term "branch of government" is not applied at the local level; however, local governments do have different branches to make and enforce laws.

Branch	Players	Responsibilities
Executive	Queen, represented by the governor general or lieutenant governor Prime minister or premier Cabinet Civil servants	Makes decisions and implements them Carries out policies and runs government departments
Legislative	Parliament (elected representatives, appointed Senate, governor general)	Introduces, debates, and passes laws
Judicial	Judges and courts	Interprets and enforces laws

FIGURE 2.4 Branches of government, the players, and their responsibilities

KEY QUESTION
How does the executive branch make decisions for Canada?

The Executive Branch

The executive branch of government is its leadership. The word "execute" means "to carry out," as in "She executed a u-turn." The executive in a government "carries out" the business of the government, including implementing laws and policies. In a school, the principal and vice-principal would be known as the executive.

THE GOVERNOR GENERAL

Because Canada is a constitutional monarchy, the queen is officially head of state. However, the constitution limits the monarch's power. Today, the British monarch is represented by the **governor general**. Until 1952, the governor general was British and came to Canada to represent the monarch. For example, Lord Stanley was governor general from 1888 to 1893. He donated the famous cup for hockey supremacy that still bears his name.

Today, the prime minister selects the candidate for governor general. Since Vincent Massey was appointed, in 1952, all Canada's governors general have been Canadian citizens.

At the federal level, the governor general

- signs all bills into law, a process known as giving **royal assent**
- officially welcomes representatives of foreign governments to Canada
- reads the Speech from the Throne (government plans in a new session of Parliament)
- promotes pride in and awareness of Canada.

The governor general is a **figurehead**, a ruler in name only. Yet he or she appoints the prime minister and dissolves Parliament. In most cases, the prime minister appointed is the leader of the party with the most seats in the House of Commons (see page 30).

THE LIEUTENANT GOVERNOR

In each of Canada's 10 provinces, it is the **lieutenant governor** who represents the monarch. The lieutenant governor is appointed by the prime minister, usually for a term of five years. Provincial duties include signing bills into law, reading the Speech from the Throne, and promoting the province.

FIGURE 2.5 Ontario's recent lieutenant governors reflect Canada's diversity. (Left to right:) Hamilton politician Lincoln Alexander was the first black Canadian to become lieutenant governor in 1985. Hilary Weston became Ontario's second female lieutenant governor in 1997. James Bartleman became the first Aboriginal lieutenant governor in 2002.

THE PRIME MINISTER AND CABINET

The prime minister and the **cabinet** hold the real power of the federal executive branch.

The prime minister is the leader of the political party with the most elected representatives, or **members of Parliament** (MPs), in the **House of Commons** (see Figure 2.6). A political party is an organization of people with similar ideas (discussed in Chapters 4 and 5).

Following an election, the prime minister chooses a group of advisers known as the cabinet. In most cases, the prime minister chooses cabinet ministers from MPs from his or her party. The cabinet is part of the executive team. As with most teams, the prime minister selects the best "players" for positions in the cabinet. In choosing these MPs, the prime minister must also reflect Canada's diversity and strive for gender equality.

Most federal cabinets include 20 to 30 members. Aside from advising the prime minister, cabinet members look after departments or **portfolios**

CivicStar

KEN DRYDEN

Ken Dryden has served Canada in many ways. In 1972, Dryden the goaltender helped Canada win the hockey Summit Series against the Soviet Union. In 2004, Dryden became the member of Parliament for the riding of York Centre (in Toronto). As minister of social development, Dryden heads a portfolio that provides social support for seniors and children.

In the intervening 32 years, Dryden won a netful of hockey awards, including the Stanley Cup six times and the best goaltender award five times. He also earned a law degree, wrote books, and became president of the Toronto Maple Leafs.

Dryden comes from a family with civic dedication. His parents founded a charitable organization called Sleeping Children Around the World. It has distributed nearly three-quarters of a million bed kits to children in more than 30 developing countries.

Your Play

1. How might Dryden's hockey background have prepared him to be part of a cabinet?
2. How can teams accomplish more than individuals?
3. Find out more about Sleeping Children Around the World and how you can help at www.emp.ca/civics.

such as Finance, Justice, Health, and Defence. For example, in consultation with the prime minister,

- the minister of finance might raise taxes
- the minister of justice might change the criminal law related to marijuana
- the minister of health might ban cigarette advertising
- the minister of defence might change the size of Canada's armed forces.

As you can see, cabinet ministers have political power. This is perhaps why they occupy front seats in Parliament. Those MPs in the governing party who are not in the cabinet sit in seats behind the cabinet and are known as **backbenchers**.

The Canadian cabinet follows the British principle of **cabinet solidarity** (acting together). This means that all members of the cabinet must publicly support all cabinet decisions or resign from cabinet.

THE PREMIER AND CABINET

The premier leads the executive branch of the provincial government. Like the prime minister, he or she leads the political party elected by the people to govern the province.

Federal principles of majority support, cabinet selection, and cabinet solidarity apply provincially as well. However, there are no provincial or territorial portfolios for defence, foreign affairs, Indian affairs, or veterans' affairs. These are areas of federal responsibility.

Canada's three territories also have premiers. In Yukon, the premier leads the political party in power. In the Northwest Territories and Nunavut, however, a **non-partisan** (not affiliated with any political party) council selects premiers.

PAUSE, REFLECT, APPLY

1. What is meant by the executive branch of government?
2. What are the major responsibilities of the federal governor general and the provincial lieutenant governor?

3. Explain the importance of the cabinet at both the federal and provincial levels.
4. Identify each of the following people and something significant that each of them accomplished: Lincoln Alexander, Hilary Weston, James Bartleman, and Ken Dryden.

▶ KEY QUESTION

How does the legislative branch represent Canadians?

The Legislative Branch

In democracies, the legislative, or lawmaking, branch of government is elected by the voting public. In Canada, if the executive branch loses the support of the elected legislature, it must resign.

THE HOUSE OF COMMONS

The House of Commons is Canada's federal legislative body. It is composed of the members of Parliament elected in 308 separate **ridings** (in 2005) across Canada. Ridings are defined geographical areas.

Think of each riding as a homeroom. In a student council election, each homeroom votes for one of its members to represent the homeroom in the student "parliament." Similarly, each MP represents the interests of the **constituents** (voters and non-voters) in his or her riding. Ridings are also known as **constituencies**, and most comprise about 100,000 voters. (In Ontario, the same ridings are used in both provincial and federal elections.)

MPs assemble in Ottawa in the House of Commons to do the country's business. Most belong to political parties. If an elected representative is not affiliated with a political party, he or she is known as an **independent**. The political party with the largest number of MPs becomes the government of Canada. To pass a bill, the government needs the support of "one-half plus one" of the total MPs ($1/2 \times 308 + 1 = 155$).

After the 2004 federal election, the Liberal Party formed a **minority government**: it had more MPs than other parties, yet fewer than 155. Like all minority governments, the Liberals needed support from another party or parties to pass bills.

Ideas for new bills are usually introduced by cabinet ministers. To become law, a bill must be approved by a majority of MPs. If the government loses an important vote in the Commons—on a budget, for example—it loses the **confidence** of the House and will probably have to resign (see Chapter 4).

After a government is defeated, the governor general may call a new election or invite the **Official Opposition** (the party with the next largest number of seats) to form a government. In any case, a federal election must be held at least every five years.

1 Speaker	**13** Interpreters
2 Pages	**14** Press Gallery
3 Government Members*	**15** Public Gallery
4 Opposition Members*	**16** Official Gallery
5 Prime Minister	**17** Leader of the Opposition's Gallery
6 Leader of the Official Opposition	**18** Members' Gallery
7 Leader of the Second Largest Party in Opposition	**19** Members' Gallery
8 Clerk and Table Officers	**20** Members' Gallery
9 Mace	**21** Speaker's Gallery
10 Hansard Reporters	**22** Senate Gallery
11 Sergeant-at-Arms	**23** TV Cameras
12 The Bar	

* Depending on the number of MPs elected from each political party, government members may be seated on the opposite side of the Chamber with opposition members (or vice versa).

FIGURE 2.6 Canada's House of Commons. *Source:* Guide to the Canadian House of Commons *(3rd ed.),* Ottawa: *Government of Canada, 2005, p. 5.*

FIGURE 2.7 Liberal Finance Minister Ralph Goodale shouts at the opposition during Question Period in November 2004. Anything MPs say in the House is protected from legal action. However, if MPs use "unparliamentary language" (calling another MP a liar, or swearing), the Speaker can insist that they apologize or eject them from the House.

The Speaker of the House of Commons is an MP who acts like a referee to enforce the rules of parliamentary debate

The **Speaker of the House** is elected, by secret ballot, by all MPs. He or she is expected to be **non-partisan**, that is, not in favour of any party.

In the House of Commons, the Speaker sits at the end of a central aisle on a raised platform. Members of the party in power sit in rows to the right of the Speaker. In the front row sit the prime minister and cabinet. Across the aisle, and to the Speaker's left, are seated the opposition parties (see Figure 2.6). Members of the Official Opposition sit in the front seats directly opposite the government.

Question Period takes place each day the House is in session

For 45 minutes, opposition members can question the prime minister and cabinet during **Question Period**, or Oral Questions. The opposition usually tries to embarrass the government with queries on almost any issue. Often, cabinet ministers do not answer questions directly. They may also criticize the opposition. The period is often full of political posturing and theatrics.

Everything everyone says in the Commons is recorded and published in an official document called Hansard. MPs cannot speak directly to one another. They must address their remarks through the Speaker, referring to one another as "the Honourable member from (name of riding)."

─THE WEB ▶▶▶
Learn more about
Hansard at
www.emp.ca/civics

THE SENATE

The **Senate** is the Upper House of the legislative branch of the federal government. "Upper" suggests that it is more important than the House of Commons, which is the Lower House. In 1867, many people held this to be true. Senators were expected to be upper-class gentlemen. A major purpose of the Senate was to **veto** (block) irresponsible bills passed by the House of Commons. At that time, the idea that the democratically elected representatives of the people could run the government without help from the upper classes was suspect.

The Senate has changed. In 1930, after an important legal decision known as the "Persons Case," the first woman senator, Cairine Wilson, was appointed. Since 1965, senators have been required to retire at age 75. All bills must still pass through the Senate to become laws. Today, however, the appointed Senate rarely vetoes legislation passed by the elected House of Commons.

Being appointed to the Senate is often an example of **political patronage** (the granting of political favours). A prime minister may appoint an individual in reward for service to the party. Many senators take the job seriously and are hard-working public servants. Aside from suggesting improvements to bills, they may serve on parliamentary committees and commissions that investigate important issues such as child poverty, and make recommendations for further action or further study.

Some senators, however, have abused their privileged position. Georges-Casimir Dessaulles was appointed to the Senate at age 80 in 1907 and served for 23 years. He spoke twice during that time: once to deny that his appointment was part of a corrupt bargain, and the other time to thank his fellow senators for celebrating his 100th birthday.

▶ **DID YOU KNOW** ◀
Frank Mahovlich, member of Team Canada in the 1972 Summit Series and six-time winner of the Stanley Cup, was appointed to the Senate as a Liberal member by Prime Minister Jean Chrétien in 1998.

☐ **DISCUSSION POINT**
Many Canadians support demands for a reformed "triple E" Senate. This would require that senators be *elected*, which could help make the Senate more *effective* and *equal*. Do you agree that this would be more democratic?

THE LEGISLATIVE ASSEMBLY

The legislative branches of Canada's 10 provinces are almost mirror images of the House of Commons.

In many provinces, elected representatives are known as members of the Legislative Assembly (MLAs). In Quebec, they are members of the National Assembly (MNAs). Only Ontario has MPPs, or members of the Provincial Parliament. In 2005, Ontario had 103 MPPs, elected in 103 ridings.

Elected representatives in provincial legislatures follow procedures similar to those followed by federal MPs. There is a Speaker, the government party, the Official Opposition, Question Period, parliamentary etiquette, and so on. There is one significant difference: provincial governments have no senates.

TERRITORIAL LEGISLATIVE ASSEMBLIES

About 100,000 people in total live in Canada's three territories: Yukon, the Northwest Territories, and Nunavut. In the latter two territories, most of the people are Inuit.

Each territory has a **commissioner** (a role similar to lieutenant governor), a premier, and a legislative assembly that functions similarly to a provincial legislature. However, territories have less power than provinces in such areas as land ownership and control over school curricula. Because of an agreement between the Inuit and the federal government, Nunavut has more control over land and resources than the other territories.

The legislatures of the Northwest Territories and Nunavut maintain Aboriginal political traditions. Decisions are based on consensus, and legislatures are non-partisan. Each issue is considered on its merits, and the elected members vote to reach an agreement by the group as a whole. Elders are consulted before any policy or bill is passed into law.

LOCAL GOVERNMENT COUNCILS

The head of a municipal government in a town or city is a **mayor**. In rural areas, this person is called a **reeve**. He or she is directly elected by the people. This person leads a government of **councillors**, who are elected by the voters in geographic areas known as **wards**. In areas of low populations, councillors are elected to represent the entire municipality. Each member of the locally elected council, including the mayor or reeve, has one vote.

The federal *Indian Act* recognizes the right of certain groups of Aboriginal peoples in Canada to elect and form local governments. These **band councils** pass bylaws similar to those of municipalities and provinces and make decisions. Under the *Indian Act*, certain bylaws passed by band councils may be disallowed by the Department of Indian Affairs.

► **DID YOU KNOW** ◄

Nunavut means "our land" in the Inuit dialects of the eastern Arctic. It was once part of the Northwest Territories.

► **DID YOU KNOW** ◄

By the end of 2003, Mel Lastman's political career had spanned 34 years. His 13 terms, first as mayor of North York, then as mayor of the City of Toronto, made him the longest-serving mayor of any major city in the world.

CivicStar

PAUL OKALIK

You have trouble with authority and alcohol. You are the youngest of 10 children. In high school, the older brother you love commits suicide. In grade 10, you are expelled for drinking. At age 17, you do jail time for breaking and entering. You can't hold a job. You consider killing yourself.

Can you change your life?

Paul Okalik did. At age 20, he heard about a government job. Negotiators were working on a land claim that was to become a new territory. They needed a researcher. Okalik knew he was their person.

"Up to that point, I didn't have much faith in myself," Okalik recalled later. "After I became a negotiator, I developed enough confidence that I could probably succeed."

Okalik not only gained confidence; he quit drinking and went back to school. He knew that his brother Norman had killed himself to avoid jail. Okalik felt that the justice system had treated his people unfairly, and he made a decision. He would move to Ottawa. There he earned two degrees, one in political science, the other in law.

Paul Okalik became Canada's first Inuit lawyer. In February 1999, he was elected to the newly created Nunavut Legislative Assembly. Shortly after, Nunavut's MLAs chose him to be the territory's first premier.

Your Play

Okalik once said that a Canadian studies class he took at university helped him face some of his fears and challenges: "It forced me to learn about myself and my own family. I went back and interviewed elders. It gave me confidence in myself and my own family."

1. Have you ever had an experience that helped you realize something about yourself?
2. How did it change your life?
3. How did it help you become a better citizen?

PAUSE, REFLECT, APPLY

1. How many ridings or constituencies are there at the federal level? How many members of Parliament?
2. Describe how a government is formed, and how that government passes bills.
3. Explain the purpose of the Senate.
4. Define the following terms: minority government, Speaker, Question Period, Hansard, MPP, and patronage.
5. How does the legislative process in the territories differ from that in the provinces?

The Judicial Branch: Federal and Provincial/Territorial Levels

KEY QUESTION
How does the judiciary administer justice in Canada?

The judiciary (judicial branch) of government deals with the law courts and the administration of justice. Canada's courts are also called upon to interpret the country's laws.

Do governments have the right to regulate tobacco advertising? Does a province have the right to separate from Canada? What is meant by "freedom of expression" or "unreasonable search or seizure"? Answers to these and many other questions are provided by the judicial branch of government.

THE SUPREME COURT OF CANADA

The Supreme Court of Canada is the highest court in Canada, and the court of last appeal. That means that if you are appealing your case, the Supreme Court is your last stop. Its ruling is final.

The court consists of a chief justice and eight other judges (three from Quebec), all appointed by the prime minister. Upon request, the Supreme Court may review the criminal or civil law decision of a lower court. It may also interpret the constitution.

Among other decisions in the past two decades, the Supreme Court has declared that certain restrictions on abortion are illegal, that Sunday shopping prohibitions are illegal, and that same-sex marriages are constitutional.

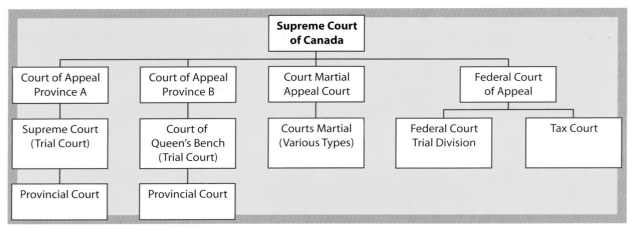

FIGURE 2.8 The structure of Canada's court system. The Courts Martial Appeal Court hears appeals from military courts.

PROVINCIAL AND TERRITORIAL COURTS

Each province and territory has courts to enforce federal and provincial laws in criminal and civil issues. Each province and territory also has a court of appeal. This court may review the decision of a lower court and interpret the constitution.

PAUSE, REFLECT, APPLY

1. Explain the role of the judicial branch at the federal level.
2. Explain the role of the judicial branch at the provincial level.
3. What do you think is the purpose of having different courts at different levels of government?

REPLAY

This chapter has informed you of these civics concepts:

1. Canada has three levels of government—federal, provincial/territorial, and local. Aboriginal self-government can occur at the local or territorial level.
2. Each level of government has different responsibilities and different sources of revenue to pay for services.
3. Canada has three branches of government—executive, legislative, and judicial.
4. Each branch of government facilitates the democratic process in a different way.
5. Canada's governments continue to evolve to reflect the diversity of its people and its heritage of democracy.

How to Locate Information

Do you need facts, figures, names, dates, opinions, pictures—information of any sort for your essay or debate? It is there for you, at your local library or on the Internet. However, using the library or the Internet is a bit like stepping into a huge information warehouse. How can you find the exact information you are looking for? Here are some tips. (All highlighted names can be accessed by visiting www.emp.ca/civics.)

At the Library

Ask a librarian to help you locate main information sources, such as books, newspapers, CD-ROMs, and videos. Ask to see the catalogue files that summarize stories and articles from local, national, and international newspapers and magazines.

Can't get to the library? Go to the 24/7 **Virtual Reference Library** for searches and assistance from a librarian at select times.

Online

Access your local newspaper archives (files of past issues) by typing the name of the newspaper into a search engine. Once you are at the paper, use its search button to search for your person or topic.

Use the **Government of Canada** Web sites. The information is reliable and accurate. For information on the laws and courts, and even actual trials, try the **Ontario Justice Education Network**. For information on voting and elections, go to **Elections Canada**, which will also send you information at no cost.

Use the **Canada Site** to find other sites of interest.

Direct Contact

Visit or e-mail local experts—community workers, politicians, government officials, and so on. Make your questions brief, to the point, and polite.

Tip

Always consider your sources. Not everything you read is factual; some of it is opinion. Some of it may not be true at all. In later Toolkits, you will learn more about biased or incomplete information, and sorting opinions from facts.

Skill Practice

1. Take an inventory of your upcoming assignments for the next month and make a list of the issues, ideas, or people that you will need to research or contact. Search the Internet. Tour the local library and ask for assistance in researching your material. Try not to focus on answering a specific question, but on becoming more independent at research.
2. What resources and methods did you learn to use by taking this advance tour?

STUDY HALL

Informed Citizenship

1. Working in small groups, find the names and pictures of the following people that represent you in government: municipal councillor, mayor or reeve, school trustee, member of your provincial legislature, premier, lieutenant governor, federal member of Parliament, prime minister, and governor general. Create a classroom display.

2. Explain why territories in Canada do not have the same rights and responsibilities as provinces.

3. Using the library or the Internet, find a story that tells you something important about the recent activities of your local government, your provincial government, and your federal government.

4. In this chapter you were introduced to Ontario Lieutenant Governor Hilary Weston, who donated her salary to job-training programs for high school students and street kids. You also read about the parents of Ken Dryden, who donated their resources to Sleeping Children Around the World. Both are examples of *philanthropy*, which means helping other people through charitable donations or work. Find another example of philanthropy in your community and explain the example to your class.

Purposeful Citizenship

5. With a partner, find out three rules in your student council's constitution that you might wish to change. Find out how this constitution can be changed (the process is called the "amending formula"). Report your findings to the class.

6. Organize a mock federal cabinet meeting. Assign roles to the prime minister and approximately 14 different cabinet ministers and their assistants. In the meeting, each cabinet minister (and assistant) argues for money to support a program in his or her department. What rules are used in the meeting? How are conflicts resolved?

7. After appropriate research, conduct a debate on one of the following resolutions:
   - The monarchy should be abolished in Canada.
   - The Canadian Senate should be abolished.

Active Citizenship

8. Invite one or more of the people profiled in activity 1 to visit your class and to speak about their concept of active citizenship.

9. Identify an issue that concerns you at the local, provincial, or federal level. Write a letter to either your municipal councillor, MPP/MLA, or MP to express your point of view. Support your point of view with evidence. Politely request a response from the person to whom you are writing.

10. Nunavut premier Paul Okalik is one of several Aboriginal leaders who have expressed concern over the high suicide rate of Aboriginal youth in certain communities. With a partner, research and present to the class measures being taken by government and non-governmental agencies to address this situation. Visit www.emp.ca/civics for links.

11. In small groups, investigate the concept of citizens paying for the services they actually use. State whether or not the idea is worthwhile, and explain your reasons. Here are some ideas:
    - the toll road Highway 407, near Toronto
    - user fees for medical services

CHAPTER 3
How Do Laws and Regulations Affect You?

A factory worker in England tests a cane in 1965. Teachers used canes to punish and discipline students. In 2004, the Supreme Court of Canada ruled that "corporal [physical] punishment by teachers is unacceptable." It also said that teachers could use "reasonable" force to restrain or remove unruly students. What do you think is "reasonable"?

What You Need to Know

- Where do you encounter laws and regulations?
- Whose beliefs and values do laws and regulations reflect?
- What happens if citizens disagree about a law?
- What is the political spectrum?
- What are the conservative, liberal, and centrist philosophies?
- Should we have more or fewer laws?
- How can you identify main and supporting ideas?

Key Terms

values	levy
beliefs	right-wing
diversity	left-wing
bylaws	political spectrum
discrimination	conservative
sexual harassment	liberal

Key Question

Are Canadians over-regulated?

Imagine a time in which a student who misbehaves is beaten with a rubber strap. A world in which a 14-year-old boy accused of killing a classmate is sentenced to hang. A society that segregates black children in their own schools and labels gay people criminals.

Imagine that it is illegal to advertise or display birth control devices, such as condoms. People do not wear seat belts in cars. The penalty for driving intoxicated (proven by the inability to walk a straight line or to touch one's nose) is a small fine. A cigarette and ashtray are offered at a parent–teacher interview. Teenagers may drive at age 16 but must wait until they are 21 to vote or drink.

How would you like to live in this world? Some of your parents and grandparents did—in Canada in the 1950s. Laws and regulations touched every area of their lives. How are things different for teenagers living today? Do laws affect you? How?

Where Do You Encounter Laws and Regulations?

It may surprise you to learn that the law affects you as much as it did your parents and grandparents. While many laws and regulations from the 1950s have been swept away, some remain, and new laws have been introduced. Today, government still plays a major role in your life.

WELCOME TO YOUR LIFE

If you were born here, your parents had to obtain a birth certificate for you. If you joined your family through international adoption or if your family emigrated to Canada, you had to obtain a Permanent Resident Card (PRC) to stay here. Later, you received a Social Insurance Number (SIN).

The food and liquids you consumed were checked and regulated by inspectors. The toys you played with and the car seat you occupied had to meet Canadian safety standards. As you grew, you had to wear a helmet when riding a bicycle. The public places you entered were smoke-free zones. At a certain age, you were required to be schooled and immunized against certain diseases. When you entered or left your school bus, other vehicles on the road had to stop to allow you to cross the street safely.

These are just some examples of how government has entered your life on a regular basis for years and years.

In some ways, government acts as a super-parent, concerned with everyone's well-being. At times, you probably disagree with your parents about rules they set. Similarly, Canadians often disagree with government about what it is doing on their behalf. However, because Canada is a democracy, citizens have a say in how government will operate.

How can you have your say? You can become informed about government by reading, viewing, and listening. You can be involved in government activities such as attending meetings and voting. If you disagree with a government, you can e-mail an elected official or attend a protest demonstration. You can support the government by taking part in recycling programs, by protecting the natural environment, by respecting human rights, and by acting to preserve Canada's heritage.

Most importantly, you can get involved by learning about which Canadian laws and regulations affect you. Knowing how far government

---

LITERACY COACH

Effective readers "preview" several paragraphs of information at a time by skimming before they read. They also draw on their own knowledge to figure out where the text is going. Where do you think this section is going? Read the first sentence again and skim the next six or seven paragraphs. Check, confirm, or revise your prediction at the end of the section.

FIGURE 3.1 Some Ontario schools ban all scarves, caps, and do-rags during class. In these schools, such items must be stowed in a locker during school hours.

reaches into your life is one of the first steps toward being civic-minded, even when you don't agree with what the government is doing.

RULES AT HOME AND AT SCHOOL

At home and school, rules are daily reminders about manners, chores, privileges, curfews, communication, and clothing. Some rules are instituted specifically for emergencies and safety. Other rules are meant to keep households and schools running as smoothly as possible. Because not all families and classrooms are the same, the rules they agree to impose also differ. Each family or classroom may have somewhat different **values** (what you find important) and **beliefs** (what you believe in), and different rules to reflect that **diversity** (differences).

In Ontario, some laws affect every student. By law, you must enter school or be home-schooled from age 7 to 16. (By the time you read this, the school-leaving age may have been raised to 18.) At secondary school, you must complete a certain number of courses in order to graduate. These are examples of laws passed by the Ontario government.

Other regulations—regarding behaviour, dress codes, and policies around lateness—are set by your school or school board. In some cases, these rules must be interpreted in order to be followed. Some schools, for example, ban T-shirts with slogans that are "offensive" or that "promote violence." If you were going to define these terms, how would you do so?

Other schools have more extensive dress codes that spell out exactly what types of jewellery, headgear, tops, pants, and shoes you can wear.

☐ **DISCUSSION POINT**
Many young people argue that a school ban on headgear is a pointless intrusion. They say their fashion choices have nothing to do with learning. What do you think?

PAUSE, REFLECT, APPLY

1. Identify six ways in which the government has affected your life to date.
2. Why do you think a government would have an interest in raising the school-leaving age from 16 to 18?
3. What is your school's dress code? How was it created? Do you ever find it difficult to interpret or follow? Explain why.
4. Develop three or four criteria for a reasonable dress code for high school students.

City and Town Bylaws

The community in which you live also passes laws. Laws passed by local governments are called **bylaws**. Different cities and towns have different bylaws.

Municipal bylaws often reach into your daily routines. There are bylaws about how much noise you can make with your garage band or stereo, and where your parents can park their car. There are zoning bylaws about how land can be used. For example, a business that features video arcades or adult entertainment cannot be established within a certain distance of schools.

STICK-HANDLING COMPLAINTS

Some communities have a bylaw that prohibits the playing of games, such as skateboarding or road hockey, on public streets. This bylaw is usually not enforced unless a citizen makes a complaint. In road hockey, for example, players get around the bylaw by stick-handling, passing, and shooting only when the roadway is clear.

What happens when a complaint is made?

In 2002, in Hamilton, Ontario, Gary Kotar and his two sons, aged 13 and 10, found out what can happen. The two boys were considered too young to be charged, but their father went to court facing a maximum fine of $2,000 for playing ball hockey on the street. Citing lack of evidence, a justice of the peace dropped the single charge against Gary Kotar. Kotar then campaigned to change the bylaw.

PET SMART

Pet lovers are also restricted by bylaws. In most communities, "pooper scooper" laws require you to clean up after your pet. Some communities ban certain kinds of pet ownership. The city of Kitchener, for example, banned pit bull dogs in 1997.

Many communities also forbid the ownership of "exotic" pets. An exotic animal is usually defined as a species that is not a dog, or a cat, or a

▶ **KEY QUESTION**
Are bylaws more concerned with protecting individuals or protecting communities?

FIGURE 3.2 Ryan and Gary Kotar, who was charged with breaking a bylaw that stops people from playing road hockey.

SOURCES

MAJOR RAMIFICATIONS AHEAD

A local take on gas emissions, also a global concern. See Sources, Chapter 11, page 197 for another view.

traditional pet, and is not native to Ontario. In Toronto, for example, it is illegal to own a snake that is longer than 3 metres.

ENVIRONMENT FRIENDLY

In recent years, municipalities have passed more bylaws related to the environment. Many ban or limit pesticide and herbicide use on lawns. They also require the separation of wastes into recyclables and landfill material. Some municipalities also have started separate collections for organic scraps or food wastes.

Local bylaws to protect the environment are often inspired by global concerns. The town of Markham, Ontario, for example, has its own Kyoto Task Force to mobilize local support for the *Kyoto Protocol*, an international program to reduce global warming. The town's Web site calls upon local governments, businesses, and residents to be "leaders in reducing emissions and set new standards for protecting the environment." In this way, local laws can reflect the widest concerns (150 countries have ratified the *Kyoto Protocol*) and can still affect you at home and in your neighbourhood.

PAUSE, REFLECT, APPLY

1. Name three ways in which local bylaws affect your daily life.
2. Have you ever encountered a local bylaw you disagreed with? What was it, and what action, if any, did you take to protest or change it?
3. Examine the cartoon in the Sources feature, above. What is a "ramification," and why does the cartoonist say major ones are ahead?

Provincial and Territorial Laws and Regulations

▶ **KEY QUESTION**
What provincial or territorial law has the greatest impact on your life?

Provincial and territorial laws also affect your daily activities. You may be aware, for example, that the province of Ontario prevents you from buying cigarettes or consuming alcoholic beverages until you are 19 years old. If you wish to drive, you must hold a beginner's driving certificate (G1) for at least eight months following your 16th birthday and pass several road tests before being granted full driving privileges. The province also insists that you pay an 8 percent sales tax on all purchases that are not essential food items, medicines, or children's clothing.

In 2004, the Ontario government announced its intention to introduce a provincewide ban on smoking. Previously, local communities had passed their own smoking regulations. With the 2006 implementation of the *Smoke-Free Ontario Act*, smoking is prohibited in all workplaces and public places, including bars, restaurants, casinos, and legion halls. This leaves only one indoor location for smokers: their own homes. The new law also restricts the display of tobacco products in stores, banning countertop displays and the "power walls" of cigarette brands behind convenience-store counters.

FIGURE 3.3 In 2001, André Fortin wrote a book on how to panhandle after living on the street in Montreal for 13 years. Had he lived in Ontario, the provincial *Safe Streets Act* would have prevented him from "aggressive" begging or asking for money in a parking lot, near a bank machine or a pay telephone, or near public transit.

ONTARIO'S *HUMAN RIGHTS CODE*

While the *Smoke-Free Ontario Act* may limit some people's freedoms, Ontario's *Human Rights Code* guarantees certain rights and protections for young and old alike. The Code is a provincial law that guarantees everybody equal rights and opportunities in specific areas such as jobs, housing, and services. The Code's goal is to prevent **discrimination** and harassment because of race, colour, sex, handicap, and age, to name some of the 16 grounds.

How does the *Human Rights Code* affect you? Under its terms, you are protected from racial jokes and insults in your workplace and at school. You are guarded from **sexual harassment**—unwanted behaviour shown to you of a sexual nature. This may include someone's staring at or making unwelcome comments about your body, making sexual requests, or displaying sexually offensive pictures. Even if it is not directed at you, sexual harassment can poison the atmosphere where you live, work, or receive services.

The *Human Rights Code*'s protection against discrimination is wide-ranging. The right to be free from discrimination and harassment applies to employment; accommodation (hotels, motels, and hostels);

FIGURE 3.4 In Ontario, you cannot be prevented from renting a property because you are pregnant or attending school. Why do you think landlords want to exclude certain people from renting their property?

housing; contracts; and membership in unions and trade or professional associations. If you are seeking an apartment, a landlord cannot reject you because you are a student, pregnant, or both. When you apply for a job, you cannot be asked whether you have any kind of criminal record. You can only be asked information that is directly related to the requirements of the job, such as whether you can lift a certain weight or have a driver's licence.

If you experience discrimination or harassment, you can inform authorities at your place of work, residence, or wherever you receive services. If the activity does not stop, you may contact the Ontario Human Rights Commission. This is the agency that hears complaints and enforces the principles of the Code.

Ontario's *Human Rights Code* also guarantees equal treatment for persons with disabilities. This applies whether the condition developed over time, resulted from an accident, or was present at birth. Because of cases brought before the Ontario Human Rights Commission, many buildings and services have been made more accessible to people with physical handicaps.

Under provincial laws, including the *Human Rights Code*, schools are responsible for taking steps to accommodate all students with disabilities. These steps include

- making the school wheelchair-accessible
- employing educational assistants
- modifying the curriculum to meet the needs of students with disabilities
- offering special technologies that aid learning.

As a result of government action, the Ontario educational system is striving to be one of the most inclusive in the entire world.

PAUSE, REFLECT, APPLY

1. List the three provincial/territorial laws that affect your life the most.
2. Do you know someone who has encountered discrimination or harassment in employment or in some other area? In your opinion, did the person have grounds for contacting the Ontario Human Rights Commission? Explain.

Federal Laws and Regulations

In many respects, you may think of the federal government as the level most removed from your life. Yet at times, it can have a dramatic impact on a young person.

CRIMINAL LAW

Criminal law is the responsibility of the federal government. It is the branch of law that deals with acts or offences against society that have been classified as crimes.

Youth Justice

The *Youth Criminal Justice Act* (2003) determines how young lawbreakers between the ages of 12 and 17 are treated. The youth justice system reflects the idea that young people are still maturing and do not yet possess the judgment of adults. In Canada, justice for youth differs from adult justice in many respects, including

- degree of accountability (to what extent the person can be held responsible for the crime)
- length of sentences
- approaches to rehabilitation.

Young people involved in the justice system are not identified by the media. Punishments may range from custody (comparable to imprisonment for adults) to extrajudicial measures (measures outside the court system). Prison sentences are less severe than those for adults and are served in youth detention centres, not adult jails. Under a variety of extrajudicial measures, the young offender may meet a Youth Justice Committee composed of community members. The committee may recommend one or more of the following:

> ◢ **KEY QUESTION**
> Should there be one set of laws for adults and another for teenagers?

FIGURE 3.5 In 1959, 14-year-old Steven Truscott was found guilty of raping and murdering his 12-year-old classmate, Lynne Harper, and was sentenced to be hanged. Eventually, his sentence was reduced, and he was quietly paroled in 1969. Truscott has always maintained his innocence. Recently, he successfully applied to the minister of justice for a review of his case. How would justice be different for Truscott today?

- restitution (paying back to the community, usually through service)
- community support for the youth
- a meeting between the victim and the young offender.

(You will learn more about the youth justice system in Chapter 7.)

According to Statistics Canada, young adults aged 18 to 24 have the highest rates of drug offences, followed by those aged 12 to 17. In 2004, the Liberal government introduced a bill that would make possession of a small amount of marijuana (less than 15 grams) no longer a criminal offence. However, offenders would face fines between $100 and $400, depending on age, circumstances, and the amount of marijuana involved. The penalty for a large-scale cannabis grower (more than 50 plants) was doubled to a maximum prison sentence of 14 years.

The Canadian Medical Association backed the government's reform of drug laws. It pointed out that a criminal record effectively bars young people from many jobs and opportunities, including getting into medical school. It called the health effects of moderate marijuana use "minimal." The Canadian Association of Chiefs of Police also advocated decriminalization, saying prosecuting people for small amounts ties up scarce resources. Other groups, such as the Canadian Police Association and Mothers Against Drunk Driving, have opposed decriminalization. They argue that it would lead to increased use of hard drugs and more cases of impaired driving.

THE *CANADIAN CHARTER OF RIGHTS AND FREEDOMS*

At the federal level, **rights** are protected by the *Canadian Charter of Rights and Freedoms*, which deals with a citizen's relationship with the government. Section 8 of the Charter states: "Everyone has the right to be secure against unreasonable search or seizure." In practice, this section means that you and your possessions cannot be searched unless police officers have a search warrant or a good reason to search. Furthermore, your dwelling place (house or apartment) cannot be searched without a proper warrant obtained from a judge.

School Searches

What about your right to privacy in an elementary or secondary school? You have fewer rights than you would in other circumstances. Teachers and other school authorities are responsible for providing a safe environment and maintaining order and discipline in the school. This may sometimes require searches of students, their lockers, and their personal belongings, as well as the seizure of prohibited items. In this sense, a student's Charter protection stops at the schoolhouse door.

Equality Rights

Section 15(1) of the Charter states:

> Every individual is equal before and under the law and has the right to the equal protection and equal benefit of the law without discrimination and, in particular, without discrimination based on race, national or ethnic origin, colour, religion, sex, age or mental or physical disability.

CivicStar

JUSTINE BLAINEY

In 1981, 10-year-old Justine Blainey was a skilled hockey player. She had just won a position on the Metro Toronto Hockey League team. Her victory was short-lived, however. League regulations did not allow girls to play. Blainey brought a complaint to the Ontario Human Rights Commission. She was shocked to learn that Ontario's *Human Rights Code* allowed sexual discrimination in sports. Blainey thought the law was discriminatory, and appealed her case before the courts.

In 1986, the Supreme Court of Canada upheld Blainey's appeal, declaring that her equality rights under the Charter (section 15) had been violated. Ontario's *Human Rights Code* was changed so that athletic organizations could no longer restrict membership on the basis of gender.

In 1988, Blainey played her first minor-bantam league hockey game. She continued playing hockey with boys until the age of 19. At the University of Toronto, she played on the women's hockey team. Blainey also fought back when the university tried to stop funding the women's team. Her "Save the Team" night raised $8,000, and the team had its funding increased.

Your Play

1. Create a flow chart to illustrate the process Justine Blainey followed, and the government bodies she contacted, to redress her situation in 1981.
2. Justine Blainey was criticized for pursuing her Charter rights. What would you have done in her situation? How would you have answered your critics?

FACE OFF   Downloading Music from the Internet

In 1999, 18-year-old Shawn Fanning invented an Internet file-sharing service. He called it Napster, after his own nickname. Fanning's invention allowed millions of users to download music from a server that was part of a Web site.

For Napster fans, technology was being used to do the same thing that had been done for years in neighbourhoods, schoolyards, and concerts: they were swapping music. What was wrong with sharing music with a friend, even if that friend was online? Young people argued that bands like Metallica made so much money from concerts that they would not miss the revenue from lost CD sales. Yet in 2000, Metallica sued Napster for copyright infringement.

> It may be hurting the music industry at this point, but my view is when consumers have the ability to learn about new and interesting music—and the barrier is lowered in a way that gives them control over how they experience it—I think those are positive things.
>
> — Shawn Fanning

The music industry saw things differently. They viewed each musical creation as their intellectual property and that of the composer, artist, and producer. Under copyright law, an artistic creation

FIGURE 3.7 Metallica guitarist Kirk Hammett appears before a US Senate Judiciary Committee about the future of digital music and to protest free music downloading.

cannot be reproduced or distributed without the owner's permission. The copyright royalties paid from radio or television broadcasts of songs and videos are the lifeblood of creative artists. Industry spokespeople charged that downloading music from the Internet was theft, pure and simple.

> It is ... sickening to know that our art is being traded like a commodity rather than the art that it is. From a business standpoint, this is about piracy, i.e., taking something that doesn't belong to you; and that is morally and legally wrong.
>
> — Metallica lawsuit against Napster

What Do You Think?

1. Copyright laws also apply to "intellectual property" other than music and videos—for example, plays, books, and sheet music. Create a table in which you list the advantages and disadvantages of copyright laws.
2. On the Internet, research the 2000 Metallica lawsuit against Napster. Summarize Metallica's arguments in an argumentative paragraph.
3. What is your opinion about free music downloading? Give two reasons for your viewpoint.

FIGURE 3.6 Who in this cartoon is the victim of crime?

While Ontario's *Human Rights Code* deals with relationships between private individuals, section 15 of the Charter deals with the relationship between the government and the individual. All provincial and territorial human rights codes are subject to the terms of the Charter. If a section of a human rights code is found to be inconsistent with the Charter, the courts can declare that section to be no longer in force.

THE CANADIAN *COPYRIGHT ACT*

Every time a radio or television station plays a song or video, musicians, composers, artists, and music companies are paid a royalty fee for their creative work. In 2004, it was estimated that 51 percent of young Canadians between the ages of 12 and 19 downloaded music from the Internet without paying a penny. Should royalties be paid for the millions of songs downloaded each year?

Canada's federal government is responsible for both communications and copyright protection. In 1998, it changed the Canadian copyright law to apply a **levy** (fee) on all blank audio recording media, including CDs, and even hard-disk–based MP3 players. The money collected is distributed to copyright holders (including artists, composers, and record companies) for revenue "lost" through Internet downloading.

In 2004, the Federal Court of Appeal ruled that the $25 fee imposed on iPods and other MP3 digital music players was illegal. That same year, the Supreme Court of Canada ruled that Internet service providers (such as Bell, Sprint, and AOL) are not responsible for paying royalties on music downloaded by users.

▶ **DID YOU KNOW** ◀
The levy on CD-Rs in 2004 was 21 cents each.

THE WEB ▶▶▶
Learn more about levies introduced because of Internet downloading at www.emp.ca/civics

PAUSE, REFLECT, APPLY

1. Explain how young people and adults receive different treatment from the Canadian justice system today.
2. Give reasons why you think that "different treatment" is a good or bad idea.
3. Describe two federal laws that you would like to see changed or adjusted. Explain why you would like the change.

▷ KEY QUESTION

Is there one "best" political philosophy?

The Political Spectrum

At every level of government, laws and regulations have some impact on your life. Sometimes you may support those laws, and sometimes you may disagree with them. Maybe you feel that pit bulls should not be banned, or that possession of small amounts of marijuana ought not to be decriminalized, and your best friend holds opposing views.

Your right to do something may also clash with what the larger group wants. For example, your "right" to keep your pit bull may conflict with your neighbour's right to feel safe. Your "right" to display a certain T-shirt slogan may ridicule a whole group of people whose race or sexual orientation differs from your own. It is the role of government and the courts to resolve conflicts. The courts often use the guideline of what a "reasonable person" would do. Section 1 of the Charter refers to **reasonable limits**" on rights and freedoms.

RIGHT, LEFT, WHAT?

You may have heard references to **right-wing** and **left-wing** in discussions about politics and society. These terms are used as convenient ways to describe bodies of beliefs. Your opinions and beliefs place you somewhere on an imaginary line called the **political spectrum**.

Being a **conservative** places you on the right side; being a **liberal** places you on the left. The concept of the right–left political spectrum dates back to the French Revolution (1789). In the French Assembly, elected conservative politicians sat to the right of the Speaker's chair; elected liberals sat to the left.

Note that the term "conservative" does not necessarily mean the same as the term "Conservative Party." Similarly, "liberal" does not necessarily mean the same as "Liberal Party." For example, in Canada, it is possible for someone to be a **centrist** (one whose political beliefs lie in the middle of the political spectrum) and a member of the Conservative Party, and it is possible for someone to have conservative views on many issues and be a member of the Liberal Party.

So what do these labels mean? Figure 3.8 lists some ways to describe the two sides of the spectrum.

◀ **Left-wing**	**Right-wing** ▶
Liberals tend to believe in	**Conservatives tend to believe in**
■ government involvement in people's lives	■ minimal government involvement in people's lives
■ ensuring equal opportunities through law	■ individuals being responsible for themselves
■ the inevitability of social change	■ maintaining traditional values and social patterns
■ generous subsidies such as welfare, medicare, and pension benefits	■ emergency relief and personal charity
■ higher taxation to guarantee social services	■ lower taxation to encourage individual spending and entrepreneurship
■ a small military, especially in peacetime	■ a strong military defence of the nation

FIGURE 3.8 The left–right political spectrum. In the centre are many people who would describe themselves as moderate, and who blend the two sides of the spectrum.

WHEN PHILOSOPHIES CLASH

When citizens clash in their political views, government's role is to address those differences. Governments try to accommodate opposing ideas by using study groups, public hearings, opinion polls, and information sessions. Citizens may express their viewpoints on an issue through e-mails, letters, and Web sites. By means of education and discussion, differing views may be understood and reconciled.

In Canada, the three levels of government follow the will of the majority, but also recognize the rights of minorities. Citizens are aware of the rights of minority groups in various ways. A Sikh citizen is permitted to wear his traditional turban and beard as a member of the Royal Canadian Mounted Police. A French Canadian citizen can communicate with government and educate her children in the French language. A citizen with physical handicaps is able to attend school, theatre, and other facilities without facing barriers.

FIGURE 3.9 Left and right, two means of protest. As citizens in Manchester, England, protest their country's involvement in the 2003 war in Iraq, a bystander displays an entirely different view, using another form of protest. Where do you think these players fall on the political spectrum? Explain your reasons.

Sometimes differences are settled in an elected parliament, sometimes in a judicial courtroom, and sometimes through a government agency such as a human rights commission or tribunal. In each setting, the opposing sides are permitted to present their ideas and philosophies. After a decision has been made, all sides accept that decision. Through the resolution of conflicts, Canadians have been able to build one of the world's most inclusive societies.

PAUSE, REFLECT, APPLY

How do you think liberals and conservatives would view each of the following issues? Examine all the characteristics of each philosophy before deciding. Offer a reason for each of your choices.

- Subsidized child care
- Same-sex marriage
- Children's rights
- Film censorship
- Guaranteed annual income for the poor
- Low taxes for business
- Environmental regulations

REPLAY

This chapter has informed you of these civics concepts:

1. Laws and regulations at every level of government affect your life.
2. Laws and regulations balance the rights of the individual with the needs of society.
3. The *Canadian Charter of Rights and Freedoms* protects individuals from unfair laws.
4. The justice system recognizes two groups of people: adults and youths.
5. The political spectrum is an integral aspect of democracy.
6. When philosophies clash, government's role is to help resolve the differences.

CIVICS ▶ TOOLKIT

How to Identify the Main Idea and Supporting Evidence

When you read information you have located, are you faced with a "wall of words"? The challenge for you is to spot the most relevant pieces of information.

The *main idea* in what you are reading is the most important piece of information. Why did the author bother writing this? The reason is usually the main idea. The details or examples that support that idea are called the *supporting evidence*.

The passage at right is about Canadian political writer Naomi Klein. Imagine that your teacher has assigned this piece for reading. The goal is to read the passage and identify the main idea and supporting evidence.

- Make sure you understand what you are looking for. Review the definitions of main idea and supporting evidence (above).
- Look for key words that tell you about the person or issue. For example, find words that express attitudes, beliefs, or decisions.
- Find a statement that expresses Klein's point of view. Then find a statement that supports that point of view. Sometimes supporting statements are specific examples.
- Be prepared to ignore information that may be interesting, but not relevant to your topic.

Skill Practice

1. Select the one statement that best illustrates the main idea of this passage. Explain why you selected this particular statement.
2. Select another statement that offers further evidence to support your choice.
3. Identify four statements that are not relevant to this particular task.

Naomi Klein, born in Montreal to American parents who came to Canada in protest at the Vietnam War, always had a love for designer labels. In her teenage years, she was a "mall rat," and in her high school yearbook she was described as "most likely to go to jail for stealing peroxide." In university, Klein, herself Jewish, wrote a newspaper article in which she urged the Jewish state of Israel to stop its occupation of Palestinian land. In 2000, she published a book, *No Logo*, that criticized large corporations such as Nike, McDonald's, and Starbucks for taking over world markets with their brand-name advertising. She expressed concern that global corporations are more interested in good appearances (logos) and profits than in real issues (workers' conditions and wages). For example, her book pointed out that Indonesian workers are paid $2 a day to make Nike running shoes that sell for $120. Although concerned about the living and working conditions in the world's poor countries, she also criticized North American "McJobs" that have low wages, no worker protection, and no future. Klein, who is married to television personality Avi Lewis, considers herself a feminist. She has succeeded in bringing attention to the manner in which large corporations take advantage of people in both developing and **developed countries** (countries that are technologically advanced and wealthy).

STUDY HALL

Informed Citizenship

1. Identify some of the ways in which a young person can become involved in government.

2. What is a bylaw? List two examples of bylaws.

3. As members of Canadian society, we have both rights and responsibilities. At the local level, we have the right of pet ownership. List at least four responsibilities associated with pet ownership.

4. Explain, with examples, three ways in which provincial laws affect young people.

5. What is section 8 of the *Canadian Charter of Rights and Freedoms*, and how does it apply to a young person's life inside and outside school?

6. What is section 15 of the *Canadian Charter of Rights and Freedoms*, and how was it applied to the case of Justine Blainey in 1986?

Purposeful Citizenship

7. a) Organize a classroom debate on each of the topics listed below.

   b) Before the debate, research your position and your opponent's position.

   c) After the debate, summarize your position on each debate topic in a well-written paragraph.

Debate topics:

- Pit bulls and other dogs deemed dangerous should be outlawed.
- Smoking should be outlawed in all public places.
- The possession of small amounts of marijuana should be decriminalized.
- There should be no restrictions on downloading music from the Internet.

8. Read about Ontario's *Human Rights Code* and the Ontario Human Rights Commission at www.emp.ca/civics. Study each of the following examples and decide whether the situation described is a legitimate case of discrimination for the Ontario Human Rights Commission. Provide reasons for your answers.

- A Chinese student is asked to move out of her apartment because the landlord believes that the tenant will expose her to SARS (Severe Acute Respiratory Syndrome), even though the tenant has not been to any hospitals, facilities, or countries associated with a high risk of SARS.
- A male student notices that he is paying five times as much for automobile insurance as a female student who is the same age and has the same driving record.
- After a complaint from a customer, a restaurant owner asks a nursing mother to breastfeed her child in the women's washroom.
- An advertisement for a receptionist's job asks for female applicants who speak "unaccented English."
- During a job interview for the position of childcare worker, you are asked to submit to a criminal record check and to supply the names of two references.

9. Select a current politician in Canada or in the world, and research that person's political ideas. In a well-written short paper, explain why the person is a conservative, liberal, or centrist.

Active Citizenship

10. With a partner, research and present to the class the measures that are being taken by your local community to improve the environment.

11. Offer some specific suggestions to improve air quality and environmental protection in your community. You may examine the efforts of some other communities at www.emp.ca/civics.

12. Outline the steps you would take to convince your community to adopt what you consider to be a new and worthwhile environmental protection measure.

CHAPTER 4

How Do Governments Make Policy?

Who is walking the tightrope? Hint: He won a minority government in 2004. "Gomery" and "Sgro" were government scandals. What do the other sharks' fins refer to? What other fins would you add?

AcmeAthletic has offered to pay half the cost to build athletic facilities on the property of Applecity High School. City council will pay the other half, as long as the facilities are open for community use on weekends and evenings. The area has no community centre and has had problems with youth gangs and vandalism for years.

AcmeAthletic and the city want the school board to donate the property. AcmeAthletic also wants the school to display its "Flash" logos. In exchange, the school can use the facilities during school hours, up to 6 p.m.

There is one problem. AcmeAthletic has used child labour in Southeast Asia to keep its costs low and profits high. Student council has been leading a consumer boycott (refusal to buy) of AcmeAthletic products. The student council has no say in the decision.

Should the school board approve this offer? Who are the winners and losers if it decides yes? If it decides no?

What You Need to Know

- What is public policy, and how is it made?
- What are the major influences on policy?
- How can you influence policy decisions?
- How do policies become laws?
- Why must policy makers recognize many perspectives?
- How can you find and identify different points of view?

Key Terms

policy	bill
platform	non-confidence
charismatic	standing committee
interest groups	youth wings
stakeholders	polls
petitions	referendum

Key Question

In a democracy, should government lead or follow public opinion?

Platforms and Policies

Policy is the plan of action of a political party or government to achieve certain goals. During democratic elections, each party promotes its **platform** to the public. This is the group of policies it promises to pursue if elected. Citizens then vote for the candidates and parties that best represent their own views and wants. The party that wins becomes the government and is then expected to turn policies into laws.

Sound simple? It's not.

DO CITIZENS REALLY WANT TO HEAR ABOUT POLICIES?

In his memoirs, Pierre Trudeau described his campaign in the 1972 federal election. Trudeau won a second term as prime minister, but the Liberal Party won fewer seats than it did in 1968:

> I described the exercise as "a conversation with Canadians." "Here's what we've accomplished in the past four years," I said to them, "and here are our plans [policies] for the next four years. If you like them— then vote for us." ... The electorate was eager for cheers and rallies, and there I was giving them calm, lucid propositions [clear ideas]. That is not how you win elections.

A different kind of leader came to power in Germany in the 1930s. Adolf Hitler was a **charismatic** speaker who inspired thousands at mass rallies by appealing to their love of Germany and their fears (see Chapter 10). Behind Hitler's stirring words, however, were hateful plans:

> It might be argued that had more non-Nazi Germans read [Hitler's autobiography, *Mein Kampf*] before 1933 [when he came to power] and had the foreign statesmen of the world perused it carefully while there was still time, both Germany and the world might have been saved from catastrophe. For whatever other accusations can be made about Adolph Hitler, no one can accuse him of not putting down in writing exactly the kind of Germany he intended to create if he ever came to power and the kind of world he meant to create by armed German conquest.

—William L. Shirer, *The Rise and Fall of the Third Reich* (1959), p. 81

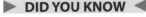

DID YOU KNOW

In 1933, *Mein Kampf* sold 1.5 million copies, making Hitler a very rich man. Every German couple intending to marry had to own a copy. Historians suggest that few people read the book very carefully.

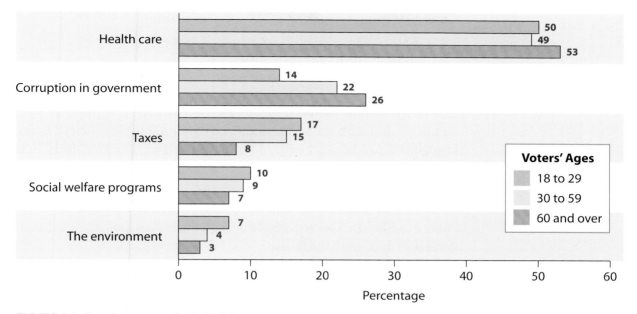

FIGURE 4.1 Canadians were asked which issues were most important to them in the 2004 federal election. What issues are important to you? *Source: Elections Canada.*

PAUSE, REFLECT, APPLY

1. a) What is policy?
   b) How does policy relate to platform?
2. a) Trudeau wrote that he nearly lost the 1972 election for what reason?
   b) Is Trudeau being insulting to voters or realistic? Explain.
3. a) List three facts you know about Adolf Hitler.
   b) List three results of Hitler's election.
4. What lessons can be learned from Hitler's ideas, election, and subsequent policies?
5. How important is it to have a charismatic leader to communicate a political party's platform?

How Are Policies Developed?

In Canada, governments spend billions of dollars collected in taxes each year. Government decisions touch every aspect of life—from homes to homelessness, from schools to threats of military attacks from outer space.

Government policies fall into several areas:

- social (health, education)
- financial (taxes, money supply)

> **KEY QUESTION**
> Why is it often difficult, complicated, and slow to pass laws in a democracy?

- international (defence, trade, foreign relations)
- public works (transportation, construction)
- resources (fisheries, agriculture, energy)
- legal (justice).

Each policy area is managed by different departments or ministries.

Policies deal with the wants and needs of our complex society. Large numbers of people are involved and consulted as opinions, facts, and information are researched.

Policies have consequences—good and bad, long-term and short-term. A policy may look good on paper. Once put into action, however, it may produce unexpectedly bad consequences. New policies must then be created to correct mistakes.

MAJOR INFLUENCES ON POLICY

Governments and political parties create policies around their core beliefs. They must also respond to many influences. Some of the most important influences are described next.

Political Party Membership

Across Canada, thousands of ordinary Canadians join and work for political parties locally. This is referred to as the **grassroots** level. Even at this level, members can strongly influence a party's goals. Members from each riding can become delegates to party conventions and conferences. Delegates can discuss policy with party leaders and elected representatives. Delegates' directions are put forward in **resolutions**. If passed, resolutions become policies.

FIGURE 4.2 Supporters of Conservative leader Stephen Harper cheer before his keynote speech at the party's 2005 convention. Conservative delegates from across the country gathered to decide the party's future direction.

Civil Service Advice

The executive branch of government employs thousands of civil servants. Top civil servants are experts and advise government on policy details. It is not enough to say, "we want everyone to have a good education." Costs must be calculated, options developed, and a plan of action devised.

Judicial Opinion

The influence of the courts on public policy has increased since the passage of the *Canadian Charter of Rights and Freedoms* in 1982. Government legislation must comply with the Charter. Courts can override laws that contravene (do not respect) the Charter. In 2004, for example, the federal government went to the Supreme Court of Canada for a constitutional opinion on proposed changes to marriage laws to recognize same-sex couples. The issue was extremely controversial.

Economic Realities

Economic conditions also affect policy decisions. Once a party is elected, voters expect it to deliver on its platform and promises. The key question: Is there enough money?

Intergovernmental Concerns

Policies in one level of government are influenced by the demands and needs of other levels of government. For example, Ontario may need federal funds to pay for more hospitals. The city of Toronto may need provincial funds to support public transit. The federal government may want municipal land to build a new airport.

International Pressures

Borders cannot keep out international influences. Foreign policy, defence, and trade all depend on relationships with other countries. Policies must reflect this reality. Most important for Canada is the relationship between its policies and the reactions of the United States, its closest ally and the world's most powerful country.

Interest Groups

In democracies, informed people can come together to pursue common causes or goals. The groups they form are called interest groups. To achieve their goals, **interest groups** try to influence policy makers. Many groups focus their efforts on the courts and interpretation of the Charter.

CONSEQUENCES OF A POLICY

Most policies are created with good intentions. Criteria to assess what "good" is would include policies that are designed to

- do what is best for the most people
- protect the weakest in society
- provide fairness and equity
- create a cleaner, healthier community.

Policies intended to improve or protect society may have the opposite effect. What is good for "most" may harm others.

For example, from 1916 to 1927, Ontario prohibited the sale and consumption of alcohol. Alcohol was seen to cause many social ills. There were social benefits to prohibition. Crimes related to drunkenness and family violence decreased. Criminals and bootleggers, however, took over production and sale of alcohol. Government taxes on liquor sales vanished.

Prohibitionists argued that by using grain for food, not liquor, Canadians were supporting the soldiers fighting in World War I. Many veterans returning from the battles of the war disagreed. They had earned the right to choose whether or not to drink. The law became very unpopular. In 1927, Ontario changed it. Alcohol could be sold, but it was controlled through the Liquor Control Board of Ontario. This is still the law.

Stakeholders

Individuals or groups that have something to gain or lose from a policy or law are known as **stakeholders**. In the case of prohibition, for example, stakeholders included liquor producers, the government, veterans, bar owners, police, drinkers, and so on. Other stakeholders included spouses and children of violent drinkers.

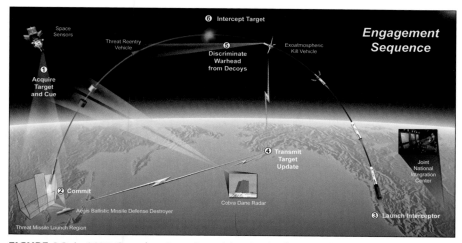

FIGURE 4.3 In 2005, Canada rejected participating in the US Ballistic Missile Defence program. Prime Minister Martin said Canada opposed putting weapons into space. Do you agree? Why or why not? What consequences might this decision have on Canada–US relations? *Source: Canadian Broadcasting Company.*

PAUSE, REFLECT, APPLY

1. Make a web diagram. In the centre, write "policy." In the outer circles, write (in one or two words each) all the stakeholders or influences that might affect policy makers.
2. Who is allowed to belong to a political party?
3. Which of the following must be democratically elected: a civil servant, a party member, a member of Parliament, a member of an interest group, a judge?
4. What is a "stakeholder"?
5. What criteria does (or should) a government use in forming a policy that will affect the interests of different stakeholders?

Interest Groups and Policy Makers

In a democracy, many individuals and interest groups try to influence parties and governments. Interest groups are diverse. Business people form interest groups; so do labour unions. Students form interest groups; so do parents and educators. Lawyers, prisoners, social agencies, ethnic and cultural groups, monarchists, artists—the list goes on.

Interest groups also use different methods and media to try to influence policy decisions: mailings, **petitions** (a written demand signed by many people), media interviews, appearances before government committees, advertising campaigns, demonstrations, meetings with government and party officials, and so on.

> **KEY QUESTION**
> How much influence should interest groups have in a democracy?

▶ FACE OFF Homelessness and Public Spaces

Policy Issue: A municipal government must decide how to deal with homeless people sleeping in public places.

Policy Background: In the 1980s and 1990s, governments adopted policies to reduce spending. Social programs were cut back. In large Canadian cities, large numbers of homeless people began to appear. This hadn't been seen in decades.

Today, across Canada, homeless people are sleeping on street grates and in building entries, parks, and public squares. The Federation of Canadian Municipalities has declared homelessness a "national disaster."

Policy Options: As many as 2,000 homeless people sleep on the streets of Anycity each night. Another 4,000 sleep in emergency shelters. More than 100 people sleep in the city hall square. City council meets to find a solution. Two sides emerge during the debate: "Tough Love" and "Have a Heart."

FIGURE 4.4 After attending classes, a 15-year-old volunteer stocks a food hamper at a Toronto homeless shelter. Which side of the debate would you say she is on?

Tough Love

- Short-term help isn't enough. Deal with the causes of homelessness (abuse, addiction, mental illness, unemployment).
- Volunteers who give blankets and food only encourage homeless people to stay on the streets.
- People have a right to walk in public places without stepping around bodies.
- Homeless people make public places unsafe and unclean.
- Homeless people victimize businesses, tourists, and residents.
- Sleeping in public places should be outlawed.
- Police should take vagrants to shelters. If vagrants refuse, they should be taken to jail.

Have a Heart

- Forcing homeless people into shelters or jail violates the rights of society's most vulnerable members.
- Forcing homeless people out of public spaces puts them at risk in unsafe hiding places.
- Government should build affordable housing or subsidize (help to pay) rents.
- Many of the homeless fear theft, fights, or disease in shelters.

- Governments must provide more medical, counselling, and social services.
- Spending 1 percent of government budgets on affordable housing would end homelessness.

What Do You Think?

1. Good policy making requires consultation. List at least 10 stakeholders that councillors should consult before making a decision. Try it alone, then work in pairs, and share your results.
2. In creating policy, politicians need to look for solutions, not arguments. Working in pairs or in groups, make three lists:
   a) List all the points on which Tough Love and Have a Heart agree.
   b) List points on which they absolutely disagree.
   c) In the middle, make a list of points where you find parts of the policy may be acceptable to both sides.
   d) Come up with a three- to five-point policy based on your "middle way."

Interest groups can also be called **lobby groups** and **pressure groups**. Regardless of the name, the goals are the same: to influence policy makers to support the group's position.

COMPETING INTERESTS

The more contact an interest group has with government, the greater its chances of influencing policy. Pressure/lobby groups compete to communicate regularly with government.

While developing its policies on the *Kyoto Protocol*, the Canadian government was lobbied by Greenpeace and the Canadian Environmental Law Association. These groups strongly supported Kyoto. The Canadian Council of Chief Executives and the Alliance of Manufacturers and Exporters also lobbied—against Kyoto. They feared that Kyoto would cost businesses billions of dollars and lead to huge job losses. The interests of both sides had to be balanced.

FIGURE 4.5 A theatrical Greenpeace protest in Ottawa in 2005 pressures the government to implement the *Kyoto Protocol.* How might polar bears be affected by global warming?

An interest group may be **non-partisan** (have no formal ties with political parties) yet include people with similar political views. The National Citizens Coalition (NCC) and the Canadian Centre for Policy Alternatives (CCPA) are two examples. Both represent large numbers of voters, but at opposite ends of the political spectrum. Both groups study policy and government very closely.

THE WEB

Learn more about the NCC and CCPA and where to place them on the political spectrum at www.emp.ca/civics

A SPECTRUM OF INFLUENCE

Some interest groups can afford to hire professional lobbyists, who make their living representing interest groups. Some professional lobbyists are former politicians or civil servants—insiders who know whom to talk to and how to contact them.

Sometimes interest groups are umbrella organizations. For example, the Insurance Bureau of Canada promotes the interests of many insurance companies. The bureau gives member companies a stronger voice influencing policies than each would have separately. Insurance companies may want limits on the amount a person can collect (liability) on a claim, or new rules on investments.

Ordinary citizens form interest groups, too. Neither rich nor powerful, these people join together to make a difference. For example, young drivers might form an organization to pressure insurance companies to lower automobile insurance rates.

LITERACY COACH

Use the "think-aloud" method as you read about CivicStar Annie Kidder or any other CivicStar in this book. To use this method, write down what you are thinking about as you read. This is a way of taking notes about the text. Here is an example:

In 1996 [I was 6] , Annie Kidder was a classroom parent volunteer [just like my mom] . When she learned that her children's school had to hold fundraisers to buy mathematics textbooks [seems unfair—textbooks are not a frill. I wonder what happened next?] ...

CivicStar

ANNIE KIDDER: MOTHER WITH A CAUSE

In 1996, Annie Kidder was a classroom parent volunteer. When she learned that her children's school had to hold fundraisers to buy mathematics textbooks, Kidder joined with others to campaign for better funding for Ontario's public schools. Without seeking funding or support from school boards or teachers' unions, Kidder organized demonstrations. These grabbed media attention and put pressure on the government.

Kidder's group named itself People For Education, or P4E. The catchy name gained instant public identification, and P4E spread across the province. Now a charitable organization, P4E receives funding from individuals and other organizations.

P4E expresses a clear, popular belief: "Public education is the foundation of a civil society." It encourages parents and students to participate actively in education. Kidder and P4E provide information about all issues affecting public education. The organization sponsors conferences, public meetings, workshops, training for immigrant parents, and a speakers' bureau. It publishes newsletters and maintains a Web site and parents' network.

A totally independent interest group, P4E conducts research and collects data. Each year it produces a Tracking Report on such things as class sizes, computer access, buildings, and portables. It checks how education dollars are spent.

Annie Kidder was a student's mother who believed in a cause. She has become a respected and sought-after voice in education. When P4E is involved, and when Annie Kidder lobbies, people listen, the government reacts, and policy decisions are influenced.

Your Play

1. What motivated Annie Kidder to take action?
2. a) What steps did she take?
   b) How effective were these steps?
   c) Why are catchy names, slogans, and logos important tools for interest groups?
3. Visit the P4E Web site at www.emp.ca/civics and check out its criteria for proper school funding. Rate your school. If it gets a failing grade, what can you do about it?

PAUSE, REFLECT, APPLY

1. What is a lobbyist?
2. Interest groups try to inform and influence the public as well as politicians. Why is this important to them?
3. What is the difference between a professional lobbyist and someone like Annie Kidder?
4. By law, all professional lobbyists in Canada must sign up on a lobby registry. This allows the public to know who is lobbying and for what.

   a) Why is this law necessary?
   b) Why might the government do what a lobby wants, even if it is not a good policy for the majority of people? (Brainstorm and record examples.)

How Policy Becomes Law

Chapter 2 described the three levels of government: federal, provincial, and municipal. The process for creating laws, carefully set out in all three levels, is similar. Only the federal government, however, has a Senate. With this background, it is possible to trace how a policy becomes a law in the provincial and federal governments by studying the federal stages.

> ▶ **KEY QUESTION**
> What safeguards are in place to make sure that policies are well thought out before becoming law?

THE STAGES IN PASSING A FEDERAL BILL INTO LAW

1. From idea to bill

Proposals for laws begin with the prime minister (PM), cabinet ministers, and sometimes private members of Parliament (MPs who are not in the cabinet). The PM and cabinet discuss and decide which policies they want as law. Cabinet ministers are then responsible to see that the policies are carefully examined by public servants in their departments. A policy on taxes, for example, would go to the finance minister.

The minister ensures that the policy is drafted and checked by government lawyers. The legal document they produce is known as a **bill**. Cabinet solidarity requires all cabinet members to support a bill, even if they personally disagree with it.

2. First reading

The cabinet minister presents the bill to the House of Commons. There is no discussion, debate, or vote.

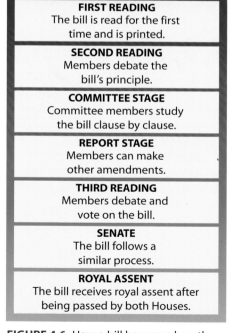

FIRST READING
The bill is read for the first time and is printed.

SECOND READING
Members debate the bill's principle.

COMMITTEE STAGE
Committee members study the bill clause by clause.

REPORT STAGE
Members can make other amendments.

THIRD READING
Members debate and vote on the bill.

SENATE
The bill follows a similar process.

ROYAL ASSENT
The bill receives royal assent after being passed by both Houses.

FIGURE 4.6 How a bill becomes law: the legislative process

3. Second reading

At this critical stage, all MPs can question the bill's purposes and consequences. The debate can take hours, days, or weeks. The government can set a time limit, but the opposition parties must agree.

4. Vote

After debate, the bill is voted on. If passed, it means that the bill is approved in principle. The bill then moves on to committee.

5. Committee and report stages

The bill is studied, clause by clause, by a **standing committee**. This group of MPs from all parties asks questions and invites public and expert input. It then reports and may recommend **amendments** (changes).

6. Voting on amendments

The bill is sent back to the House of Commons. Any amendments are introduced, debated, and voted on.

7. Third reading

There can be still more debate and more proposed amendments. Finally, a vote is taken.

8. The Senate (federal level only)

If passed, the bill goes to the Senate and goes through the same stages as in the Commons. The Senate, which is appointed, can delay or defeat the bill. In 1988, for example, the Senate refused to pass the Canada–US *Free Trade Agreement* so that a federal election could be held on the issue. An election was called, and the agreement was eventually passed. But by tradition, the Senate usually approves bills. After all, by this point bills have been approved by elected representatives. If the Senate proposes amendments, the revised bill returns to the Commons for another vote.

9. Royal assent

Finally, the governor general signs the bill, turning it into an act, and law. The assent reads, "Her Majesty, by and with the advice and consent of the Senate and House of Commons, enacts as follows … ." The governor general is appointed, not elected, and by tradition will not refuse to give assent. (At the provincial level, the lieutenant governor signs the bill.)

THE WEB ▶▶▶
Find out how a minority government can be brought down at www.emp.ca/civics

THE WEB ▶▶▶
To see different kinds of federal bills, go to www.emp.ca/civics

THE PASSAGE OF MUNICIPAL BYLAWS

Although there are different systems of municipal government across Canada, all are non-partisan. To become bylaws, municipal policies follow a similar process.

1. Elected councillors (or alderpersons) sit on various committees that oversee such areas as parks and recreation, planning and transportation, community services, and budget and finances.
2. Committees study policy proposals. Citizens are free to contact their councillors, attend committee meetings, and ask to address council meetings.
3. Bylaws pass through stages similar to the provincial and federal process: first reading; a second reading, with debate and public input; committee; final reading; vote. There is no Senate or royal assent.

PAUSE, REFLECT, APPLY

1. Why is a bill more likely to be defeated in a minority than in a majority government?
2. Who is responsible for the formal writing and preparing of a policy into a bill?
3. Who is responsible for presenting a bill to the House? What is this stage called?
4. A "standing committee" is basically the same in all three levels of government. Describe it.
5. The Senate has been called the "house of sober second thought." Do you think that this is a benefit in the passage of bills? Explain.
6. Based on the quotation from the royal assent (page 70), who might you think makes law in Canada?

Where Do I Come In?

Some people feel that one must be part of a larger group in order to be heard. They are mistaken. Here are some strategies you can use to be heard by governments.

> **KEY QUESTION**
Can ordinary citizens still influence government policies after elections?

CONTACT YOUR REPRESENTATIVE

The most direct access to government is through your local elected representative. You can contact him or her in various ways. Many organizations offer advice on how to do this effectively. Here are a few tips:

1. E-mails and faxes are easy to send (and easy to ignore).
2. Handwritten or typed letters to federal and provincial representatives are more personal and more effective:
   - Briefly and clearly relate your experience and concern.
   - Identify the specific law, regulation, policy, or program, and how you want it addressed.
3. Copy your letter to the minister or councillor responsible for the area that concerns you. He or she has great political power and needs to hear from citizens directly.

GET INVOLVED AT THE GRASSROOTS LEVEL

How can young people change the system, improve opportunities, or fight injustice if only older people pick the leaders—and are the leaders?

Earlier in this chapter, the grassroots membership of political parties was identified as a major influence on policy. It is a route that is open to all citizens, including youth. Most major political parties in Canada accept members from the age of 14.

Most parties have **youth wings**. These are meant to increase access for young members into the party. They can also focus youth power within the larger party. As convention and conference delegates, young members can influence leadership choices. They can also put forward resolutions.

Members of youth wings often become party leaders. Former prime ministers Brian Mulroney and Jean Chrétien—and Stephen Harper, current leader of the Conservative Party—were all members of youth wings.

THE ROLE OF PUBLIC OPINION POLLS

To win elections, parties like to know what citizens want. One way to do that is through surveys, or public opinion **polls**. Compas, Ekos, Environics, and Ipsos-Reid are among Canada's best-known polling companies and are often quoted in news reports.

By contacting as few as 1,000 people, pollsters can get an accurate snapshot of how all Canadians feel on an issue. The sample (the people interviewed) must be selected at random (not biased or skewed). **Random sampling** statistically ensures that each individual in a population has an equal chance of being selected.

Poll questions must be carefully designed. They must not lead people to respond in a certain way. To test the popularity of Prime Minister X, a pollster might ask: "Who is your favourite politician?" or "Do you prefer

THE WEB ►►►
For extensive federal and provincial contact information, go to www.emp.ca/civics

THE WEB ►►►
Find links to youth wings of major parties at www.emp.ca/civics

LITERACY COACH

Whenever you read poll results, check the questions asked, the sample size, and the margin of error.

X, Y, or Z for prime minister?" or "How would you rate X's effectiveness as prime minister: very good, good, fair, or poor?"

Polls have a **margin of error**. For example, a poll shows that party leader X has 52 percent approval and Y has 48 percent. The margin of error is plus or minus 5 percent. In other words, X might actually have 47 percent to Y's 53 percent! It is wise to view polling data as having a range.

A poll is very different from an election or a **referendum** (a direct vote on an issue or policy). Polls do not involve ballots, and governments are not obliged to make laws based on poll results.

THE WEB ▶ ▶ ▶
For more information on pollsters and polling, go to www.emp.ca/civics

---

CivicStar

FIGURE 4.7 Lester Pearson at a Montreal Expos baseball game in 1970

LESTER PEARSON: SUPERMAN IN A BOW TIE?

Lester Pearson (1897–1972) was often modest in person. But as a Canadian diplomat, policy maker, and politician, he was a world giant.

The government under Prime Minister Lester Pearson (1963–1968) achieved the extraordinary. It showed politicians taking account of different perspectives and popular opinion and still making major policy decisions based on principles.

Pearson never led a majority government. His policies had to win support from at least one other party. Usually, this was the New Democratic Party.

Pearson governed at a time when groups that had felt powerless were speaking out. Francophone Canadians, Aboriginal peoples, and women were all demanding political change. Immigration was overturning traditions. Canada was becoming multicultural.

Already a Nobel Prize–winning diplomat, Pearson was trained to listen and to try to satisfy all stakeholders. That can be a superhuman challenge in politics. Pearson was criticized for being indecisive or too easily influenced.

In 1963, Pearson set up the Royal Commission on Bilingualism and Biculturalism. Eventually, it opened up opportunities for francophone Canadians in the public service, society, business, and education. Pearson brought prominent Quebeckers into cabinet, such as Pierre Trudeau.

The 1967 Royal Commission on the Status of Women sought to give "women equal opportunities with men in every aspect of Canadian society."

Pearson introduced major new social welfare policies, including the Canada Pension Plan and the Canada Assistance Plan. Most controversial of all, the *Medical Care Act* provided medical coverage for every Canadian. Today, universal health care is as much a part of the Canadian identity as the Maple Leaf flag.

Facing fierce opposition, Pearson unified the Canadian navy, army, and air force into the Canadian Armed Forces. Finally, under Pearson, and after furious debates, Canada adopted the Maple Leaf flag, replacing the British Union Jack.

Pearson retired in 1968. At the Liberal leadership convention that year, he said, "[A leader is] expected to be a combination of Abraham Lincoln and Batman, to perform instant miracles. Then, when the poor chap can't live up to this, the process of demolition begins so that another superman can be erected in the ruins."

Your Play

List Pearson's new policies. Beside each, describe three stakeholders that were affected, and explain in what ways.

Government by Numbers?

Would government based on polls be good government? Chapter 1 described how majority opinion does not always lead to achieving the common good. Besides, public opinion changes, sometimes overnight. Polls cannot predict how people will feel in the future.

In the end, citizens expect parties and governments to stay informed about issues. Then, representatives and leaders must do what they feel and reason is right—even if it is unpopular. As US President Harry Truman once advised a young politician: "Always do right. This will please some and surprise the rest."

PAUSE, REFLECT, APPLY

1. Find the names of your municipal, provincial, and federal elected representatives.
2. Why is a letter more effective than an e-mail in getting the attention of a member of Parliament or a cabinet minister?
3. a) What is a public opinion poll?
   b) What features ensure a poll's accuracy?
4. Identify two major differences between a poll and a referendum.
5. Politicians use polls to see what voters like and dislike. Why are non-politicians interested in polls?
6. Search the Web sites of the polling companies named on page 72. Select one or two polls being reported. Describe what the information says to you about an issue or policy.

REPLAY ▪ ▫ ▪ ▫ ▪ ▫ ▪ ▪ ▪ ▪ ▪

This chapter has informed you of these civics concepts:

1. Effective policy makers consult large numbers of stakeholders and experts.
2. Government policies are affected by many influences.
3. Policies are seldom a choice between right and wrong; they are usually a choice between what is better under the circumstances.
4. Bills pass into law in the federal, provincial, and municipal levels of government through a series of steps.
5. Citizens can use a variety of means and strategies to influence government.

CIVICS ▣ TOOLKIT How to Look for and Detect Different Points of View

When looking for information about an issue, it is important to know the points of view of the sources you find. Consider this ancient parable (story) from India.

Six blind people were asked to describe an elephant by touching the elephant's body. Each one touched a different part: the side, the tusk, the trunk, the leg, the ear, and the tail. In turn, each declared the animal to be like a wall, a spear, a snake, a tree, a fan, and a rope. The moral of the parable? Though each person was partly right, all of them were wrong.

All sources have a perspective and thus some **bias** (one-sidedness). You cannot eliminate it. However, you can recognize the perspectives of your sources. You can also look at an issue from many different perspectives.

Here is a checklist to help you find different perspectives:

- Identify a variety of stakeholders.
- Locate different reports and source different media.
- Find sources from different regions.
- Opinions change over time; look at sources from different time periods.

Here is a checklist to assess perspective and bias:

- What do stakeholders have to gain or lose?
- How knowledgeable is the source?
- What is the source's reputation?
- Is the source connected to a political party or group?
- Do an Internet search to check the credentials of unfamiliar sources.
- Is the source *primary* (original) or *secondary* (interpretive or analytical)?
- Is the perspective *subjective* (opinion) or *objective* (unbiased, fact)?
- Check where and when news items were written.

Skill Practice

1. Review the Face Off feature on page 66. Identify the stakeholders. Playing the role of a reporter, identify a new stakeholder that you would wish to speak to. Explain that new perspective.

2. In 1995, the federal government introduced Bill C-68 in response to the 1989 mass killing by a gunman of 14 female students in Montreal. Enacted in 1995, the *Firearms Act* requires all people in Canada who own firearms to register them. The original cost of the gun registry was estimated at $119 million. It has cost more than $2 billion. Describe the possible perspectives of these stakeholders on the *Firearms Act*:
   a) an MP
   b) a gun collector
   c) a hunter
   d) the sister or brother of one of the women killed in Montreal
   e) the Canadian Association of Chiefs of Police
   f) the Law-abiding Unregistered Firearms Association.

3. Find three very different perspectives on a current news event from very different sources. Consider using news media, Web sites of parties and interest groups, and so on. Identify different viewpoints. Think: why do these differences occur?

STUDY HALL

Informed Citizenship

1. Explain the relationship among policy, platform, bill, and act.

2. Identify five different factors that influence policy decisions. Explain how each factor exerts influence.

3. A municipal bylaw to force street people to sleep in shelters has been proposed. As a municipal councillor, write a) an argument in favour of the policy and b) an argument opposed to the policy.

4. a) What is a lobby group?

   b) Why does the government have a lobby registry that is accessible to the public?

5. a) Review the stages of passing a bill into law. At what points do you, as a citizen, have the best opportunity to be heard?

   b) What would you have to do to be heard?

   c) How would you know if anyone was listening?

Purposeful Citizenship

6. Canadian society faces the same issues again and again. Using one of the following issues, prepare a two- to three-minute speech or audio-visual presentation. The topic: "How do policy choices we face today compare with policy decisions made in the past?" Research the issue using your history texts, the library, and the Internet. State your position clearly. Use the past as an example of a policy's good or bad consequences.

Issues

- (80 Years Ago) Should marijuana use be decriminalized today? Compare today's debates with prohibition debates in Ontario from 1916 to 1927. What can be learned from the past?

- (70 Years Ago) What policies are needed to deal with the homeless today? How do they compare with homeless policies during the Great Depression of the 1930s?

- (40 Years Ago and Recent) What should Canada's policy be regarding participation in US missile defence? Compare the decision of Paul Martin's government in 2005 with the Bomarc debates of 1963. Compare the positions of Lester Pearson, John Diefenbaker, and Tommy Douglas with those of Paul Martin, Stephen Harper, and Jack Layton. Compare Canadian attitudes to President John F. Kennedy and President George W. Bush. How did these influence policy decisions?

Active Citizenship

7. Conduct a poll in two classes other than your own. Try two questions: a *closed question*, such as, "Should students be able to elect their principal?" and an *open question*, such as, "If an election were held today, whom would you vote for as principal of your school?" Select a scale and make a graph of the poll results. Do you believe that the school board would follow your wishes?

8. Your instructor will divide the class into three groups: Liberal, Conservative, and New Democrat. You and the other members of your group must use the Internet or telephone to contact a party, youth wing, or riding association. Find out

   a) how to join

   b) membership requirements

   c) youth group activities

   d) how young members and youth groups get their issues into party platforms.

   A possible followup: Write a letter to the party leader about whether your research experience was helpful or unhelpful in finding out about the party's policies.

UNIT 2

Government and the People

CHAPTER 5
How Do Citizens Elect Governments?

Iraqi villagers line up to vote in spite of the threat of attacks by insurgents intent on disrupting the election.

What You Need to Know

- How does government share power to meet citizens' needs and resolve conflicts?
- How are governments elected in Canada?
- What is the role of political parties in the parliamentary process? How do the roles differ for majority and minority governments?
- How can your beliefs and values shape your participation in civic life?
- How can citizens participate to resolve public issues?
- How can you ask questions to find information and detect bias?

Key Terms

representative democracies
direct democracies
chief electoral officer
constituency
franchise
majority government
minority government
first past the post (FPTP)
proportional representation (PR)
bias

Key Question

Do elections produce governments that truly represent the people?

On January 30, 2005, the people of Iraq voted in their first election since the overthrow of dictator Saddam Hussein in 2003. Iraq suffered under Hussein's brutal authoritarian rule for many years. US and British forces invaded Iraq, defeated the Iraqi military, and occupied the country. When elections were held for the new, democratic government, people turned out to vote in surprisingly large numbers, under conditions of great danger.

In such a state of civil disorder and violence, will Iraqis be able to establish and maintain the democracy they want?

Voting

Democracy is the process by which people choose the man who'll get the blame.
                    —Bertrand Russell (1872–1970), English philosopher

Voting in an election has been called the single most important act of political participation in a democracy. Democracies today are **representative democracies**, not the **direct democracies** first developed in the small cities and towns of ancient Greece. Modern nations are too large to assemble all citizens to debate and vote on all laws affecting them. Instead, citizens elect representatives to exercise their power of debate and policy making. That power includes sending their citizens to war, as the US president and Congress did when they committed their nation and thousands of troops to the invasion of Iraq. What checks are there on the great power given by citizens to their representatives in a democracy?

CHECKS ON REPRESENTATIVES' POWERS

Candidates make promises to the electorate during election campaigns. Not all such promises will be kept. It is important that elections be held frequently to ensure that representatives are responsive to the electorate. Canadian federal and provincial representatives must hold an election at least every five years. Municipal politicians are elected every three years.

Additional methods have been suggested to make our representatives more accountable. These will be considered later in the chapter. First, let's look at how elections are run today.

THE ELECTION PROCESS

The prime minister (in the case of a federal election) or premier (in a provincial election) chooses the best time to call an election within the five-year limit. Elections also occur when a minority government is defeated in the legislature (see Majority and Minority Governments, page 86).

For a federal election, the prime minister asks the governor general to call a general election. It must be held within 36 days of that announcement. Election day is always on a Monday unless there is a statutory holiday, which moves it to a Tuesday.

The **chief electoral officer**, who is head of Elections Canada, mobilizes thousands of permanent and temporary workers to prepare for the election. Voting locations are reserved in schools and community centres, individuals are hired to supervise voting, and ballot boxes are sent out to the 308 ridings across Canada.

Notices are delivered or mailed to voters telling them where to go to vote. Instructions on where to vote are included for people who may be travelling on Election Day and wish to vote ahead of time in advance polls. Canada has a permanent voters' list drawn from government income tax information, driver's licences, and other sources containing citizens' addresses.

The campaign begins in earnest as the candidates and their political parties use newspapers, radio, and television advertisements to promote their platforms (the policies they will introduce if elected). Party leaders travel the country to support their candidates, speak at rallies in towns and cities, and engage in television debates.

On Election Day, polling stations are open for 12 hours. By law, all employees are allowed three consecutive hours to vote with no loss of pay. After showing some identification, voters are given a ballot by the

☐ **DISCUSSION POINT**

Should Canadians be given the right to vote at age 16?

FIGURE 5.1 A prisoner in the Montreal Detention Centre casts his ballot in the 2004 federal election. All inmates in federal and provincial prisons have the right to vote.

deputy returning officer who is in charge of the polling station. A poll clerk strokes the voter's name off the voters' list. The voter moves to a booth and chooses one of the candidates by marking an X on the ballot. The voter then drops the ballot in a ballot box in full view of the poll clerk.

After the polls close, the votes are counted by the deputy returning officer and poll clerk. Scrutineers—members of political parties whose candidates are on the ballot—are present to witness the count.

The candidate with the most votes becomes the member of Parliament (MP) for that riding. If the vote is especially close between candidates, the ballots may be recounted.

Who Can Vote?

Qualifying to vote in a federal election is simple: one must be a Canadian citizen over the age of 18. The same rule applies to provincial elections, with the further requirement that the citizen be a resident of the riding or **constituency** where the vote is taking place.

PAUSE, REFLECT, APPLY

1. Who, in theory, has the power to call a federal election? Who actually makes the decision?
2. What circumstances might require a voter to use an advance poll?
3. Why is a voters' list necessary for a proper election?
4. All ballots are numbered with a set number given to each polling station. Why is this measure necessary?
5. What purpose is served by scrutineers?
6. All ballots judged to be spoiled (improperly marked) are kept in case of a recount. What kinds of mistakes might a voter make in marking a ballot, causing it to be judged spoiled?
7. Are Canadian elections fair and free of fraud? Do they produce a government that represents our wishes? Give your opinion from what you have studied so far.

Elections in Canada

Compared with today, voting at the time of Confederation was undemocratic, and election practices were corrupt. In 1867 the vote was limited to male, British citizens over the age of 21 who owned property. This excluded large numbers of people—women, renters, minorities, and Aboriginal peoples—who can vote today.

> **KEY QUESTION**
>
> Is Canada a vigorous democracy with widespread voting participation, and political parties that excite and engage Canadians?

FIGURE 5.2 Important events in the franchise in Canada

■ **1867**
—all property-owning males of British ancestry may vote
—provinces produce voters' lists (women, minorities, Aboriginal peoples cannot vote)

■ **1885**
—federal government takes control of national vote, removes property qualification
—provinces continue to exclude some people from voting

■ **1916**
—women gain vote in provinces of Manitoba, Saskatchewan, Alberta

■ **1917**
—women related to soldiers, Aboriginal soldiers gain national vote
—national vote taken from central Europeans

■ **1918**
—all women gain national vote

■ **1920**
—citizens over 21 years of age gain vote
—first chief electoral officer appointed
—Asians and Aboriginal peoples on reserves cannot vote

■ **1934**
—Inuit lose vote

■ **1948**
—Asians gain vote

■ **1950**
—Inuit gain vote

■ **1960**
—Aboriginal peoples on reserves gain vote

■ **1982**
—right to vote embedded in new constitution

■ **1987**
—citizens over 18 years of age gain vote

■ **1993**
—prisoners serving less than two years, mentally disabled gain vote

■ **2002**
—Supreme Court strikes down law barring penitentiary inmates from voting in federal elections

There were also several voting days across Canada instead of one. The first election day would be chosen by the government in ridings where it stood the best chance of winning. The idea was to spread the news of the government's win to other areas to encourage voters to elect government candidates! In addition, balloting was not kept secret. Because the number of voters in a riding was small—about 750 on average—candidates knew most voters personally and could influence their vote.

Denying the right to vote (the **franchise**) was used as a weapon several times against minorities in Canada. In 1885, Asians were denied the right to vote. During World War I (1914–1918), the government extended the vote to groups likely to support its policy of conscripting men for war, and took it away from groups likely to oppose it. Women were finally permitted to vote in federal elections in 1918, but various provinces took longer to grant them that right. Hindus, Chinese, and Aboriginal Canadians were excluded from voting for the first half of the 20th century.

Today, the vote has been extended to all Canadian citizens over 18 years of age, to all prison inmates, and to the mentally challenged. Voting stations everywhere must have facilities to allow blind and disabled citizens to exercise their right to vote.

CANADA'S RECENT VOTING RECORD

The percentage of Canadians voting in federal elections has been in steady decline for a number of years.

Mandatory Voting

Following the 2000 federal election, Canada's chief electoral officer said that Parliament might have to pass a law requiring citizens to vote if the Canadian voter participation rate continues to fall.

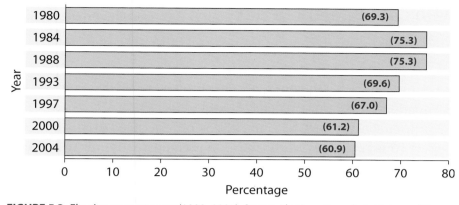

FIGURE 5.3 Election turnout rates (1980–2004). *Source: Elections Canada,* A History of the Vote in Canada.

Voter turnout for the 2004 election was little more than 60 percent, the lowest in Canada's history. Such a dismal participation rate gives Canada one of the worst records among the 29 industrialized countries in the Organisation for Economic Co-operation and Development, ahead of only Poland, Switzerland, and the United States.

According to a 2004 study published in the *Canadian Parliamentary Review*, the participation rate in Australia, where voting is mandatory, is 94 percent. Voting is also compulsory in Belgium and Greece, where the turnout rates are 92 percent and 80 percent, respectively.

▶ **DID YOU KNOW** ◀

Women did not receive the right to vote in Quebec provincial elections until 1940, more than 20 years after they received the right in other provinces.

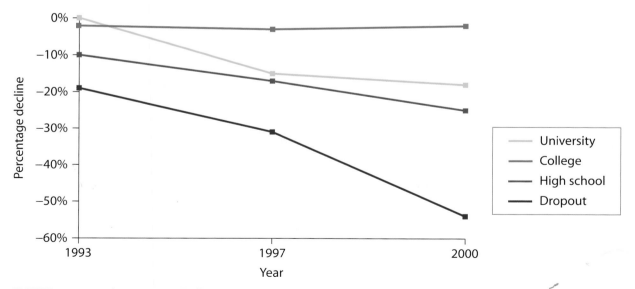

FIGURE 5.4 Turned out or turned off? Percentage decline in youth participation in voting, by level of education. The turnout in 1993 among those with some college education is used as the benchmark. *Source: Elections Canada,* Electoral Insight, *July 2003, p. 10.*

☐ **DISCUSSION POINT**
History books talk about the Fathers of Confederation in 1867. Why were there no Mothers of Confederation?

WHO CAN RUN FOR OFFICE?

Any Canadian citizen can run for political office. The candidate

1. must be 18 years of age or older
2. must collect the signatures of at least 100 other citizens on the nomination form
3. must deposit $1,000 with an election official called a returning officer (this amount is refundable if the candidate submits receipts for allowable election expenses)
4. does not have to live in the riding or constituency he or she intends to represent
5. does not have to be a member of a political party. However, most candidates are, and must show proof of their official party nomination. A candidate who is not a member of a political party is classified as an independent.

WHAT DO POLITICAL PARTIES STAND FOR?

A political party has a central core of beliefs that define it. The terms "left," "right," and "centre" are used to define the differences in beliefs among political parties. A good way to understand the differences between these positions is to consider their attitude toward change.

A party on the left is dissatisfied with the present conditions of society (the status quo). It sees inequalities of income between people as too great. It believes that government should actively reduce these inequalities, regulate business behaviour, and provide more social programs.

A party on the right is cautious about change, particularly when it comes to government spending and regulation. It values social order and tends to support traditional institutions such as the conventional family, religion, the military, and the police.

A party at the centre combines beliefs from both left and right, depending on the issue. It is generally satisfied with the status quo, but will advocate change it deems beneficial. Parties on the left criticize centrist parties for not going far enough for needed changes. Parties on the right criticize centrist parties for going too far for change.

FIGURE 5.5 The Canadian political spectrum

Left		Centre		Right
◀ NDP	Bloc Québécois		Liberal Party	Conservative Party ▶

No Canadian political party can be placed on the extreme left or right. In fact, the policies of the main parties often overlap. (See also Figure 3.8 on page 55.)

PAUSE, REFLECT, APPLY

1. a) Consider requirements 1, 2, 3, and 5 governing who can run for political office. Think of a reason why each requirement helps ensure that only serious candidates run for office.
   b) Give your opinion on requirement 4. Should candidates have to live in the riding they seek to represent?
2. Predict where a party of the left, right, or centre might stand on each of the following issues:

   a) a nationally funded daycare system
   b) lower tuition fees for postsecondary students
   c) same-sex marriage
   d) lower business taxes
   e) greater search powers for police.

3. Does having a choice of political parties help citizens elect governments that truly represent their wishes? What if there were no political parties?

Political Parties in Canada

> **KEY QUESTION**
>
> Is Canadian democracy better served with several political parties, or with two? Does our electoral system need to be changed?

Political parties are organizations that try to elect individuals to public office to control the machinery of government. A person nominated by a party receives publicity, campaign workers, and financial help in an election. Parties are not mentioned in the constitutions of most democracies. Their powers do not come from laws but from the support of voters. Voters can eliminate a party in an election, or create new parties. Canada has done both.

For most of Canada's history, two political parties dominated federal politics: the Liberals and the Conservatives. The Conservatives held power for most of the period from Confederation in 1867 to the beginning of

FIGURE 5.6 Seats in Parliament as percentage of vote, 2004 federal election

Liberals (leader, Paul Martin)	135 seats	
Conservatives (leader, Stephen Harper)	99 seats	
Bloc Québécois (leader, Gilles Duceppe)	54 seats	
New Democratic Party (leader, Jack Layton)	19 seats	
Independent	1 seat	
Total	308 seats	

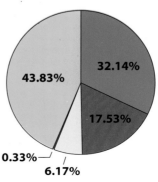

□ **DISCUSSION POINT**
After the 1993 election, the federal Parliament was nicknamed "the pizza Parliament." Why did the nickname stick?

the 1900s. For most of the 20th century, the Liberal Party has held power. A smaller party, the Co-operative Commonwealth Federation (CCF), later renamed the New Democratic Party (NDP), was formed in the 1930s. Then in the 1993 election, two new parties—the western-based Reform Party (later the Canadian Alliance) and a Quebec-based separatist party, the Bloc Québécois—won over 50 seats each, while the Progressive Conservatives won only two. Until 2004, there were five major political parties (with the Liberals holding the majority of seats). Today, four major political parties contend for power at the federal level.

MAJORITY AND MINORITY GOVERNMENTS

To form a **majority government**, a party must win one-half of Canada's 308 ridings, plus one more (155). With this number, the party forms the government and has enough votes to pass legislation it wishes to see made into law. Most of the time party members vote to support their party's legislation. If important legislation proposed by the government is defeated in Parliament, the prime minister and cabinet must resign (see **non-confidence**, Chapter 4, page 70). Majority governments are seldom forced into an election.

Because Canada has several major parties, it is possible for one party to win more seats than each of the others, but not win a majority of seats.

FIGURE 5.7 What statement is the cartoonist making about minority governments?

This is exactly what Canada faced after the 2004 election. The Liberals had 139 seats, 16 short of a majority. They had a **minority government**, one that governed and proposed legislation, but was dependent on the support of other parties. The legislation that the Liberals proposed could be opposed by one of the supporting parties, leading to defeat, resignation, and another election. As you can see, minority governments lack the stability of majority governments.

TWO-PARTY AND MULTIPARTY SYSTEMS

If Canada had only two parties, every government would be a majority government (the chances of a tie with an even number of seats out of 308 are remote). A two-party system has the advantage of offering a clear choice between two leaders and two party platforms. It offers stability by avoiding the uncertainty of a minority government. The United States, Britain, New Zealand, and Australia have two-party systems.

The multiparty system, however, offers the public a wider choice of policies, even if it produces less stable minority governments. But there is another argument used against both two-party and multiparty systems. It is that our voting system, called **first past the post (FPTP)**, is unfair and undemocratic and should be replaced by a **proportional representation (PR)** system (see Face Off, page 91).

Interest Groups

Voting in an election is not the only way that citizens can make changes in a democracy. Another way is to form a pressure or interest group. This is a group of citizens who hold a common goal (such as Greenpeace, which pressures government to pass laws to preserve the environment) or are members of a particular occupation (such as the Canadian Medical Association, which represents Canadian doctors on health care issues). Pressure groups try to influence governments to pass laws favouring their goals or interests. (See also Chapter 4, pages 67–68.)

Interest groups hold private meetings with top civil servants in government, send representatives to parliamentary committees, and advertise in the media to try to influence government.

Supporters say that interest groups provide specialized information that representatives need to make important decisions and pass laws. Critics say that some groups are too powerful and enjoy unfair influence on government decision making.

CIVICSTAR

JOE OPATOWSKI

Joe Opatowski ... walked away from a troubled home life to inspire tens of thousands of schoolchildren to help change the world. ... [He] criss-crossed North America for Leaders Today, a group associated with Free the Children, an organization founded by Toronto-area activists Craig and Marc Kielburger. ... He had just given a speech [in October 2004] to schoolchildren in Buffalo, New York when, driving home ... , he died in a car accident. ... In one year alone, Opatowski is estimated to have spoken before 100,000 children... .

His message was repeated again and again: The young people of today have an obligation to care for one another and to care for the less fortunate.

> — Excerpted from Phinjo Gombu, "He Changed Himself: Then He Started Changing the World" (obituary), *The Toronto Star*, November 4, 2004

Joe Opatowski's story is perhaps best told in his own words:

Riverton, Jamaica. I'm bouncing down a country road in a bus with a group of volunteers, ready to "get involved"... . On either side of the bus were piles and piles of garbage. Suddenly one of the piles moved. A flap opened and out climbed a young boy and an old man. The flap of garbage was the front door to their home. ...

Out of breath and seriously thirsty, I wandered over to a street vendor and bought a carton of juice. As I raised it to my mouth, I noticed a small boy with big shining eyes staring up at me. ... Guilt quickly kept me from drinking the juice. I handed him the carton. ...

I expected a look of gratitude, but instead I watched ... him walk toward the other children, carton in hand. I couldn't believe my own eyes as I saw this ... poor little boy making sure that each of his friends had an equal sip. ...To this day, I am left with the fact that I, a kid from North America, took a sip of that juice before a 6-year-old kid who lived in a garbage dump.

I quickly realized that it wasn't all about me, after all. I wasn't the only victim. ... [I]n this case, ... a poverty-stricken little boy—wasn't just surviving. He was *aliving*. This was a lesson I would never forget.

> — From "My Story: Joe Opatowski," in *Me to We: Turning Self-Help on Its Head*, compiled by Craig and Marc Kielburger (Toronto: Wiley, 2004, pp. 187–189)

Your Play

1. In your own words, explain why meeting the Jamaican child confirmed Joe Opatowski's activism. Do you think Opatowski's difficult background played any part in turning him into the **activist** that he was?
2. What contribution do people such as Opatowski make in dealing with large problems such as child poverty around the world?
3. Do you think that people such as Joe Opatowski can help the situation of the world's poor children? What other steps must be taken?
4. Suggest other inspirational individuals or groups who help mobilize opinion on social injustices.

PAUSE, REFLECT, APPLY

1. a) How do political parties help candidates become elected?

   b) Why does an independent candidate find it difficult to win an election?

2. a) State the difference between a majority and minority government in terms of numbers.

   b) Why do multiparty systems sometimes produce minority governments?

3. Minority governments are sometimes criticized for being weak. Others say they are more responsive to the electorate as a whole. What do you think?

4. What is one advantage of a multiparty system? a two-party system?

5. What is an interest group? What value do interest groups have to the democratic process?

Electoral Reform

Since the 1990s, groups such as Fair Vote Canada, Every Vote Counts (Prince Edward Island), and Mouvement pour une démocratie nouvelle (Quebec) have effectively lobbied for electoral reform. A number of factors have contributed to Canadians' dissatisfaction with the first-past-the-post voting system:

- *Lack of representation.* Since the 1993 federal election, many political parties have competed for Canadian votes. Critics argue that voters who choose to support one of the smaller parties are not fairly represented in Parliament.

- *Declining voter turnout.* Voter turnout at federal elections has been declining steadily since 1988. An Elections Canada survey found that many people did not vote because they felt the election result was already decided. Supporters of electoral reform believe that people would be more likely to vote if they felt that the number of seats a party held more closely represented its percentage of the popular vote.

- *Controversial election results.* British Columbia's progress in election reform was fired by voter anger over the controversial results of the 1996 provincial election. In that election, the New Democratic Party won a majority of seats and formed the government despite the fact that the Liberal Party received a higher percentage of the popular vote. Similarly, the Parti Québécois won the 1998 Quebec election, even though the Liberal Party had a higher percentage of the votes.

- *Ineffective opposition.* The call for electoral reform has sometimes been a response to "landslide" election victories. Some voters feel unrepresented when the winning party is left to govern without effective opposition in Parliament. In the 1987 New Brunswick election, the Liberal Party won all 58 of the province's seats. In the 2000 election in Prince Edward Island, the Progressive Conservatives won 26 of 27 seats.

In October 2004, the federal government promised to examine the issue of electoral reform. In November of the same year, the Ontario government announced that it would appoint citizens to study the province's electoral system and to make recommendations for reform. The province of Quebec is expected to introduce electoral reform legislation in 2005.

THE BC INITIATIVE

In 2003, the BC provincial government established an independent commission of citizens to examine the province's electoral system. The British Columbia Citizens' Assembly studied the province's existing electoral system (first past the post) as well as alternative systems. It held public consultations to decide whether to keep the current system or to recommend a new system compatible with Canada's Parliament.

In December 2004, the Citizens' Assembly delivered its report. It proposed a new electoral system—proportional representation. The Citizens' Assembly felt the new system would produce more proportional results, give voters more choice and control, and strengthen local representation.

THE WEB ▶▶▶
Learn more about BC's Citizens' Assembly at www.emp.ca/civics

REFERENDA

A referendum is a form of direct democracy because it allows voters, rather than elected representatives, to vote on a particular issue. A referendum can take the form of a single question (requiring a yes or no answer) or a number of alternatives (from which voters must choose). Dramatic examples are the Quebec referenda in 1980 and 1995. The Parti Québécois asked the Quebec electorate to decide—Yes/Oui or No/Non—whether to separate the province from the rest of Canada. The referendum campaigns were emotional and hard fought. In 1980, over 60 percent of Québécois voted No/Non, but in 1995, the margin of victory for the No/Non side was less than 1 percent.

▶ FACE OFF   **A New Electoral System for Canada?**

A study by the Institute for Research on Public Policy released in July 2000 found that 49% of Canadians find the current voting system unacceptable, compared to 23% who favour the current system.

> — Democracy Watch,
> www.dwatch.ca/camp/voterpt.html

Should Canada change its method of electing members of Parliament? Canada has always used the first-past-the-post (FPTP) election system, but criticism of it is mounting. Here is the problem. Suppose in a school with 500 students, four students ran for president of the Student Council. Candidate A received 200 votes; Candidate B received 100 votes; Candidate C received 125 votes; and Candidate D received 75 votes.

Under a FPTP system, Candidate A wins the election. He or she has the most votes and is first past the post, like the lead horse in a race. However, A has won only 40 percent (200/500 × 100 = 40%) of the votes cast. Sixty percent of the students did not vote for A (who does not have a majority of the votes, but still wins). Is this fair?

Critics say that FPTP is unfair. When there are more than two parties running, one party gains the majority of seats with less than a majority of the total votes cast—just as in the school election. These critics advocate replacing FPTP with proportional representation (PR).

> In the 24 federal elections since World War I, only three have resulted in majority governments that were actually elected by a majority of the votes cast!
>
> — Democracy Watch,
> www.dwatch.ca/camp/voterpt.html

A PR system divides up the seats according to the total percentage of votes each party receives. Voters must vote for a party, not a candidate. A party that receives 20 percent of the vote receives 20 percent of the seats. Then the party chooses candidates from party lists to fill those seats. In effect, MPs are chosen not by voters in ridings, but by the parties.

> Having been in New Zealand at the time of their first election under proportional representation, I am disappointed that some in Canada are advocating the same system, which would see MPs chosen, not by voters in ridings, but from closed party lists. This is an insult to the intelligence of voters.
>
> — Letter to CBC during 2004 federal
> election, www.cbc.ca/canadavotes/
> yourview/letters_w5.html

British Columbia is thinking of combining the FPTP and PR systems. The ballot will allow voters to choose candidates, but the governing party will be the one with the greatest percentage of the total votes cast throughout the province.

> Electoral reform proponents believe switching to an electoral system that uses ... [PR] will produce a fairer result and help voters feel that their vote matters. Today, most of the world's democracies use PR.... .
>
> — From "What Else Can Be Done to
> Encourage Canadians to Vote,"
> www.mapleleafweb.com/features/
> electoral/voter-turnout/
> what-can-be-done.html

What Do You Think?

1. Why is a PR system unnecessary if only two candidates or parties run in an election?
2. Explain how a PR system appears to be fairer when more than two parties are running in an election.
3. Some FPTP defenders say that PR encourages the formation of smaller parties and, thus, minority governments. Explain the link between the two. Do you think this is an argument in favour of PR or against it?

Critics argue that referenda

- undermine the authority of elected representatives in Parliament who are entrusted to make the laws of the country, subject to removal in the next election
- simplify complex issues to a yes or no answer, making compromise difficult
- can be used to convince the rest of the world that the electorate supports the government (the government obtains the referendum result it wants by using propaganda and intimidation)
- can be used against minorities in the name of majority sentiment. For example, in Quebec, the northern Aboriginal population believes that Quebec's separation from Canada would be illegal because it would include lands they claim belong to them.

PAUSE, REFLECT, APPLY

1. a) What does a voter vote for in a PR system?
   b) Whom does a voter vote for in a FPTP system? Which system do you think is fairer?
2. Why are referenda a form of direct democracy? Do you think they should be used more frequently or not?

REPLAY

This chapter has informed you of these civics concepts:

1. Frequent, fair elections are a check on the power that citizens give to their elected representatives to make decisions for them.
2. The standardized, careful procedures followed by election officials ensure that Canadian elections are fair and free of fraud.
3. Canada has evolved into a multiparty system expected to produce more minority governments than it has in the past.
4. Although the struggle to extend the vote to all Canadian citizens has been largely won, voter turnout is declining.
5. Voters are growing dissatisfied with the current (first-past-the-post) voting system and are considering other systems, such as proportional representation.

How to Identify Bias

Suppose you were given a civics assignment to cover a public meeting about the use of the local arena by minor hockey leagues. The issue is controversial, and public interest is high. The local cable television station and the local newspaper cover the meeting. You want to cover the story without **bias** (the slant or emphasis on certain facts that a news story or person expresses).

Sources can reflect bias in

- choice of headline to draw attention to the story
- placement of a story (front page or back pages)
- choice of visuals
- omission or inclusion of certain facts
- unwarranted or unsupported assumptions
- omission or labelling of some individuals or groups.

You write your account of the meeting as you saw it. Afterwards, you compare your account with the television and newspaper coverage. You might find that your memory and account differ from the other two sources. All three accounts reflect bias.

Bias can be intentional or unintentional. Unintentional bias sometimes happens because of the nature of the medium. Television is biased in favour of a good visual story, or evidence of conflict between individuals. Newspaper stories are biased in their choice of headline and their selection of facts in the lead paragraph intended to capture readers' attention. A newspaper editorial may go further, being intentionally biased in its selection of facts to support the point of view of the publishers.

With practice and awareness, you can learn to choose sources that give the fair and balanced coverage you need to make informed decisions.

Skill Practice

1. Bias can occur in news accounts by choice of words. Contrast the bias demonstrated by each of the following pairs of statements:
   a) "a handful of people protested the speaker's remarks" versus "loud jeers occurred when the speaker stated..."
   b) "a former convict was nabbed" versus "an individual charged a number of years ago for an offence was arrested"
   c) "a group of terrorists attacked a compound" versus "a group of rebels engaged in a fight with government forces"
2. Arrange with a classmate to buy two different newspapers on the same day. Compare the headlines and coverage of three events. Identify the slant or bias that each paper brings to the story.

STUDY HALL

Informed Citizenship

1. Consider the following quotation: "The people as a body cannot perform the business of government for themselves .... Limiting the duration of rule is ... an old and approved method of identifying the interests of those who rule with the interests of those who are ruled." (James Mill, English political philosopher, 1825)

   a) Explain Mill's statement in your own words.

   b) Who actually has the power to make decisions—the people or their representatives?

2. How are frequent elections a check on the power that voters give their representatives?

3. Pick out several procedures from the election process that are intended to ensure that elections are free from fraudulent practices.

4. Explain how the requirements for candidates in an election are intended to exclude individuals who are not truly serious about political office.

Purposeful Citizenship

5. The 2002 decision granting the vote to all prisoners was highly controversial. What is your opinion on it?

6. Consider a mock riding with 10,000 voters and four candidates representing four different parties. Show how a candidate could win with fewer than 5,000 votes.

7. Polls are taken often during election campaigns to estimate the percentage of voters supporting a party or candidate at that time. Do you think polls tend to influence voters? If so, should they be limited or banned? Give a reasoned opinion on this issue.

8. Politicians are often criticized for not keeping their election promises once they are elected. Their defence is that sometimes circumstances change after they come to office. What do you think? Do voters have the democratic right to insist that politicians carry out all their promises?

9. Voting in Australia is compulsory for all citizens. A fine is levied on non-voters who are unable to present a reasonable excuse. What do you think of this idea, considering that only 60 percent of Canadians eligible to vote did so in the 2004 federal election?

10. Most polls indicate that a majority of Canadians favour capital punishment. Yet the practice was abolished in 1976 by Parliament, and most observers agree it would never be reintroduced. Do you think all citizens should decide on capital punishment in a referendum? Make a case for or against this way of deciding the issue.

Active Citizenship

11. Elections Canada is active in many new democracies, supervising or helping people to organize a free and fair election. Imagine you are part of an election team sent to a new democracy in a developing country. These are the conditions:

    a) Many citizens cannot read.

    b) Villages are remote, and few citizens own transportation.

    c) People are intimidated by authority and authoritarian figures.

    d) Women's votes are subject to male influence.

    e) Local citizens have difficulty obtaining information about each candidate.

    Is the situation hopeless for a democratic election? Suggest ways you believe some of these problems could be overcome.

CHAPTER 6

What Are Rights and Responsibilities?

A land of freedom? You're kidding, right?

What You Need to Know

- What are the origins of rights and responsibilities?
- What are Canadians' rights and responsibilities?
- Why are rights and freedoms limited?
- What are Canadians' Charter freedoms?
- What are Canadians' Charter rights?
- What happens when the rights of two or more people clash?
- How can you break down information from books, newspapers, and reports?

Key Terms

freedoms	reasonable limits
privacy rights	common good
rights	democratic rights
responsibilities	equality rights
mobility rights	disability rights

"A land of freedom? You're kidding, right? I'm pierced, my hair's blue, and I get hassled all the time about my jeans hanging too low on my backside. My friend Dave got suspended for getting a tattoo. That's unfair—you can cover them up! Another friend, Karla, got a $110 fine for supposedly smoking on school property. Last month, police dogs did a sniff search of our lockers. On our way into the school dance last Friday, we were actually searched by a teacher! I do my school work, and I get Level 3 marks, but I don't get much respect. We live in a dictatorship."

— Deborah, a grade 10 student in an Ontario high school

Are Deborah's complaints about lack of freedom valid? Why or why not? Why do you think there are restrictions on her **freedoms**?

Key Question

How should government be involved with people's rights and freedoms?

Where Do Rights and Responsibilities Originate?

Canada, like other democracies, has developed a framework for the rights and responsibilities of citizens. All democracies have a tradition of respecting citizens' rights and encouraging responsibility through civic participation.

In Canada, citizens' rights are written down in the *Canadian Human Rights Act*, provincial human rights codes, and, most importantly, the federal *Canadian Charter of Rights and Freedoms*.

Canadians' **privacy rights** are covered under the federal *Privacy Act* and the 2001 *Personal Information Protection and Electronic Documents Act*. Privacy rights limit the ability of others to enter your private spaces, take your property, or collect personal information about you. Privacy is not explicitly addressed in Canada's constitution. However, it is considered a fundamental human right and an important part of a democratic society.

The responsibilities of Canadians are less well defined. However, they exist through a common appreciation of what it means to be Canadian and belong to Canadian society.

The government of Canada outlines Canadians' rights and responsibilities as shown in Figure 6.1.

What Are Rights?

A **right** is something to which a person is morally or legally entitled. At home, young people should have the right to safety, the right to food, and the right to be treated with dignity. In Canada, the government protects these rights. In extreme cases, the government removes a child from a parent's home in order to protect the child's rights.

In school, you have the right to an education and the right to be treated with respect. In the larger community, you have the right to express an opinion, the right to drive a car, the right of mobility, and the right to privacy.

WHAT ARE RESPONSIBILITIES?

In the democratic tradition, rights always carry **responsibilities** (something you are accountable for). For example, along with the right to be

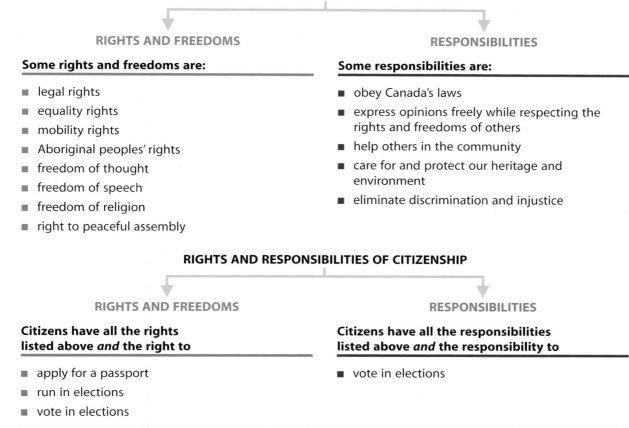

RIGHTS AND RESPONSIBILITIES

RIGHTS AND FREEDOMS	RESPONSIBILITIES
Some rights and freedoms are:	**Some responsibilities are:**
■ legal rights	■ obey Canada's laws
■ equality rights	■ express opinions freely while respecting the rights and freedoms of others
■ mobility rights	■ help others in the community
■ Aboriginal peoples' rights	■ care for and protect our heritage and environment
■ freedom of thought	■ eliminate discrimination and injustice
■ freedom of speech	
■ freedom of religion	
■ right to peaceful assembly	

RIGHTS AND RESPONSIBILITIES OF CITIZENSHIP

RIGHTS AND FREEDOMS	RESPONSIBILITIES
Citizens have all the rights listed above *and* the right to	**Citizens have all the responsibilities listed above *and* the responsibility to**
■ apply for a passport	■ vote in elections
■ run in elections	
■ vote in elections	

FIGURE 6.1 The rights and responsibilities of Canadians

treated with dignity in your home and school comes the responsibility to treat others respectfully. The right to drive a car carries with it the responsibility to pass a test and follow the rules in the driver's handbook. **Mobility rights** (to move about as you wish) come with the responsibility to obtain a passport for certain travels. A parent's right to choose a child's education includes the responsibility to oversee the education in a school or home setting.

RIGHTS IN CONFLICT

At different times, rights conflict. For example, a child's right to security may clash with a parent's right to exercise authority. Your right to freedom of expression may clash with someone else's right not to be exposed to certain words and sentiments.

FIGURE 6.2 Do you think this forehead sticker should be allowed? Why or why not?

THE *CANADIAN CHARTER OF RIGHTS AND FREEDOMS*

At the federal level, your rights are protected by the *Canadian Charter of Rights and Freedoms*. The Charter deals with a citizen's relationship with the government. It lists many rights and freedoms, some of which are discussed in this chapter. Legal rights are addressed in more detail in Chapter 7, and Aboriginal rights are examined in Chapter 9.

When you deal with other people in areas such as housing, employment, and services (non-governmental areas), you do not need to invoke your Charter rights. In these situations, you are protected by either the Ontario *Human Rights Code* or the *Canadian Human Rights Act*.

APPEALING TO COURTS TO PROTECT RIGHTS AND FREEDOMS

If you feel that you have been unfairly treated, you have the right to take your complaint to a court or human rights commission. (See Chapter 3, CivicStar: Justine Blainey, page 51.) If you lose your case in a lower court, you may seek to have a higher court hear your case. A higher court can overrule a lower court, just as a school principal can overrule the decision of a teacher. The highest court of appeal is the Supreme Court of Canada.

"REASONABLE LIMITS" ON RIGHTS AND FREEDOMS

In a democratic society, individual rights and freedoms need to be balanced with the needs of society. In other words, rights and freedoms are not absolute; they have **reasonable limits** (as stated in section 1 of the Charter). Your freedom of expression, for example, does not allow you to yell "fire" in a crowded movie theatre. Your right to privacy ends when you enter the customs zone of an airport.

PAUSE, REFLECT, APPLY

1. a) Why are there limitations on our rights?
   b) Give three examples of authorities limiting rights. In each case, explain why you agree or disagree with the limitation.
2. List three rights and the responsibilities attached to those rights.
3. Nelson Mandela has said, "[O]vercoming poverty is not a gesture of charity. It is an act of justice." In many major Canadian cities, there are numerous homeless people. Should everyone have the right to a basic standard of living?

What Are Charter Freedoms?

As you just read, rights impose duties on the government. The government has a duty to set up voting stations so that you can vote. It also has a duty to protect you against unlawful searches. Freedoms may be viewed as rights that do not impose this kind of duty on the government. For example, you have freedom of religion and freedom of expression.

The Charter also describes freedom of the press, of peaceful assembly, and of association. You are free to live without persecution, and you are free to criticize and oppose government policies. You are free to do anything not prohibited by law. Moreover, you can ask the government to come to your aid if your freedoms are threatened.

FREEDOM OF RELIGION

Freedom of religion means the freedom to practise the faith of your choice. It also means that society cannot impose any one religious faith on citizens.

Until 1985, retail stores in Canada were closed on Sunday, the Christian day of rest. Until 1988, public schools in Ontario started the day with Christian prayers. Court decisions ended these practices. Citing section 2(a) of the Charter, the courts ruled that non-Christians' "freedom of conscience and religion" was disturbed by Sunday closing laws and school religious exercises.

In 1994, the Quebec Human Rights Commission ruled that public schools cannot forbid Muslim students to wear the Islamic veil or *hijab*. In this case, individual freedom was protected from government interference.

However, if a religious practice threatens the well-being of citizens, religious freedom may be limited. For example, seriously ill children have been removed from the custody of Jehovah's Witnesses parents who refused permission for life-saving medical treatments on religious grounds. Once in the care of the state, the children receive the treatments. In this situation, courts have decided that to limit religious freedom is "reasonable."

FREEDOM OF THOUGHT AND EXPRESSION

You are free to think whatever you like. And you are free to express your thoughts and beliefs. However, our laws and courts place "reasonable limits" on freedom of expression. For example, cigarette companies cannot advertise their products in Canada. Liquor companies are limited in

KEY QUESTION

Do Canadians have too few or too many freedoms?

▶ FACE OFF Freedom of Religion versus Right to Security

What happens when religious beliefs clash with other people's right to security?

Khalsa Sikhs pray every morning and evening and forgo alcohol and tobacco. They observe the five Ks: *kesh* (uncut hair), *kanga* (comb), *kara* (bracelet), *kachha* (undergarment), and *kirpan* (dagger). Each "K" has spiritual meaning for believers. The sheathed *kirpan* stands for justice and inner strength. It has been compared to the Christian cross in significance.

In 2001, 12-year-old Gurbaj Singh was banned from his Montreal school for wearing a *kirpan*. A year later, the Quebec Superior Court ruled that Singh could wear the *kirpan*—as long as it was wrapped and checked by school officials. Under police escort, the boy returned to school. His arrival prompted dozens of parents to remove their children from the school.

The school appealed to a higher court, arguing that the blade posed a danger to other students. Quebec's highest court, the Court of Appeal, agreed with the school and ruled that the ban was a reasonable limit on religious freedom. In 2005, the case moved to the Supreme Court of Canada for a final decision.

Some commentators see Singh as a victim of racism. The *kirpan* is sewn into a sheath and would make a poor weapon. Singh's lawyer argued that it was no more dangerous than a geometry compass. British Columbia's Surrey School District, a board with almost 80 percent Sikh enrollment, allows *kirpans* in the classroom. So does Ontario's Peel board.

Others argue that zero tolerance of weapons in schools means all knives, including ceremonial daggers. They argue that a *kirpan* could be seized by another student and used as a weapon. The steel *kirpan* should be replaced by a plastic version. The safety of all children is more important than the religious beliefs of a minority. *Kirpans*

FIGURE 6.3 Gurbaj Singh returns to his school in Montreal in April 2002.

have been banned on airlines, and should also be banned in schools.

What Do You Think?

1. If you were a member of the Supreme Court, how would you decide the case of Gurbaj Singh? Give legal arguments for your decision.

2. In 2004, France banned the wearing of religious symbols such as headscarves, skullcaps, and large crosses in public schools. The government stated that it wanted to promote equality and prevent religious conflict. Many of France's 5 million Muslims saw this as an attack on their beliefs. Do you think Canada should adopt a similar law?

▶ **DID YOU KNOW** ◀

There has been no incident of *kirpan*-related violence in a Canadian school in 100 years. In Surrey, British Columbia, more than 200 Sikh students wear *kirpans*.

the kind of advertising they can use. Producers of pornography cannot sell their products everywhere. They can also be prosecuted for producing certain types of pornography.

Parliament and the courts impose limitations on expression in order to protect the **common good** of society. Because cigarette smoking and alcohol consumption can be hazardous, their advertising is restricted. The depiction of sexuality in a violent or degrading manner is also limited because it creates a harmful environment.

Teachers are also limited in what they may say in the classroom. Jim Keegstra was an Alberta high school teacher who consistently made anti-Semitic (anti-Jewish) remarks to his history students. When he was charged with promoting hatred, Keegstra claimed he had a Charter right to freedom of expression. In a 1990 decision, the Supreme Court declared that he and others do not have the right to say absolutely anything they desire. For the greater good of society, there is a reasonable limit to what anyone can say.

> **DID YOU KNOW** ◄
>
> Quebec bans all advertising aimed at children under the age of 12. It is the strictest provincial law in Canada. This law has been judged a reasonable limit on toy manufacturers' freedom of expression.

☐ DISCUSSION POINT

A 16-year-old Ontario youth was arrested and spent 34 days in jail after writing a fictional short story about a teen who tries to blow up his school in revenge for bullying. He read the story, "Twisted," in his grade 11 drama class in November 2000. Police said the story included death threats. Do you think the boy should have been arrested? Was his right to freedom of speech infringed?

School Powers and Freedom of Expression

Most schools allow students as much self-expression as possible, especially in student publications. However, in certain cases, censorship occurs. If the school administration thinks that a story or editorial poses a threat to the safety of students or to the positive climate in the school, it can cut the articles.

Dress is a form of self-expression. The courts have confirmed that schools have the power to create dress codes. Schools can set reasonable limits on certain freedoms. For example, your school most likely has a policy prohibiting you from downloading violent, racist, or sexual images on a school computer.

School boards also have a say about the types of books taught as part of the curriculum. However, their power is not absolute. In 2002, the Supreme Court of Canada ruled that a British Columbia school board should not have banned kindergarten and grade 1 books that depicted same-sex parents.

SOURCES

Jeremy Patfield spotted Governor General Adrienne Clarkson in the hall at Rideau Hall and wondered aloud: "Is that the woman that spends the money on the Queen when she comes?"

That comment was enough to get the Whitby youth and about 60 of his grade 8 schoolmates kicked out of the governor general's residence.

Even though Clarkson didn't hear the question, asked during a tour of the official residence, the guide immediately cut short the 45-minute tour and escorted out the students from John Dryden Public School in Whitby. To make matters worse, Jeremy said, he was told he was suspended from school for three days, starting that day.

"I guess it was [Clarkson's] house," Jeremy said, after returning from Ottawa. "But still, they basically treated me like a criminal, like I ran in there and assaulted her or something."

He added that he feels like he is "being punished for my freedom of speech."

Since she was appointed governor general in 1999, Clarkson has been criticized for her spending, including using government planes to fly to her Georgian Bay cottage and spending millions of dollars on allegedly exorbitant trips—such as $5.3 million in 2003 for a three-week trip through Russia, Iceland, and Finland.

One day after the newspaper story appeared, Governor General Clarkson telephoned Jeremy to apologize and to invite him to a special tour of her residence. There are no inappropriate questions, only inappropriate answers, said the Queen's representative in Canada. At the same time, the school lifted Jeremy's three-day suspension.

Source: Unnati Gandhi, "Pupils Get Vice-Regal Ejection," *The Toronto Star*, February 17, 2005.

PAUSE, REFLECT, APPLY

1. Why do governments and courts limit our freedom of expression? Give three examples of limits on freedom of expression. In each case, explain why you agree or disagree with the limitation.
2. Why do you think the Supreme Court in 1985 declared the Sunday store closing law unconstitutional (not in keeping with the Charter)?
3. Should a student be able to ask any question in school or on a school excursion? If your answer is no, indicate what sorts of questions a student should not be able to ask.
4. In Canada, do we have too much or too little freedom? Give specific examples.

◗ KEY QUESTION

How much power should courts have in interpreting Charter rights?

What Are Our Charter Rights?

Among the rights addressed by the Charter are democratic rights, mobility rights, legal rights, equality rights, minority language rights, and Aboriginal rights. Many of these rights are discussed in different sections of this text.

While the Charter outlines your basic rights, Canadian courts, especially the Supreme Court, clarify those rights. The courts interpret the

Charter to determine exactly what those rights mean. For example, what is meant by the right of "security of the person," the right "not to be subjected to any cruel and unusual treatment or punishment," or the right to "the equal protection and equal benefit of the law"? By responding to the cases brought before them, Canadian courts have been answering these questions since the Charter was created in 1982.

DEMOCRATIC RIGHTS

The **democratic rights** of Canadians are outlined in sections 3, 4, and 5 of the Charter. These rules guarantee Canadians a democratic government and the right to elect their representatives. These rules apply to federal, provincial, and territorial elections.

The voting age in Canada used to be 21. Based on a decision of the Supreme Court of Canada, the right to vote (franchise) has been extended to almost every Canadian citizen over the age of 18. Most recently, the franchise has been extended to all inmates in Canada's prison system, including those with life sentences.

LEGAL RIGHTS

Your legal rights (sections 7 to 14 of the Charter) ensure that you are treated fairly when dealing with the justice system. Section 8, for example, guarantees you "the right to be secure against unreasonable search." Section 9 says you have "the right not to be arbitrarily detained."

In most cases, searches are conducted because someone in authority suspects that a law or rule has been broken. When the person searching you is a police officer, the search is legal if there is

- a search warrant
- an arrest
- reasonable cause.

In a school, the principal or vice-principal is considered to be acting in place of your parents. This gives them the authority to search your person, your bag, or your locker if they have a good reason for doing so. School officials have this authority (backed by court decisions) so that they can maintain order and safety in schools.

FIGURE 6.4 Would it be legal for a school official to search your locker just because it's messy and he or she wants to check to see what's inside?

If there is no good reason for the search, school authorities can be punished for invading students' privacy. In 1998, in a high school in Kingsville, Ontario, 19 grade 9 boys were strip-searched after a classmate reported $90 missing from a gym bag. The incident grabbed media attention. Eventually, the vice-principal and the gym teacher who ordered the students to remove their clothes were suspended without pay for 10 days and reprimanded by the school board. The $90 was never recovered.

In some circumstances, it is legal to detain people, even if they are not suspected of committing a crime. For example, during highway spot checks, any driver can be detained to determine if he or she has consumed alcohol. Because alcohol-related traffic accidents are frequent and deadly, the Supreme Court has decided that spot checks are a reasonable limit on the right not to be detained.

EQUALITY RIGHTS

The rights of all Canadians to be treated equally are guaranteed by the Charter. Governments are prohibited from discriminating against anyone on specific grounds, as listed in section 15(1) of the Charter:

> Every individual is equal before and under the law and has the right to the equal protection and equal benefit of the law without discrimination and, in particular, without discrimination based on race, national or ethnic origin, colour, religion, sex, age or mental or physical disability.

Equality rights are meant also to ensure that everyone can access opportunity equally. How? Supreme Court Justice Rosalie Abella has said that "equality is not a concept that produces the same results for everyone. It is a concept that seeks to identify and remove, barrier by barrier, discriminatory disadvantage."

Equality Rights and Sexual Orientation

Some rights protected by the Charter are not explicitly stated. However, the Supreme Court of Canada has identified similar grounds for protection in addition to those listed in section 15(1). Among these grounds is sexual orientation.

▶ FACE OFF   **To Spank or Not to Spank?**

"Ouch! You didn't have to hit me! And you didn't have to hit me that hard!"

Are children's equality rights being violated when they are spanked? Do parents, guardians, and teachers have a right to strike children? Federal law states that they do—so long as the force used is "reasonable." That law, first written in 1892, is intended to permit children to be disciplined.

Some people argue that government rules have no place in family matters. They say that parents should not be charged with assault for spanking a misbehaving child. Similarly, a teacher should not be arrested for physically restraining a disruptive student. After all other means have failed, physical correction may be the only answer. At times, this may also be the only way to ensure safety in the classroom.

> Spanking was good for me; I turned out OK. It should be good for my children.
>
> — Caller to a phone-in radio program

Others argue that spanking is always wrong. Corporal (bodily) punishment, they say, is just a nice term for physical abuse. Spanking is an act of violence. Young people who are spanked get the idea that violence is permissible. Laws should protect children from physical assault, just as adults are protected. The Charter speaks about the right to "security of the person" (section 7), the right to "the equal protection and equal benefit of the law" (section 15), and the right not to be subjected to "any cruel and unusual treatment or punishment" (section 12).

> Children are the only remaining Canadian citizens who can be legally assaulted for their correction.
>
> — Catholic School Board spokesperson, London, Ontario

The Supreme Court ruled in 2004 that children had limited rights and that parents can apply

FIGURE 6.5 After some Ontario children were removed from their family because they were spanked, members of their church congregation protested.

"reasonable force." The court banned the use of corporal punishment for children under age two and over age 12. It prohibited the use of instruments such as rulers and belts, or striking a child on the face or head. Teachers can no longer use corporal punishment. The court saw the new interpretation as achieving a balance between the needs of parents and the rights of children.

What Do You Think?

1. With reference to specific sections in the Charter, explain how children are not given full rights under the *Canadian Charter of Rights and Freedoms*.
2. Explain why you agree or disagree with this denial of full Charter rights.

▶ DID YOU KNOW ◀

In 2004, 12 European countries had "anti-smacking legislation." In most cases, the laws were intended to educate parents rather than punish them.

After the 2004 Supreme Court of Canada decision, a lawyer noted: "I can remember being strapped by my principal, and that was entirely acceptable by society 30 years ago. Attitudes are changing. In 20 years all spanking of children will be outlawed."

FIGURE 6.6 In 2002, 17-year-old Marc Hall (left) took the Durham Catholic District School Board to court after it ruled that he could not take his boyfriend to the high school prom. The board stated that Hall's action would violate Catholic teachings on homosexuality. Hall's lawyer argued, successfully, that the board's decision violated Hall's Charter rights to equality, freedom of expression, and freedom of association.

The basic goal of section 15 is to protect human dignity. It does this by ensuring that the law treats all Canadians as equal in value and worth. In a series of court decisions, gay and lesbian Canadians have been guaranteed equal treatment under the Charter. This means that lesbian and gay Canadians are protected from discrimination in accommodation and employment. Same-sex couples are also entitled to the same benefits (such as pensions and support payments) as heterosexual couples. By June 2005, courts in eight provinces and one territory had recognized same-sex marriage. By the end of July 2005, the *Civil Marriage Act* became law, recognizing same-sex marriage across Canada.

Disability Rights

Disability activists fought hard to have **disability rights** included in the Charter. Their victory was considered a significant achievement for the disability movement. Since then, many legal challenges have ensured that people with physical or mental disabilities have access to a full range of services. Access to buildings and facilities has also improved. In one landmark case, a person in British Columbia who was deaf won the right to communicate with health care providers using a sign language interpreter provided by the government.

Tracy Latimer: Equality Rights or the Right to Die?

Tracy Latimer was a 12-year-old girl living with severe cerebral palsy in rural Saskatchewan. She could not move her limbs and communicated only by means of facial expressions, laughter, and crying. Tracy enjoyed music from a radio, which she controlled with a special button. However, she was in constant pain.

When Tracy faced further painful surgery in 1993, her father, Robert, made a decision. He placed her in his pickup truck while her mother and siblings were at church. He then inserted a hose from the exhaust pipe into the cab. Tracy died from carbon monoxide poisoning.

CivicStar

STEVEN FLETCHER

He clicks his mouse by means of an infrared remote attached to his forehead. He moves about in a high-tech wheelchair. He is Steven Fletcher, a Conservative MP who cannot move his body below the neck.

At age 23, Fletcher was a mining engineer. Driving home one day, he had an accident. A moose crashed through his windshield. Fletcher's life changed in a second. As a result of a spinal cord injury, he cannot feel hunger, pain, or pleasure. Yet his head works just fine.

Fletcher adapted to his condition. He returned to university. He earned a business degree and was elected student president. Several years later, he became leader of the Manitoba Progressive Conservative Party. In the 2004 federal election, Fletcher ran as a Conservative candidate in a Winnipeg riding, won the seat, and was appointed his party's health critic.

The Parliament buildings also had to be adapted to accommodate Fletcher, Canada's first quadriplegic MP. In Ottawa, Fletcher has continued to advocate for *community living*—the integration of physically or mentally challenged individuals into society. He has said, "Community living is better for the individual for sure, better for their families, and in most cases—not all—it's better on the taxpayer too."

Fletcher's words express his optimism: "I'd rather be paralyzed from the neck down than the neck up." In his determination and accomplishments, Steven Fletcher tests and strengthens Canada's commitment to equal opportunity and equal treatment for all members of society.

Your Play

1. How would your home or school have to be adapted in order to be accessible to Steven Fletcher?
2. Fletcher has observed that politicians in Parliament had no real grasp of what it means to be seriously physically disabled before he arrived. He says there's a difference between dealing with "issues" and dealing with people. Describe what you think that difference involves.

The legal case pitted Tracy's equality rights against her father's claim that he was releasing her from a life that was too painful. At trial, he was convicted and sentenced to one year in jail and one year of house arrest. A higher court, however, ruled that he was guilty of second-degree murder. He would have to serve the same sentence as anyone else: life, without parole for 10 years. Latimer defended his action as euthanasia, or "mercy killing." He argued that it would be "cruel and unusual treatment or punishment" (section 12 of the Charter) to incarcerate him for an act of compassion.

Disability activists disagreed, passionately. The Charter, they said, gives no one the freedom or right to kill anybody. Instead, section 15 guarantees equal protection of the law "without discrimination based on ... mental or physical disability." Canada's Supreme Court agreed. In 2001, it ruled that Latimer had other options. For example, he could have placed Tracy in a group home.

PAUSE, REFLECT, APPLY

1. Rights are clustered under different categories within the Charter. What are those categories, and how do they differ?
2. Justice Abella said that "equality is not a concept that produces the same results for everyone. It is a concept that seeks to identify and remove, barrier by barrier, discriminatory disadvantage." Write a two-paragraph opinion piece on the meaning of these comments. Use examples from real life to illustrate your point of view.

REPLAY ■ ■ ■ ■ ■ ■ ■ ■ ■ ■

This chapter has informed you of these civics concepts:

1. Democracies have a tradition of rights and responsibilities.
2. Canadians' rights are protected in human rights codes, in the *Canadian Charter of Rights and Freedoms*, and in privacy law.
3. Rights always imply responsibilities.
4. There are reasonable limits on individual rights in order to protect the needs of society.
5. If you feel you have been treated unfairly, you may take your case before a human rights commission or the courts.
6. When individual and societal rights clash, courts interpret which rights will prevail.

CIVICS ◼ TOOLKIT

How Can I Break This Down?

To analyze means to break something down into its parts. Keep this in mind when analyzing information from books, newspapers, reports, and so on. It's a good idea to read the whole item first. Then approach the item as you would a puzzle.

Start by doing the following:

- Take your time.
- Look up unfamiliar words in a dictionary.
- Use an Internet search engine to learn more about unfamiliar phrases, concepts, or people.
- Examine all the parts. For example, with a statistical table, make sure you know exactly what is being measured. Look at all the labels. Check the legend, if there is one. If it is a report, scan the headings to get a sense of the main structure. Use the headings to zero in on the information that is pertinent to your research. Examine photographs and captions.

Next, go a little deeper:

- Try to grasp the purpose of the piece. Why did the author write it? The answer to that question is usually the "big idea" of the piece.
- In a written piece, examine the first and last sentence of a paragraph for clues about the main idea.
- Look for chronology (time order) as an organizing principle. That way, you can sometimes jump to particular events that interest you or relate to your research.

- Look for the arguments the author makes, as well as evidence to support those arguments. What cause-and-effect claims does the author make?
- Remember that words and images may have a symbolic meaning. In political cartoons, the artist often uses symbolism or exaggeration to make a point.
- Remember that words in italics can be the names of published works, the names of ships, or phrases from a language other than English.

Skill Practice

1. Read Face Off: Freedom of Religion versus Right to Security on page 100. Identify points of comparison between different views. Identify cause-and-effect sequences (one thing happens because of something else).
2. Read the Sources feature on page 102. What is the main message of the article? Identify and explain key words and phrases that reporter Unnati Gandhi uses to get her message across to the reader.
3. Find a political cartoon in this book or in a magazine or newspaper that you think is very effective. Analyze the techniques that the cartoonist has used to give the political message humour or impact.

STUDY HALL

Informed Citizenship

1. Distinguish between a freedom and a right. Use an example for each.

2. Locate a copy of the *Canadian Charter of Rights and Freedoms* (for example, at http://laws.justice.gc.ca/en/charter). After reading the following sections of the Charter, find an example in this chapter of how each of the sections has been applied by Canadian courts: 1, 2(a), 2(b), 3, 7, 8, 12, and 15(a).

Purposeful Citizenship

3. In small groups, decide whether a right has been violated in each of the cases described below. If a right has been violated, explain the right and its relationship to the *Canadian Charter of Rights and Freedoms*.

   - Derek is an atheist. At Derek's public school, a short religious message is read after the national anthem each morning.

   - Mary is contacted by someone selling funeral arrangements. The person obtained Mary's name from a clinic list of cancer patients.

   - Seventeen-year-old Timothy is a suspect in a murder. In an effort to locate Timothy, police publish his photograph in a local newspaper.

   - With her parents out of town, Ella is having a party at home. Police knock on the door. Upon learning that the parents are absent, police enter the home and charge five teens with underage drinking.

   - Sheema is suspended for a day because she refused to remove her *hijab* (headscarf worn by many Muslim women) in her physical education class.

   - Dina, who is deaf, goes to the hospital to deliver her baby. She is not provided with a sign language interpreter.

   - A police dog is brought into Dave's school. As a result of the dog's sniffing, Dave's locker is searched by the school administration.

4. Paula refuses to stand for the playing of "O Canada!" during her school's opening exercises. She says she disagrees with the values in the song. It is male-oriented ("True patriot love in all thy sons command"), contains a militaristic flavour ("we stand on guard for thee"), and is religious ("God keep our land glorious and free!"). Paula believes in feminism, pacifism, and atheism. She has been told that according to Ontario law, the national anthem must be played each morning, and she must respect the song by standing. If she does not comply with school rules, she will be suspended for three days.

   In small groups, decide what rights and responsibilities are present in Paula's protest. Attempt to resolve the apparent conflict of rights and responsibilities in this scenario.

Active Citizenship

5. Posters at your school encourage students to visit a certain Web site. The site preaches hatred against Muslim Canadians, African Canadians, and Jewish Canadians. What steps could you take to make certain that Canadian rights and freedoms are protected in this situation?

6. Organize a classroom debate on the topics listed below. Before the debate, research your position and your opponent's position. After the debate, summarize your position on each debate topic in a well-written paragraph.

   - All spanking of children should be made illegal.

   - Doctor-assisted suicide under certain circumstances should be legalized in Canada.

7. Interview a person with a disability in your school or community. Find out how the disability has affected his or her rights and freedoms.

CHAPTER 7

How Does the Judicial System Work?

Led away in handcuffs

What You Need to Know

- What safeguards in the judicial system protect the rights of people accused of crimes, the victims of crime, and society?
- What roles should the police and the courts play in a democracy?
- How is civil law different from criminal law?
- How has Aboriginal justice affected the judicial system?
- How can you organize information before writing a paper or delivering an oral report?

Key Terms

burden of proof	Crown
prosecution	adversarial system
Aboriginal justice	incarceration
young offenders	defendant
Youth Criminal Justice Act	restorative justice
warrant	

It was a beautiful fall night when a local gang severely beat two 15-year-olds walking in the park. Residents in a nearby house heard the disturbance and called 911. When police arrived, many young people were at the scene. Several were led away in handcuffs. One girl kept saying she was glad someone had finally made the victims "shut up for being so dumb."

Police suspected that more teens were involved in the incident. They knew they would be gathering more evidence in the coming weeks. Two teens were eventually arrested and charged with the beatings. You will meet them in the following pages. Before you read their stories, predict what might happen to them.

Key Question

How much should government interfere with people's rights and freedoms?

Canada's Judicial System

The Canadian judicial system tries to achieve two goals. First, it must ensure that society operates in a peaceful and orderly manner. Pedestrians and motorists need to know, for example, that drivers will stop at red lights. Homeowners must be assured that people will not trespass on their property. Everyone in society needs to know that people who harm others will be prosecuted for their offences.

Without such assurances, society would be chaotic and unpredictable. To quote 17th century political philosopher Thomas Hobbes, life would be "nasty, brutish, and short." Law is the glue that holds society together by ensuring social order.

Second, the judicial system tries to balance the need for social order with respect for the individual rights of the citizen. Not all societies do this. As you learned earlier, authoritarian governments impose social order through harsh laws and the use of police and military force. Individuals can be arrested and imprisoned without trial.

☐ **DISCUSSION POINT**
Why do democracies balance the rights of individuals and society?

FUNDAMENTAL LEGAL RIGHTS

In a democracy, all citizens are equal before the law and accountable under the law for their actions. No citizen is above the law, and neither is any government. As you learned in Chapter 1, this guiding principle is called the **rule of law**.

Fundamental legal rights are clearly stated in the *Canadian Charter of Rights and Freedoms*. Canadians have

- the right to be free from unreasonable searches or seizures
- the right on arrest or detention (put in custody) to be told of the reasons
- the right to be represented by counsel (a lawyer)
- the right to have a court decide if the detention is lawful
- the right, on being charged with an offence, to be told the details of the offence
- the right to a trial within a reasonable time
- the right to be presumed innocent until proven guilty (this **burden of proof** in a criminal trial rests on the **prosecution**, the lawyers working for the state, not on the person charged)
- the right not to be denied **bail** (temporary release from custody) without just cause

- the right not to have to testify against themselves (appear as a witness in their own trial)
- the right not to be subjected to cruel and unusual treatment or punishment.

THE CHANGING JUSTICE SYSTEM

Canadian society is constantly changing, and the legal system must change with it. Laws and legal procedures are always under review. Old laws may become outdated because of changing social values and new technologies.

In the past, the courts did not have to deal with crimes involving the Internet and high-tech digital information. There was no such thing as "theft of personal electronic information." Few people talked about decriminalizing marijuana possession. Concepts such as **victims' rights** (the rights of those people hurt by a criminal offence) and **Aboriginal justice** (a justice system managed by Aboriginal peoples) were unknown. Where the law goes next will depend on developments in the 21st century.

The justice system also has to deal with a growing case load. Many more cases are coming before Canadian courts today than in the past. It can take months to bring criminal cases to trial, and often years before civil disputes are settled. The judicial system is experimenting with newer ways to settle disputes and with ideas drawn from Aboriginal justice (see pages 124–125).

ATTITUDES TOWARD THE LAW

In many democracies around the world, confidence in the justice system has waned. There are many reasons for this. As democratic societies become more open and less authoritarian, citizens are less inclined to trust their institutions. Also, several high-profile trials around the world have exposed corruption or mismanagement in police departments and in the courts.

Sometimes a case can highlight people's attitudes about a law, or a proposed change in law. On March 4, 2005, four RCMP officers were shot and killed while trying to repossess a pickup truck at an Alberta farm. The owner of the farm was also running an illegal marijuana growing operation.

FIGURE 7.1 At the funeral for the four slain RCMP officers, the fiancée of one officer accepts his Stetson hat from a fellow officer.

The event shocked Canadians. It was the worst attack on the RCMP since the Riel rebellions of 1885. Flags flew at half-mast across Canada. Many politicians and citizens called for tougher sentences for marijuana growing operations. Others said that if marijuana had been made legal, such a violent standoff would never have occurred and five lives could have been saved. The event highlighted public attitudes toward three cornerstones of the Canadian justice system: the police, the courts, and the laws themselves. Most citizens have strong opinions about all three.

As you can see from Figure 7.2, many Canadians are confident in the justice system, but a sizable number are not. If you add the last three numbers together, you find that 46 percent of Canadians express confidence in the justice system. Those in the mid-range (22 percent) feel neutral about the justice system, while 32 percent (numbers 1–3) indicate a lack of confidence in the justice system.

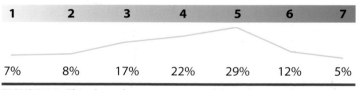

1	2	3	4	5	6	7
7%	8%	17%	22%	29%	12%	5%

FIGURE 7.2 This chart shows responses of Canadians to the question, "How much confidence do you have in the justice system?" 1 represents "no confidence"; 7 represents "a great deal." *Source:* Confidence in Justice: An International Review, *Table 4.1; www.kcl.ac.uk.*

The study's researchers found even lower levels of confidence in European nations and the United States. Is the justice system in trouble in Canada and other democratic countries?

The authors of the study, *Confidence in Justice: An International Review*, concluded the following:

- Most people believe that the crime rate is rising and blame the criminal justice system.
- Police receive the highest confidence rating; the courts and the parole system receive the lowest.
- Correctional authorities do a better job at supervising prisoners than supervising offenders in the community.
- People do not know much about the criminal justice system. They are often exposed to unique stories of failed prosecutions, lenient sentences, and wrongful convictions, and think these are the norm.
- People respect police officers more than they respect the courts and correctional authorities because they know them better.

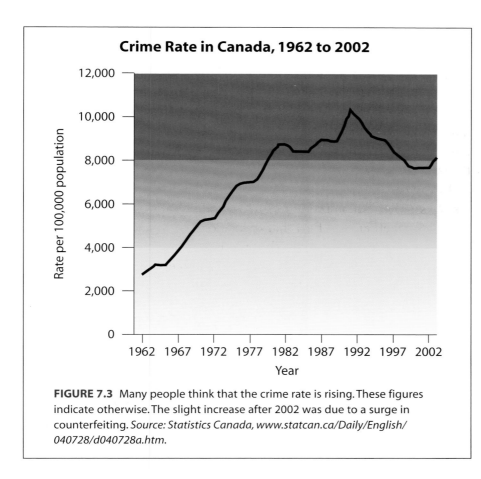

FIGURE 7.3 Many people think that the crime rate is rising. These figures indicate otherwise. The slight increase after 2002 was due to a surge in counterfeiting. *Source: Statistics Canada, www.statcan.ca/Daily/English/ 040728/d040728a.htm.*

Trust in the justice system is important for Canadians. If the public loses confidence, then citizens are more reluctant to report crimes, act as witnesses, or serve on juries. These are all responsibilities that citizens in a democracy must be willing to perform if the justice system is to work properly.

WRONGFUL CONVICTIONS

The Canadian justice system is based on the principle that a person is innocent until proven guilty. However, sometimes this principle is over-looked when the system is busy pursuing someone it believes to be guilty.

David Milgaard and Guy Paul Morin are two Canadians who were convicted of serious crimes they did not commit. Milgaard was convict-ed of the rape and murder of nursing assistant Gail Miller in Saskatoon, Saskatchewan. He spent the next 20 years in prison for this crime. Morin was convicted of the murder of nine-year-old Christine Jessop in

Queensville, Ontario. After two trials, he was sentenced to life in prison. In both cases, the new science of DNA testing exonerated the men. They received government compensation for their time in prison. It was also later revealed that the police and the prosecution in both cases had a single theory about the crime that prevented them from considering alternative theories and suspects.

CivicStar

THE INNOCENCE PROJECT

What would you do if you were sitting in jail knowing that you were innocent?

You could contact the Innocence Project, a unique legal clinic associated with York University, Toronto. Under the supervision of the project directors, law students might investigate your case. If your case includes biological evidence, new DNA tests could be ordered to reveal the identity of the people at the crime scene. Or, the team might agree to delve into lost evidence or false testimony. How much help could you get?

Consider the case of Romeo Phillion, who spent 31 years in prison after being convicted of the homicide of Ottawa firefighter Leopold Roy. Phillion was actually in Trenton, Ontario, getting his car fixed the night Roy died. There was even a report confirming his alibi, but it was kept hidden. The volunteer work of students on the Innocence Project revealed that Phillion's defence lawyer never had a chance to see the document. The Innocence Project freed Phillion after three decades.

Canada's Innocence Project is part of a network of organizations in the United States, Britain, and Australia. In December 2004, its co-founder, Dianne Martin, died. Remembered by her colleagues as a staunch fighter for justice, Martin is sorely missed by her colleagues, students, and one man in particular—Romeo Phillion.

About Martin's commitment, Phillion said, "She rescued me and saved my life. I could never say enough about this woman. She was the enemy of injustice. She was my hero."

FIGURE 7.4 Romeo Phillion with his cat Tiger, who lived with him in prison

The Innocence Project cooperates with another Canadian initiative—the Association in Defence of the Wrongly Convicted. This organization came to the aid of both David Milgaard and Guy Paul Morin (see pages 115–116).

Your Play

Dianne Martin once described three classic features of wrongful conviction cases: a tragic event, a suspect who lacks power or authority, and suspicious evidence. Explain how you think these three factors might combine and lead to a wrongful conviction.

YOUTH CRIMINAL JUSTICE

Canadians between the ages of 12 and 17 who commit an offence are sometimes called **young offenders** and fall under the *Youth Criminal Justice Act*. This Act recognizes that a youth must be held accountable for criminal activity, but not to the same extent as an adult. The Act emphasizes rehabilitation so that the youth can become a productive member of society.

Young offenders are not always arrested if they commit an offence. Police have options. A young shoplifter may be persuaded to return goods. Police might contact parents when a young person disturbs the peace. If the offence is serious, however, the police must arrest the youth suspected of the crime.

All the rights of adults upon arrest (see pages 112–113) apply to young offenders. Some special provisions apply. A youth must be told in clear language that he or she has the right

- to have a parent, guardian, or other adult present during questioning
- to have a lawyer, with one supplied by legal aid if necessary
- not to make statements that could be used against him or her.

One reason that a youth's rights must be spelled out so clearly is that young people are often unaware of their rights. A young person who is frightened and confused during an arrest may make statements that he or she does not really mean.

PAUSE, REFLECT, APPLY

1. a) What are the two goals that the Canadian judicial system tries to achieve?
   b) Which of the two is more important, in your opinion?
   c) How do these two intentions sometimes conflict with each other?
2. Define the term "rule of law." Why is it essential for a democracy to work on a basis of equality?
3. Why do people have less confidence in the courts than in the police? In what sense is lack of knowledge about the judicial system as a whole a problem?
4. How would you rate your confidence in the judicial system?
5. Refer to Figure 7.3 on page 115. Offer some reasons why people perceive the crime rate to be going up when in fact it is going down.
6. Do you think that a particularly disturbing crime sometimes places too much pressure on the police to solve it, possibly leading to a wrongful conviction? Explain.
7. a) What differences are there between the arrest procedures for teenagers and for adults?
   b) Are teenagers given more rights than they deserve, or are they given enough? Explain your answer.

▶ **KEY QUESTION**
Why are there procedures for investigating crimes and trying defendants?

The Criminal Justice Process

Carl, 18, and his friend Matt, 16, are suspected of being part of a gang that severely beat up two youths. Each will be tried in a different justice system—one as a youth and one as an adult. Let us follow both.

THE CRIMINAL INVESTIGATION

FIGURE 7.5 Carl, age 18

FIGURE 7.6 Matt, age 16

Acting on information from witnesses, police obtain **warrants** (legal documents) for arrest from a judge. This empowers them to arrest Carl and Matt. The police are also allowed to take each suspect into custody, search his home and person, ask him questions, and seize evidence. As we have seen, Carl and Matt have legal rights. No matter what the police believe about their guilt or innocence, Carl and Matt are innocent until proven guilty in a court trial.

Both suspects are charged with committing an **indictable offence**. This is a serious offence, one that involves, for example, violence or theft over a certain amount. Minor offences are called **summary offences**. Carl, as an adult, is informed of the charge, told that he may consult a lawyer, and brought before a judge. The judge decides whether there is enough evidence to proceed with the case, and whether bail can be granted. Carl is then released to await trial.

As a youth, Matt is handled differently. The charge is carefully explained to him in language he can understand. He is told that he can contact a parent or other adult to assist him at the police station. He does not have to make a statement that might be used against him in court. The police fingerprint and photograph him and release him into the custody of his parents.

THE COURTS

Carl's trial takes place in a provincial superior court. He can be tried before a judge alone, or before a judge and jury. On his lawyer's advice, Carl chooses a jury trial. The jury is selected from a large number of citizens who have received notices requiring them to appear for jury duty. Each of the 12 jurors in a criminal case must be approved by the defence lawyer and the **Crown** (prosecution).

Matt's case will be decided in a different court—a Youth Justice Court. This court was created by the *Youth Criminal Justice Act* to deal with youth aged 12 to 17.

In the Youth Justice Court, a judge normally conducts a trial alone, although an accused may request a trial by judge and jury if the offence is very serious. The rules are the same as in adult court, and the trial is public. Because the offence is serious, Matt's name could possibly be made public. Usually, however, young offenders' names are not publicized. While sentences in the Youth Justice Court are lighter than those in adult court, a youth court judge may, in certain circumstances, impose a stiffer, "adult sentence."

THE TRIAL

Whether Carl or Matt is found guilty will be decided in a clash between two adversaries: the prosecution and the defence. This system is called the **adversarial system**. It is based on the idea that when two opponents argue their case to the best of their ability, one will be stronger than the other and the truth will emerge.

As stated earlier, the burden of proof rests upon the prosecution. This means that the prosecution must prove the defendant's guilt. The prosecution must be able to show that the defendant is guilty beyond a reasonable doubt.

The quality of the evidence against Carl and Matt is a major concern. **Hearsay** evidence is not allowed. "Hearsay" applies to things witnesses have heard other people say, not what they have personally observed. Witnesses are not allowed to comment on Carl and Matt's character or any past problems that either may have had with the law. The judge can also rule evidence **inadmissible** (unable to be considered). This is likely to happen with any evidence that was gained through violation of the defendant's rights, such as unreasonable search and seizure. Finally, Carl and Matt cannot be forced to give evidence. It is up to each to decide whether to take the stand and testify.

VERDICT AND SENTENCING

Carl's trial involves a jury. The jury hears evidence and retires to make its decision after lawyers for the defence and the prosecution make their final arguments. The jury must also hear the judge's **charge to the jury**. This is the judge's review of the facts of Carl's case, and an explanation of the law that applies to it.

> ## SOURCES
>
> This is what the Manitoba justice ministry has to say about jury duty:
>
> Trial by jury is the foundation of our judicial system. Now, and for centuries past, trial by jury has been the process through which facts of cases are uncovered and determined. Through jury duty, members of the community actively share in the delivering of justice. To serve on a jury is your democratic right, your civic responsibility, and a great honour.
>
> Source: www.gov.mb.ca/justice/court/jury.html.
>
> Which of the three reasons for serving would prompt you to serve on a jury?

Once the jury has decided whether Carl is guilty or not guilty, the judge either allows him to leave immediately (if he is found not guilty) or sentences him (if he is found guilty).

Sentencing is based on several ideas:

- **punishment** of the offender to a degree that the public understands that the offence is serious
- **deterrence**, or discouraging the offender from repeating the offence
- **protection** of the public from dangerous people
- **rehabilitation** of the offender so that he or she can rejoin society as a law-abiding, productive citizen.

The sentence itself can take different forms. It may be a combination of two or more alternatives—fine, probation, suspended sentence, community work, or jail.

Matt's case proceeds in the same way as Carl's, but without a jury. If the judge decides that Matt is guilty, he or she will pass an appropriate sentence. As a young person, Matt is considered to have a better chance of being rehabilitated than an adult. The judge may consult with youth workers and probation officers. Often, the judge will draw upon school records and interviews with parents and others before deciding on a sentence. The sentence may range from a reprimand to community service, **open custody** in a group home, or **secure custody** in a prison separate from adults.

Both Carl and Matt have the right to appeal their verdicts if they and their lawyers believe them to be unfair.

▶ FACE OFF Young Offender or Young Adult?

In 1997, Canadians were shocked after 14-year-old Reena Virk was beaten and left to drown by a group of teenagers under a bridge in Victoria, BC. The case focused national media attention on teen violence and the youth justice system.

The brutal killing raised a serious question: Should teenagers be treated as adults when they commit crimes of violence?

Some people think that teens should be treated as adults by the justice system. They say that violent crimes show a shocking disregard for human life. Anyone who commits such a crime should be punished severely. Victims of violent crime feel diminished when a young offender gets a light sentence. Shorter sentences also give society the message that young people will be excused for their behaviour. Some people point out that teenagers often want to be treated as adults.

> Teens ask to be treated like adults by their parents, but not the courts. ... it doesn't make sense, they want the responsibility at home, but nowhere else. ... HELLO—treat them like the adults they want to be!!!
>
> — Internet debater, www.lawyers.ca

Other people say that youths need special rights and consideration. Teenagers are not adults and may not understand their rights upon arrest. They may waive (give up) their rights without understanding what they are doing. Moreover, the lighter sentences often given to youths reflect the idea that they are more likely to be rehabilitated than adults. Teenagers should not be sent to adult prisons, where they may be surrounded by hardened criminals.

> Sending a kid to an adult prison is not a disciplinary measure intended to reform and teach—it's about revenge. If you want to cut back on youth criminal activity then you should focus on prevention and intervention (like counselling, not jail) for at-risk youth ... .
>
> — Internet debater, www.lawyers.ca

What Do You Think?

1. In the discussion above, list the arguments from strongest to weakest in favour of
   a) treating young offenders as youth with special rights
   b) treating them as adults.
2. Which do you think is the better approach to the problem of teenage violence—harsher penalties or prevention and rehabilitation programs?

FIGURE 7.7 Reena Virk's mother talks to reporters following the trial of one of the defendants in her daughter's case.

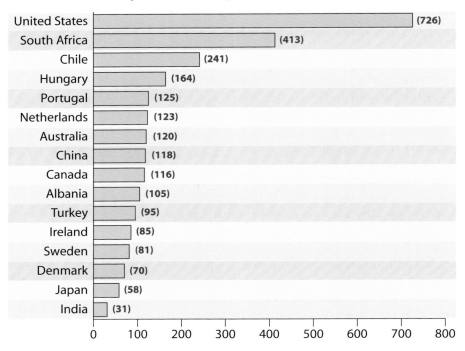

Number of People in Prison (per 100,000 population), 2005

United States	(726)
South Africa	(413)
Chile	(241)
Hungary	(164)
Portugal	(125)
Netherlands	(123)
Australia	(120)
China	(118)
Canada	(116)
Albania	(105)
Turkey	(95)
Ireland	(85)
Sweden	(81)
Denmark	(70)
Japan	(58)
India	(31)

FIGURE 7.8 The number of people sent to prison varies a great deal around the world, as this graph shows. What else would you want to know about the countries with high or low rates of **incarceration** (imprisonment)? *Source: www.prisonstudies.org.*

PAUSE, REFLECT, APPLY

1. Why does the law insist that police use search and seizure procedures carefully?
2. Why is Matt fortunate that his case is tried in a youth court?
3. Can you think of any reasons why a jury is not normally used in youth court?
4. Why do you think each juror has to be approved by the defence and the prosecution?
5. What is meant by the "adversarial system"? Do you think that it is the best way to "get at the truth" of innocence or guilt?
6. Explain how the rules regarding types of evidence in a trial serve to protect the rights of Carl and Matt.
7. Which of the four sentencing principles do you believe is the most important for a judge? Do you agree with the emphasis on rehabilitation for Matt if he is found guilty?
8. Why is the right of appeal an important right?

Civil Law

Civil law is different from criminal law in an important way. Criminal activity is a public offence against society. The police must arrest and charge anyone who has broken the *Criminal Code*, and a court must hear the case.

Civil law is concerned with private disputes between individuals. An individual who feels wronged by another in some way can **sue** (take legal action against) that person. Police are not involved, and there is no arrest. Civil law deals with claims resulting from accidents, all kinds of contracts, property ownership, and family matters.

PROCEDURE IN CIVIL CASES

Suppose you are hurt because you fall into a ditch while crossing a farm. You believe that the owner has been negligent (careless) in not posting a warning about the ditch, which is almost impossible to see. If you decide to sue, you are known as the **plaintiff** in the civil case. The owner, or the party you are suing, is the **defendant**.

Plaintiffs file a plea with the court outlining their complaint and the **remedy** (what they expect to receive in compensation). The court considers the information, issues a document with the court's seal on it, and delivers it to the defendant.

Defendants must reply by providing the court with a statement of defence. If they do not do this, the court will assume that the facts presented by the plaintiff are true. In this case, the defendant will be liable (responsible) for **damages** (a fixed amount of money).

Defendants may call upon a lawyer for help, and the case can be settled out of court. If there is no out-of-court settlement, the two sides participate in an "examination for discovery." This allows both sides to examine the evidence that each will bring to the trial.

At the trial, the plaintiff must prove that it is more probable than not that the defendant is liable. This is less of a burden of proof than is required at a criminal trial. (At a criminal trial, the prosecutor must prove that the defendant is guilty beyond a reasonable doubt.)

Civil cases can be decided before a judge alone or before a judge and jury. Civil juries usually have only six jurors.

KEY QUESTION

How does civil law differ from criminal law?

FIGURE 7.9 Warning signs need to be visible. This one is clear and visible from a distance.

DECISIONS IN CIVIL CASES

Decisions in civil cases can take several forms. If the plaintiff is successful, the judge will order the defendant to pay damages. Another type of decision is called a **declaratory order**. In this situation, the court outlines or declares the rights of the two parties who are having the dispute. For example, the court might say who can do what according to a contract, or who will get what according to the terms of a will. A third type of decision is an **injunction**. This requires the defendant to stop doing something, such as making noise, or to do something, such as removing an ugly sign from a property.

PAUSE, REFLECT, APPLY

1. Identify the following terms as part of either criminal law procedures, civil law procedures, or both:

   - plaintiff
   - accused
   - defendant
   - statement of defence
   - prosecution
   - damages
   - sentence
   - injunction

2. Why do police not become involved in civil cases?

3. State a reason why most civil cases are decided out of court.

> **KEY QUESTION**
>
> What can be learned from Aboriginal justice?

Aboriginal Justice

There are approximately 1.2 million Aboriginal people in Canada, including First Nations, Inuit, and Métis. In many parts of Canada, Aboriginal groups operate separate justice systems and their own police forces.

One reason for the Aboriginal justice system is the high number of Aboriginal men and women in the prison population. Both Aboriginal leaders and the Canadian government are concerned about this situation. About 18 percent of male inmates and 29 percent of female inmates in federal prisons are Aboriginal. The figures are even higher in the prairie provinces. In Manitoba, for example, more than 50 percent of inmates are Aboriginal. Social and economic inequalities are a contributing factor, but the criminal justice system itself must bear some of the blame.

Canada's criminal justice system is European in origin. It relies on the state to punish the offending individual as an example to the community. Aboriginal tradition is different. It views the offender as disturbing the harmony of the community. This harmony can be restored only when the offender understands what he or she has done, admits to the hurt inflicted, and asks for forgiveness.

The Aboriginal justice system uses both sentencing circles and healing circles.

In a **sentencing circle**, the offender is brought before the victim and other members of the community, or band. The victim confronts the offender, and conveys the hurt he or she has suffered. The circle of band members decides on an appropriate sentence. This could range from banishment for a specified time to community service.

In a **healing circle**, the offender admits guilt and seeks forgiveness from the victim. The offender works toward reconciliation with the rest of the community.

These methods have been used successfully in Aboriginal communities since "time immemorial." They have also been adapted by Canada's mainstream justice system on an experimental basis. Many Canadians believe that victims of crime receive too little attention and no compensation for their suffering. One method, called **restorative justice**, allows victims, their families, and offenders to meet in a kind of healing circle. Here, the offender can understand the effects of the crime, and possibly compensate the victim in some way.

FIGURE 7.10 Garrette Courchene finds healing in drumming and singing at Winnipeg's urban sweat lodge. The program was started to help Aboriginal gang members sever ties with their gangs.

PAUSE, REFLECT, APPLY

1. How does the Aboriginal concept of justice differ from the European idea? In what way does it reflect the traditional way of life of Aboriginal peoples?

2. Why do Aboriginal peoples in Canada have the right to manage their own justice? In your view, is this system fair? Explain your opinion.

3. What is the value of restorative justice for the offender? For the victim? Can you think of situations in which restorative justice would not be appropriate? Outline these situations as you see them, and state why this method would not be an option.

REPLAY

This chapter has informed you of these civics concepts:

1. The justice system tries to balance the need for social order with the need to guard individual rights.

2. The rights of a person when arrested and tried flow from the basic idea that a person is innocent until proven guilty.

3. Young offenders have the same rights as adults along with special provisions. They can be transferred to adult courts for very serious offences.

4. Civil law concerns the settlement of differences between individuals.

5. Aboriginal justice brings offenders and victims together in community sentencing and healing circles. This approach is being adapted to Canada's judicial system.

CIVILS TOOLKIT   How to Organize Information

Organizing the information that you have gathered is an important step before writing a paper or delivering an oral report. This step will show you

- how much information you have gathered on each aspect of your topic
- whether your information is useful or relevant
- areas where you need more information.

There are several ways to organize information so that it is clear and usable. Suppose the topic for investigation is: Should marijuana possession be decriminalized? You could cluster your information in a fairly straightforward outline that uses categories and subcategories:

1. Marijuana in general
   - past and present laws
   - penalties
     - for possession and use
     - for growing, smuggling, selling
   - medical, scientific evidence regarding effects
2. Attitudes
   - past attitudes
   - changing attitudes
3. Law enforcement
   - difficulties in enforcing law
   - problems with growing operations
   - role of organized crime
4. Options
   - legalize growing and using?
   - legalize using, regulate growers?
   - don't change the law?

Another way to organize information is to use a sequence chart. This is particularly effective when looking for the connections among a series of ideas or events. For example:

past attitudes about marijuana ▶ known as harmful substance ▶ harsh laws ▶ changing attitudes ▶ seen as less harmful ▶ widespread flouting of law ▶ difficulties for courts, police

As you can see, a sequence chart can go on indefinitely.

A third information organizer is the mind map. This can reveal how one part of a topic fits in with another. (See Figure 7.11 as an example.)

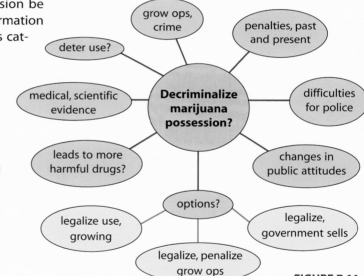

FIGURE 7.11

Skill Practice

Identify the method above that you think would be best for organizing information for writing or giving an oral report on

1. the development of laws dealing with youths from past to present
2. Aboriginal justice methods and their impact on the Canadian judicial system
3. actual crime rates and public perceptions.

STUDY HALL

Informed Citizenship

1. a) What rights must the police have in order to perform their duties efficiently?

   b) The police can obtain court approval to tap a suspect's telephone line, yet wiretap evidence cannot usually be admitted as evidence in court against the accused. Why do you think this contradiction exists? Should wiretaps be allowed as evidence, or should they be forbidden entirely?

2. Why are each of the following rights important for a citizen charged with an offence?

   ■ right to hear the charge immediately

   ■ right to a lawyer

   ■ right to bail

3. Which of the following acts would result in a) a summary offence or b) an indictable offence?

   ■ theft over $5000

   ■ bank robbery

   ■ disturbing the peace

   ■ gang fight

   ■ speeding 60 km/h over the speed limit

   ■ carrying a concealed weapon

4. Distinguish among punishment, deterrence, protection, and rehabilitation as goals of sentencing.

Purposeful Citizenship

5. How can the need for social order conflict with the need to protect individual rights? Give three examples.

6. Which result do you think is more likely to occur because of the rights extended to a person accused of a crime: an innocent person would be wrongfully convicted, or a guilty person would be set free? Be specific in referring to the rights of an accused person.

7. What factors should lead a youth court judge to sentence a convicted youth as an adult?

Active Citizenship

8. "Violent crimes deserve longer sentences than are currently given out." Do you agree with this statement? Make a list of arguments either for or against, and share it with the rest of the class.

9. The United States has one of the highest incarceration rates in the world. What do you think are the reasons for this? Consider:

   ■ social or economic factors

   ■ gun control laws

   ■ length of sentences

10. The use of cameras in schools, stores, and streets to record illegal behaviour has become commonplace in many communities. Some people believe that cameras are an invasion of citizens' privacy; others see them as an effective means of law enforcement. What do you think about this issue?

11. Research the reasons that the *Young Offenders Act* of 1984 was changed to the *Youth Criminal Justice Act* in 2002, and highlight the major changes.

CHAPTER 8

Government and the People: Issues and Solutions

George Orwell wrote *1984* long before the Internet and advanced computer technology. Today, is Big Brother watching you? Or are you watching Big Brother?

"At one end of [the hallway] a coloured poster ... had been tacked to the wall. ... BIG BROTHER IS WATCHING YOU, the caption beneath it ran."

— From *1984*, by George Orwell

When the novel *1984* was written in 1948, its description of a nightmare future was shocking. In Oceania, "Big Brother" monitors everything citizens say, read, and think. Big Brother is the central government. It knows and sees everything.

1984 raised serious questions that are still debated: How much privacy and personal decision-making power do citizens really have? Do citizens care if government becomes too powerful, as long as they get what they think they need?

"For the ordinary man is passive," wrote Orwell. "So far from endeavouring to influence the future, he simply lies down and lets things happen to him." Do you agree?

As you read this chapter, look for evidence to support the argument, "George Orwell is wrong. Ordinary people are not passive and helpless. They take action and do not simply let things happen to them."

What You Need to Know

- What forms of negotiation has Canada used to address social issues and concerns?
- How can Canadians resolve disputes outside the court system?
- Besides government, what individuals, agencies, and organizations address social issues and needs?
- How do personal and social values influence legislation?
- What limits are there on the right to dissent?
- How can citizens express their beliefs and values effectively?
- How can you prepare an effective speech?

Key Terms

compromise	civil disobedience
sovereignty	ombudsman
secession	activist
conscience	trade unions
pluralistic society	strike
dissent	collective bargaining

Key Question

Is decision making as open and democratic as it should be in Canada, in your province, and in your school?

LITERACY COACH

Different people can have very different positions on the same issue. One way to understand both sides of an argument (not just the side you support) is to take a position you personally disagree with. Now try to argue that position by bringing forward the very best evidence to support that claim. It's difficult, isn't it? By going through this exercise, you can understand the opposing viewpoint better and also expose flaws in your own reasoning.

Canadian Issues and Conflicts

As members of society, we interact with many people. We often run into differences, and we negotiate agreements on a personal level. On a government level, negotiation would not be necessary if everyone always agreed. But this is impossible. Negotiation would also be unnecessary if one person or central authority made all decisions, but this would be undemocratic.

NEGOTIATION AND COMPROMISE: THE CANADIAN WAY

Canada became a country not through civil war but through negotiation and **compromise**. During the Charlottetown, Quebec City, and London conferences (1864–1866) that led to Confederation in 1867, all sides gave up some things to get other things. Confederation thus created a federation (alliance) of provinces from former independent colonies.

Compromises led to two levels of government (see Chapter 2). The federal government deals with national and international areas, such as defence, trade, and so on. Provincial governments deal with local social, political, cultural, and economic matters. To this day, both levels dispute who has more power in overlapping areas, such as health care and the economy.

Constitutional Complexities

Negotiation and compromise also shaped conferences leading up to the *Constitution Act, 1982*. Satisfying all governments was not simple. For example, the federal and provincial negotiators had to devise several formulas for amending the constitution:

- *The basic 7/50 amending formula:* the federal government plus seven provinces (representing at least 50 percent of the population) must agree
- *Unanimity:* the federal and all provincial governments must agree to a change—for example, a change in the amending formula or the use of English or French as official national languages
- *The federal government and provincial government(s) that are involved in a change:* for example, to change provincial borders or official language(s)
- *The federal government alone:* changes to the Senate or House of Commons

Quebec: Compromise and Clarity, or the End of Canada?

Quebec did not sign the constitution in 1982. It has held two referenda (in 1980 and 1995) asking Quebeckers for the power to negotiate separation from "the rest of Canada." In both cases, a majority of Quebec voters chose to remain within Canada (59.56 percent in 1980 and 50.58 percent in 1995).

Even though a Yes vote would have ended Canada as we know it, the Quebec referenda were peaceful. Quebec **sovereignty** (complete independence from outside control) and **sovereignty-association** (independence with close economic ties to Canada) remain key issues in Canada.

Two federal–provincial efforts have tried to get Quebec to sign the constitution. In 1987, federal and provincial leaders negotiated the Meech Lake constitutional amendments with the goal of getting Quebec to sign. However, the Meech Lake Accord failed to get the required unanimous agreement.

In 1992, provincial and federal leaders negotiated new amendments to have Quebec sign the constitution. This was the Charlottetown Accord. In a national referendum, citizens in a majority of provinces, including Quebec, rejected the accord.

Although the federal government promoted Canadian unity, it did not dispute Quebec's right to hold the referenda. The federal government did criticize the 1995 Quebec referendum's wording and passed the *Clarity Act* (2000).

The *Clarity Act* lays out rules to govern the **secession** (formal withdrawal) of any province. Any referendum on separation must be based on a clear question and win a "clear majority." The Act states that "it would be for elected representatives to determine what constitutes a clear question and what constitutes a clear majority."

► **DID YOU KNOW** ◄

Only three national referenda have been held in Canada: in 1898, on prohibition; in 1942, on conscription; and in 1992, on the Charlottetown Accord. Why do you think national referenda have been so rare?

THE WEB ►►►

Read the preamble to the *Clarity Act* at www.emp.ca/civics

FIGURE 8.1 Passion or politics? A seven-year-old from Guelph, Ontario, cheers for Canadian unity at a Montreal rally just before the 1995 Quebec referendum. Businesses across Canada gave discounts for people to travel to Quebec. Was this fair to Quebec? Explain.

THE WEB ▶▶▶
Learn about the sometimes deadly confrontations between Aboriginal activists and police at Oka, Quebec; Ipperwash, Ontario; and Gustafsen Lake, BC, at www.emp.ca/civics

SUBJUGATION, CONFRONTATION, NEGOTIATION: AN ABORIGINAL PERSPECTIVE

Debate, negotiation, court cases, constitutional conferences, land agreements, violent confrontations: these are some of the processes that have been used to deal with disputes between Aboriginal peoples and the governments of Canada (see also Chapter 9).

The *Constitution Act, 1982* recognized that Aboriginal peoples have basic rights as Canada's first inhabitants. These rights pertain to land and to Aboriginal cultural traditions. For the first time, the Act also recognized the right of Aboriginal peoples to participate directly in the constitutional process. This promise was followed up by a First Ministers' Conference on Aboriginal Rights (1983–1987).

Later, in 1996, the Royal Commission on Aboriginal Peoples affirmed the right to some forms of Aboriginal self-government (see Chapter 2). Aboriginal leaders believe that this power will help them negotiate and solve many social and economic problems.

SOURCES

"I found the Indians suffering, deprived of responsible government and public liberties. We have made petitions to the Canadian government; we have taken time. I have done my duty."

— Louis Riel, Métis politician and rebel leader, on trial in July 31, 1885 (Riel was found guilty of treason and hanged)

"We are denied a voice in our own land. Our peoples have the right to live in a world where our Nations are recognized as nations. For seven generations our Nations have been under attack. ... I believe in using the courts, the media, the judicial system. I know when to fight and when to negotiate."

— Matthew Coon Come, former National Chief of the Assembly of First Nations, 2002

PAUSE, REFLECT, APPLY

1. What significant constitutional compromise was negotiated in a) 1867? b) 1982?
2. What is the meaning of the "7/50 amending formula"?
3. Describe the federal government's position during the Quebec referenda.
4. What rights for Aboriginal peoples were recognized in 1982?
5. What was the major recommendation of the Royal Commission on Aboriginal Peoples?
6. The *Clarity Act* says a successful referendum on secession would require a "clear majority." In your opinion, what would that be?
7. a) Compare the quotations in Sources, above.
   b) How many years separate them?
   c) What does this span indicate to you?

What Beliefs Should Guide Elected Representatives?

In Orwell's *1984*, citizens do not make decisions. They have no choices and no power. In Canada today, both citizens and politicians are daily called upon to make choices and decisions.

KEY QUESTION
On what basis should elected representatives make decisions that involve questions of conscience?

MORAL ISSUES AND CONTROVERSIES

Like all citizens, legislators have personal values. Sometimes these conflict with their public roles. Capital punishment (the execution of people convicted of certain crimes), euthanasia ("mercy killing"), the "right to die" (assisted suicide), abortion, the age of consent—the list of controversial issues is long.

All legislators and voters will face this decision many times: Which is more important: not to impose personal beliefs on others, or to stand up for one's beliefs—even when to do so is unpopular?

During elections, voters can ask candidates about issues of **conscience** (personal sense of right and wrong). If elected, would the candidate vote on policy and legislation according to

- personal beliefs?
- religious teachings?
- the party's position?
- the will of the majority?

Or, would the candidate look at each case individually?

Canada is a **pluralistic society**. This means that diverse religious and cultural groups must coexist peacefully. Answering questions such as the above will challenge candidates and elected representatives.

FIGURE 8.2 Marcel Tremblay was suffering from a painful and crippling terminal illness. He held a press conference in 2005 and announced he would end his own life—while he still could. Reporters waited outside his home. Inside, Tremblay placed a helium-filled bag over his head and died of suffocation. He was surrounded by family, but no one helped or tried to stop him. Tremblay believed that terminally ill people need access to assisted suicide. How might his public action change social values?

Would you vote for someone who acts only according to personal conscience, whether or not that person's view differs from your own? Would you vote for someone whom you consider to be honest and intelligent, and trust that person's choices?

Personal and Social Values

Each of us has personal beliefs and values. We also have social values. In a democracy, these interact. For example, some people believe that schools and parents should have the right to use corporal (physical) punishment to discipline children. Canadian social values say this is no longer appropriate. One may personally believe that it is wrong to work on a holy day, but socially believe that the choice should be an individual one.

Changing social and personal beliefs about human sexuality also create controversy. Same-sex marriage is one example.

> **FACE OFF** **Church? Conscience? Constitution? The Same-Sex Marriage Debate**

After courts in most provinces ruled that the traditional heterosexual definition of marriage was unconstitutional, the federal government studied the issue. In 2005, Liberal Prime Minister Paul Martin introduced Bill C-38 to redefine marriage to include same-sex partners. Many MPs believed that this was the correct thing to do. Others believed that it was morally wrong.

Some churches and religious authorities in Canada supported the bill; many opposed it. The Roman Catholic Church instructed Catholic legislators to vote against Bill C-38. The Congregation for the Doctrine of the Faith, the source of the Church's legal and moral teaching, stated on June 3, 2003:

> It is one thing to maintain that individual citizens are free to behave in a certain manner [homosexual behaviour]; this falls within the civil right to freedom. It is quite different to give these activities legal recognition. ... Where legislation in favour of the recognition of homosexual unions is proposed for the first time in a legislative assembly, the Catholic law-maker has a moral duty to express his opposition clearly and publicly vote against it. To vote in favour of a law so harmful to the public good is gravely immoral.

In Vatican II's *Document of Religious Liberty*, the Catholic Church also advised that a person knows the will of God through his or her own conscience:

> He is bound to follow his conscience faithfully. ... He must not be forced to act contrary to his conscience.

Prime Minister Paul Martin is a devout Catholic. He introduced Bill C-38 to the House of Commons in February 2005, saying this:

> Religious leaders have strong views both for and against this legislation. They should express them.

Certainly, many of us in this House, myself included, have a strong faith, and we value that faith and its influence on the decisions we make. But all of us have been elected to serve here as Parliamentarians. ... [W]e are responsible for serving all Canadians and protecting the rights of all Canadians. ... [W]e must not shrink from the need to reaffirm the rights and responsibilities of Canadians in an evolving society.

What Do You Think?

1. In your own words, define a) a moral decision, b) civil law, c) faith, and d) evolving society.
2. On what grounds does the Congregation for the Doctrine of the Faith oppose laws that would recognize homosexual unions?
3. How did Prime Minister Martin justify promoting the same-sex marriage bill?
4. Using the Internet, research churches and religious leaders that supported Bill C-38. Summarize their positions.

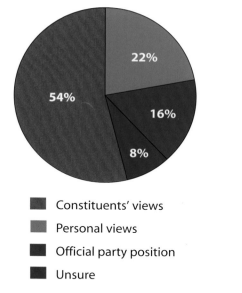

■ Constituents' views
■ Personal views
■ Official party position
■ Unsure

FIGURE 8.3 Canadian opinion on how MPs should vote on same-sex marriage (based on a 2005 poll). *Source: SES Research, "Same-Sex Marriage: A Nation Divided," February 6, 2005.*

PAUSE, REFLECT, APPLY

1. What does "pluralistic society" mean?
2. How does pluralism complicate legislators' decisions?
3. What is the difference between "personal beliefs" and "social values"?

4. Clearly explain why elected representatives should vote on issues based primarily on
   a) conscience
   b) the wishes of constituents
   c) party policy.
   Is there a way in which all three concerns can be addressed?

How Can Citizens Act on Their Beliefs and Values?

The very first clause of the Charter guarantees freedom of thought, belief, opinion, and expression "subject only to such reasonable limits prescribed by law as can be demonstrably justified in a free and democratic society." Citizens discover what those "reasonable limits" are when they **dissent**, or disagree, with government.

▶ **KEY QUESTION**
What limits, if any, should be placed on citizens' ability to respond to issues?

FIGURE 8.4 British singer Pete Doherty performs at a Unite Against Racism concert on May Day in Trafalgar Square in London, 2005. The concert concluded the union-based International Workers' Day March in London. What steps can you take to oppose racism?

THE CANADIAN CIVIL LIBERTIES ASSOCIATION

The Canadian Civil Liberties Association (CCLA) is a non-profit, non-governmental organization. Funded by thousands of ordinary Canadians, it supports the democratic right to dissent—even when views are unpopular or offensive.

The CCLA works to keep "reasonable limits" as broad as possible. Its philosophy is that the best protection against unjust government is an atmosphere of free and open debate.

For the CCLA, the right to dissent is the foundation of all freedoms.

The CCLA uses public forums—such as trials, government committees and rallies, and the media—to identify and oppose attempts by governments and courts to infringe upon citizens' rights. In the view of the CCLA, it is better to **censure** (criticize) offensive people through the media than to **censor** (gag or repress) them by law. That belief is easy to put into words but difficult in practice.

PEACE, ORDER, GOOD GOVERNMENT— AND PROTEST?

How far does the right to dissent go?

In April 2001, 25,000 people protested the Quebec Summit of the Americas. They believed that international trade policies were being made secretly and that these would hurt poorer nations. Riots erupted, and police and demonstrators accused each other of using unnecessary force. The two sides disagreed on "reasonable limits."

A police spokesperson explained: "We have full intentions of allowing the democratic right of people to demonstrate, but if personal behaviour becomes violent, the police will respond."

In September 2002, Jewish organizers invited former Israeli Prime Minister Benjamin Netanyahu to speak at Montreal's Concordia University. Concordia has many Jewish, Palestinian, and Arab students.

Ongoing conflict in the Middle East had created tensions between the pro-Israeli and pro-Palestinian factions on campus.

Many students objected to Netanyahu's policies and organized a protest. Police were called in when it turned violent. Netanyahu's speech was cancelled. Later, a speech by an anti-Israel critic was cancelled for fear of retaliation by pro-Israel students. The university banned any future events related to the political climate of the Middle East.

Intimidation and Freedom of Expression

Groups such as the CCLA say public demonstrations are one of the few ways that disadvantaged people can be politically active. Protests, however, should be used to criticize, not intimidate. How democratic is it when scare tactics stop a person from speaking?

In contrast to the CCLA, groups such as the Ontario Coalition Against Poverty (OCAP) endorse **direct action**—the use of disruptive behaviour in marches and protests. They also advocate **civil disobedience** (passive resistance to government and peaceful breaking of laws). These tactics are seen as necessary tools of dissent against unjust governments and social inequalities. Direct action and civil disobedience are justified on the grounds that large banks, corporations, and businesses run the economy and influence government policy yet are not democratic institutions.

> **THE WEB** ►►►
> In "Big Mountie Is Watching You," the CCLA warns police against "targeting democratic radicals." Read the warning at www.emp.ca/civics

OTHER WAYS TO STAND UP FOR YOUR RIGHTS

In an attempt to reduce court time and costs, federal and provincial governments set up agencies, boards, and tribunals to deal with disputes that concern citizens. Some of the areas covered include

- human rights
- accommodation
- conservation
- environmental assessment
- liquor control
- immigration and refugees
- parole
- labour relations

FIGURE 8.5 An Ontario Coalition Against Poverty protestor bites a police officer after being pepper-sprayed during a demonstration outside a Liberal Party barbecue in Toronto in 2004. How could both police and demonstrators justify their actions?

THE WEB ▶▶▶

Check out Ombudsman Ontario's "How to Complain Effectively" at www.emp.ca/civics

Many provinces also provide an **ombudsman**, a public official who deals with complaints about government departments and agencies. For example, the office of the Ontario Ombudsman investigates and resolves thousands of complaints each year. Alternatively, it directs complainants to appropriate agencies or boards.

PAUSE, REFLECT, APPLY

1. Explain the difference between a) "censure" and "censor," and b) "criticize" and "intimidate."
2. What is the CCLA, and why do citizens support it?
3. a) How do the CCLA and OCAP differ in their attitudes toward the use of direct action?
   b) How would each organization justify its opinion?
   c) Which position do you agree with? Explain.

4. Why did protestors at the Quebec Summit and Concordia feel justified in their actions?
5. a) Describe whether you have the right to dissent in your school, home, and any organizations to which you belong.
   b) If not, why is dissent not allowed?
   c) If dissent is allowed, how can it be expressed effectively?

▷ **KEY QUESTION**

Aside from participating in government and protests, how can you express your beliefs and values and make a difference?

☐ **DISCUSSION POINT**

How does the message of the starfish story differ from that of Orwell's *1984*?

Finding Positive Ways to Effect Change

This story is often used in civics classes and volunteer groups:

A man walking along a beach sees a local woman picking up starfish, one at a time, and then throwing them into the water. Washed up on shore, the starfish are dying from lack of oxygen. The man points out that there are thousands of starfish on the beach. This is happening at thousands of beaches. "You can't possibly make a difference," he says. "Made a difference to that one," replies the local as she throws another starfish out to sea.

PEOPLE TAKING ACTION TOGETHER

There are thousands of individuals and not-for-profit, non-governmental groups in Canada. Their goal? To save the world, one person, one project, at a time. They and their causes cover the political spectrum. Here are some examples.

1. Leaders Today

Marc and Craig Kielburger (who founded the organization Free the Children) run workshops that train students in organizational and leadership skills. They also provide opportunities to volunteer globally—while participants are still in high school! (See the Chapter 5 CivicStar feature on Joe Opatowski, page 88.)

2. Centre for Social Justice

This organization is more politically **activist** (more aggressive) than Leaders Today. It educates the public about social and economic inequities. At summer camps, university students work with people from various backgrounds to learn how to lead and dissent more effectively.

3. Habitat for Humanity (H4H)

H4H is ideal for the non-political person who wants a hands-on way to make a difference. H4H acquires land and materials; then a band of volunteers works with families to build affordable homes. H4H does not eradicate homelessness—it reduces it, one house at a time.

SERVICE CLUBS

Service clubs allow citizens to socialize and, at the same time, contribute to society. Goals can vary, from providing scholarships to funding shelters for street youth. This year, about 6.5 million volunteers will help 180,000 charity organizations operate across Canada. Membership fees and fundraising—not government funding—keep them running.

THE WEB ▶▶▶
Find links to hundreds of volunteer sites at www.emp.ca/civics

FIGURE 8.6 Organizations use logos to get their missions and messages across. Can you match these logos to the club or organization mentioned in this chapter? Check them out at www.emp.ca/civics

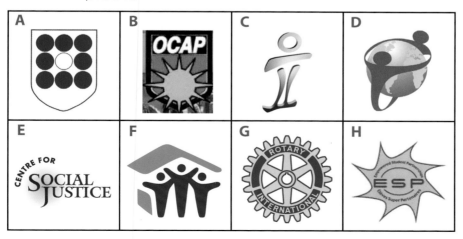

Every community in Canada has service clubs such as the Kinsmen, Knights of Columbus, Shriners, Lions, Kiwanis, YM/YWCA, Civitans, Elks, B'nai Brith, Zonta—to name just a few. Each aims to create community spirit by working on local and global projects.

1. Rotary International

This network has 31,000 clubs in 166 countries with a total of 1.2 million members. Its global PolioPlus Campaign set 2005 as a target to eradicate polio. Starting in 1988, Rotarians raised $500 million and more than 1 billion volunteer hours for global immunization. By press time, it had achieved a 99 percent reduction in polio.

2. Empowered Student Partnerships

This group unites students, the police service, and the Canadian Safe Schools Network to deal with community problems including bullying, gossiping, drugs, and drinking and driving. ESP also works on building healthy relationships, food drives, environmental protection, and outreach programs.

COMMUNICATING, CELEBRATING, AND COMMEMORATING

Canadians communicate their beliefs, values, opinions, and priorities in many different ways. The following options are not available in all societies, particularly in countries with authoritarian governments:

- Submit letters, articles, and opinions to local and national media, including newspapers, magazines, radio and television phone-in shows, Web logs (blogs), and so on.
- Participate in walk-a-thons, marathons, bike-a-thons, wheelchair marathons, hunger strikes, and sit-ins.
- Attend meetings, join school councils, join in rallies and marches, distribute pamphlets.
- Wear signs, labels, buttons, poppies, and hats.
- Wear ribbons and other symbols to express sympathy, remembrance, solidarity, and support. There are white ribbons (men against male violence against women), red ribbons (AIDS; MADD), green ribbons (environmental action), blue ribbons (campaign against second-hand smoke), and purple ribbons (remembrance of victims of the 1989 Montreal massacre).

CivicStar

JEAN VANIER AND L'ARCHE

Attitudes toward people with mental disabilities reveal society's values. At one point, people with mental disabilities were confined in institutions in Canada.

Eugenics (the study and use of controlled pro-creation to "improve society") was embraced by many authorities around the world, starting in the 1920s. Eugenics was core policy in Nazi Germany, a way to eliminate "inferior" people and create a superior race. In Alberta, under the *Sexual Sterilization Act, 1928*, doctors sterilized mentally ill or "retarded" people without their knowledge or consent. The law was in effect until the 1970s.

Jean Vanier, son of former Canadian Governor General Georges Vanier, stands for a different choice. In 1964, he purchased an old house in France, which he shared with two mentally disabled men. From there he began "L'Arche," a community for people with learning and developmental disabilities. Today there are L'Arche communities in 30 countries, nine in Ontario alone.

L'Arche is a community, not an institution. It is composed of core members and assistants—not patients, clients, and staff. Each community member has a role and makes contributions, all according to his or her skills. Hundreds of volunteers also assist in teaching life and vocational skills, sharing household chores, and creating a world where everyone is treated with respect.

Vanier believes that social order is often based on fear—even of the poor, weak, and disabled. If citizens are not watchful, society will create an order where "the rich and powerful are at the top, and at the bottom are the weak, the fragile, and the crushed."

"The aim of L'Arche is not to change the world, but to create little places where love is possible," says Vanier.

Your Play

1. Describe how Jean Vanier put his values into practice in the world.
2. Research the organization and the meaning of the word "L'Arche." Vanier had a strong religious background. Why might he have used that title?
3. How do Vanier's values and beliefs contrast with social beliefs and policies based on eugenics? (You may want to research eugenics and Nazism; see Chapter 10.)

Canadians also express beliefs and values by choosing people and events to commemorate and celebrate. Some examples: Labour Day, Remembrance Day, National Day for Remembrance and Action in Violence Against Women, International Day for the Elimination of Racism, Raoul Wallenberg Day, Sovereign's Birthday (Victoria Day), A Day of Commemoration of the Great Upheaval (Acadian Exile), Constitutional Proclamation Day, Multiculturalism Day, Saint-Jean-Baptiste Day, Aboriginal Day, Flag Day, Heritage Day, and, of course, Canada Day.

PAUSE, REFLECT, APPLY

1. a) Create a comparison chart of organizations described above. Show what all have in common and how each is different.
   b) Who are the "starfish" that each organization is helping?
2. More people in Canada volunteer than take part in protests. Why might that be?
3. What criteria would you use in deciding how best to take a stand on a social problem?
4. Research volunteer organizations using the Web feature on page 139.
   a) With which organization(s) would you volunteer?
   b) What criteria would you use to make that decision?
5. Identify groups in your school that are similar to ESP. Do you belong to any of them? Explain your reasons.
6. Create a table, poster, or display of federal, provincial, and civic flags, symbols, flowers, animals, and logos.
7. Which of these communications options (table, poster, display) do you feel would be most effective in the following situations?
   a) fundraising
   b) changing a school rule
   c) getting a candidate elected
   d) getting a traffic light installed on your street
   e) raising student awareness of drug abuse.

▶ **KEY QUESTION**

What options are available to workers and employers, other than the courts and legislatures, to resolve conflicts?

THE WEB ▶▶▶

The Canadian Union of Public Employees and the Canadian Auto Workers are two of the largest unions in Canada. Find links to them and many other unions at www.emp.ca/civics

☐ **DISCUSSION POINT**

Labour strikes make headlines. Peaceful negotiations between workers and employers usually do not. Why do you think this is so?

Labour Negotiations and Strikes

Workers in Canada have a legal right to negotiate with employers for better wages and working conditions. Working conditions include work hours, workplace environment, provisions for sickness and injury, job expectations, protection against being laid off or fired, health and pensions benefits, and so on.

Some groups of workers form **trade unions**. As union members, workers elect representatives to negotiate with employers collectively on their behalf. Government regulates how workplaces unionize. In 2004, 30.5 percent of all workers in Canada belonged to unions.

Generally, unionized workers have the right to **strike** (refuse to work) if the employer does not bargain seriously during contract negotiations. Employers have often resisted union activity because it may interfere with how they run their businesses, affecting labour costs and profits.

METHODS OF LABOUR NEGOTIATION

Provincial and federal laws set out rights and protections for all workers regarding working conditions, minimum wages, and conditions under which a worker can be fired or laid off. In Ontario, employers and employees can take disputes to the Ontario Labour Relations Board for a hearing to settle grievances. Ontario's *Labour Relations Act, 1995* also sets out the rules and procedures for negotiating and settling labour disputes.

► FACE OFF   Essential Services and Teacher Strikes

Not all unionized workers can strike. Some services are considered essential and cannot be legally shut down. The Ontario *Crown Employees Collective Bargaining Act, 1993* describes essential services as those that are necessary to prevent any danger to life, health, or safety. But there is no official list of essential jobs. During labour negotiations, union and employer representatives must agree which workers, if any, are essential.

Which jobs do you consider essential? Most people would say police, firefighters, and doctors; other jobs are open to debate. What about garbage collectors, transit workers, snow removers, airport workers, or ambulance drivers?

What about teachers? Are they so essential that they should not be allowed to strike? Two teams face off on this issue:

No Strikes for Teachers

Think of the innocent victims: students trying to graduate and poor and single parents who cannot take time off work to look after their children during the day. Teachers are professionals, like lawyers and doctors. They lose respect when they go on strike. If a business has a strike, consumers can buy elsewhere—students have no alternatives when teachers strike. Taxes pay teachers' salaries—during a strike, taxpayers get nothing in return.

Let Teachers Strike

Teacher strikes endanger nobody's safety. They are disruptive, but that is the point. Strikes allow teachers to put public pressure on government to bargain seriously. Besides, being inconvenient is not the same as being essential. If government forbids strikes because of inconvenience, no strikes would be allowed. And if arbitration is imposed, the media may not pay attention to problems in the education system that teachers want to expose. Forbidding strikes only creates frustration and anger.

What Do You Think?

1. According to the definition in the *Crown Employees Collective Bargaining Act*, would you consider teachers an essential service?
2. Should teachers be permitted to strike? Why or why not?
3. Should any of the other services mentioned above be listed as essential based on the criteria of the Act?

Methods of reaching agreement include:

1. **Collective bargaining**: Employer and employee representatives meet to negotiate between what the workers want or need and what the employer is willing or able to afford.
2. **Mediation**: If collective bargaining fails, an impartial person is brought in to re-examine the issues and suggest solutions. Mediators cannot impose a solution.
3. **Arbitration**: A mutually agreed upon or government-appointed impartial person (or panel) studies the dispute and draws up a solution. Arbitration may be binding (must be accepted) or non-binding.

FIGURE 8.7 Wal-Mart is the world's largest retailer and prefers to deal with individual workers, not unions. In Jonquière, Quebec, workers voted to make their store the first unionized Wal-Mart in North America in 2004–2005. In April 2005, Wal-Mart closed the store, saying it was no longer profitable. In this ad, Wal-Mart explained its decision. How might the closing affect attitudes toward Wal-Mart? Toward unions?

PAUSE, REFLECT, APPLY

1. Describe collective bargaining, mediation, and arbitration in your own words.
2. What areas are included in "working conditions"?
3. What is the role of the Labour Relations Board?
4. a) Why would workers feel it necessary to form unions?
   b) Why would many businesses oppose unions?
5. Research the situation of Wal-Mart in Jonquière, Quebec, and produce a list of arguments for both sides.

REPLAY

This chapter has informed you of these civics concepts:

1. Canada's constitution has been developed through conflict, negotiation, and compromise.
2. Political policies and social values are influenced by personal values and beliefs.
3. Canadians use many different agencies and processes in politics, the community, and the workplace to address injustices and conflicts.
4. Canadians can express their values and beliefs in a variety of democratic ways through words and actions.
5. One of our greatest freedoms is the right to dissent. One of our most common practices is negotiation.

CIVICS TOOLKIT

How to Be Heard: Preparing an Effective Speech

Anyone who wants to present a dissenting point of view will probably need to speak publicly. The problem is, public speaking terrifies most people. Effective oral communication, however, is a fundamental literacy skill. Like most skills, it can be learned.

There are three basic types of speeches:

- an impromptu talk (1–2 minutes, little or no preparation)
- a prepared speech (2–5 minutes, lots of preparation)
- a major address, such as a valedictory speech (even more preparation)

Here are some speech-making tips:

- *Know the purpose of your speech.* Is it to present information, or to persuade? Do you want to make a specific point, or to amuse? If you are not clear in your own mind what you are intending to do, chances are your audience won't know, either.
- *Know your audience.* Are they peers, friends, family? What are their ages? How much do they know on this subject? This will help you decide on the amount of information and the level of vocabulary to use.
- *Research.* Know your subject; know your facts. This will improve your speech and your self-confidence. Locate and include compelling data, examples, illustrations, quotations, and sources.
- *Don't drown them in data.* If it doesn't relate to your main point, drop it. Otherwise, you run the risk of boring your audience.
- *Make a "speech burger":*

  Tell them what you are going to tell them

  Tell them what you want them to know

  Tell them what you told them

- *Make an outline.* Prepare a summary of your main points and crisp, clear, concluding remarks. What do you most want them to remember? How do you want them to respond?
- *Get their attention.* Hook listeners with a catchy introduction, and clearly describe what your speech is for and about. Avoid clichés.
- *Be brief.* After your introduction, limit yourself to three or four main points. Speakers often use the words "First," "Second," "Third" to keep their thoughts in order. Speeches need unity and coherence.
- *Be witty.* When appropriate, include humour or a personal anecdote (story).
- *Practise your delivery.* Ideally, videotape yourself giving the speech. Review the tape with a partner or someone with public speaking experience. During playback, look for
  - vocal clarity and projection
  - vocal variation in tone and emphasis
  - pronunciation and enunciation
  - eye contact with the audience
  - stiffness, fidgeting, over-reading of notes
  - appropriate hand, body, and facial gestures
  - sincerity.

Skill Practice

1. Prepare a three- to four-minute persuasive speech.
2. Your topic is *either* a) "teachers provide an essential service and should not be entitled to go on strike" or b) "students must participate during strikes to support teachers."
3. Videotape your speech away from the classroom and submit it on tape.
4. Have it assessed by peers or the teacher in preparation for your end-of-chapter assignment.

STUDY HALL

Informed Citizenship

1. a) Explain how the federal system and the amending formulas are examples of negotiated compromises in Canada's constitutional development.

    b) Why were these deals necessary?

2. a) What types of powers and recognition are Aboriginal peoples asking for in negotiations with Ottawa and the provinces?

    b) Why do Aboriginal leaders insist on achieving these goals?

3. a) What rights do Canadians have under the Charter to hold public protests?

    b) What is meant by the right to dissent?

    c) What restriction is put on the freedom of expression?

4. What is the role and purpose of the provincial ombudsman?

5. Define the following terms and concepts: dissent, civil disobedience, activist, eugenics, binding arbitration, and essential services.

Purposeful Citizenship

6. Select a volunteer organization from this or another chapter and research its structure and work. Create a newsletter, brochure, pamphlet, or computer presentation that clearly and effectively promotes the group and asks for public donations to support its work.

7. Holding a referendum has been suggested as a way to settle the issues of Quebec sovereignty, Aboriginal land claims, and same-sex marriage. Referenda have also been strongly opposed. Give reasons why a referendum is a) acceptable and b) unacceptable as a method to deal with each issue. Consider these criteria: minority rights and majority rule; public participation; level of public understanding; clarity of the question.

8. Employees and employers can negotiate using collective bargaining, mediation, arbitration, and strikes.

    a) Use a table or another graphic organizer to show both the benefits and the drawbacks of each method.

    b) Of the methods, which would be the ideal way to negotiate and settle issues? Why?

Active Citizenship

9. In groups of four, work as an imaginary team of assistants to a member of Parliament. A vote is to be held on whether to allow assisted suicide. You are to compile three lists: a) all groups and viewpoints to be considered; b) all arguments for assisted suicide; and c) all arguments against assisted suicide. Don't forget public opinion polls. Finally, you must advise the MP on how to vote. Research the issue. (Go to www.emp.ca/civics for some good links.) As a bonus, submit your material to a class vote.

10. Select any issue from this chapter and prepare and deliver a three-minute speech on it. Consult with your teacher. Referring to the Civics Toolkit (page 145), conduct research and prepare your speech. Record your speech on video for evaluation, using the guidelines.

11. Set up a class or school calendar highlighting commemoration dates in Canada from this chapter and elsewhere. Each class member should

    a) select one date and research its history

    b) simply and accurately explain the history of the date

    c) prepare a series of 30-second infomercials for the morning announcements in your school celebrating Canada's democratic achievement.

12. Create a two-column list of examples from this chapter that support and oppose George Orwell's premise that the ordinary person is simply a victim of events. Choose one side, and research more evidence to support your point of view. *Alternative*: You and a partner each prepare a speech, pro and con.

13. Research a group such as Empowered Student Partnerships that is not represented at your school. Attend a meeting and find out why the group is absent. See if you can start such a group at your school. If there is one, what evidence can you find to show that it is a worthwhile activity?

14. Is Big Brother watching you? Through observation and discussion in class, at home, and at work, brainstorm and list the ways in which governments or other authorities can track what you do. Do you find this surveillance threatening or comforting? Explain your view.

UNIT 3
Citizenship in Action

CHAPTER 9

How Do You Define Citizenship?

"Our differences make us strong."

What You Need to Know

- What are the unique characteristics of Aboriginal citizenship?
- What are the historical roots of bilingualism in Canada?
- What are the forms of bilingualism in Canada today?
- Why did Canada change its immigration policies?
- What is multiculturalism, and what forms does it take?
- What is the meaning of Canadian citizenship?
- How can you organize and write a formal essay?

Key Terms

Iroquois Confederacy
First Nations
Inuit
Métis
United Nations Human Development Index (HDI)
Official Languages Act
United Empire Loyalists
republicanism
Holocaust
refugees
points system
multiculturalism

Key Question

How has the past influenced Canadian citizenship?

"Well, as the saying goes: 'I am Canadian.' What does that mean to me? Lots of different things. For one thing, my family speaks French; we moved here from Tunisia in the early 1990s. We are also Muslim, and I use the prayer room at school. Being Canadian might be different for you, though, because there's no cookie-cutter shape. You can be many things and still share this idea—of Canada, and of being Canadian. Our differences make us strong. I like that."

— Samira, a grade 10 student in Quebec

In many ways, Canada contains the globe within its borders. Built by three founding peoples—the Aboriginal peoples, the English, and the French—Canada has offered citizenship to people from all corners of the world. What does being Canadian mean to you? Do you think our differences make us strong? Why or why not?

Citizenship and the Aboriginal Peoples of Canada

The Aboriginal peoples were the first inhabitants of the land that is now Canada. Before the arrival of the Europeans, they had established a variety of governmental systems. On the West Coast, some hierarchical societies evolved with top-down decision makers. In the East, the **Iroquois Confederacy** emphasized decision making by consensus and diplomatic relations with neighbouring nations. The Confederacy also had its own constitution, which was based on many democratic ideals.

WHO ARE THE ABORIGINAL PEOPLES?

According to section 35 of the *Constitution Act, 1982*, the term "Aboriginal peoples of Canada" includes the **First Nations**, **Inuit**, and **Métis** peoples of Canada. "First Nations" refers to those nations who first met the Europeans; it does not include the Inuit of the North or the Métis, who are the descendants of European explorers and the local Aboriginal peoples.

☐ **DISCUSSION POINT**
Why do the Aboriginal peoples have a unique position in Canada?

ABORIGINAL RIGHTS

Historically, Canada mistreated the Aboriginal peoples. At the end of the 19th century, Aboriginal children were forced from their homes and sent to residential schools. Authorities wanted them assimilated (absorbed) into mainstream Canadian culture. Approximately 100,000 children attended these schools over the decades. Under the 1927 *Indian Act*, Aboriginal peoples could not form political organizations.

Today, Aboriginal peoples have the same rights as other Canadians. Most importantly, existing "treaty or other rights" are protected under section 25 of the *Canadian Charter of Rights and Freedoms*. In many cases, this means eligibility for certain benefits conferred by existing treaties, as well as the right to self-government. These rights are basic to "citizenship" for the Aboriginal peoples in Canada.

Despite guaranteed rights, Aboriginal peoples still do not share in Canada's general prosperity. This injustice is considered by many to be a result of mistreatment. The **United Nations Human Development Index (HDI)** measures economic status, literacy, education, life expectancy, and other factors of human well-being yearly. Since 1990, Canada has ranked first in the world eight times. However, compared with other Canadians, Aboriginal people live shorter lives, receive less education, make less money, more often live in inadequate housing conditions, experience more health problems, and face a much higher rate of imprisonment.

ABORIGINAL CITIZENS: MEETING THE CHALLENGE

The Assembly of First Nations (AFN) is anxious to resolve some of the issues facing First Nations people in Canada today. This organization brings together representatives from over 600 bands across Canada. Today, one of the AFN's top priorities is improving the state of First Nations education. In Ontario, for example, a recent survey of Aboriginal schools found that books and other learning resources were in short supply, that most schools were understaffed, and that literacy rates were lower than the provincial average.

Two-time national chief of the AFN Phil Fontaine has said that the solution to issues is not just increased funding, but "the empowerment of First Nations teachers, principals, and school boards to exercise the necessary decision-making power to end discrimination and inequality in educational opportunities."

Fontaine's runner-up in the 2003 AFN election, Mohawk lawyer and former chief Roberta Jamieson, has worked to improve Aboriginal access to law and medical schools. To reflect the population base, she says, Ontario needs an additional 350 Aboriginal physicians. As head of the National Aboriginal Achievement Foundation (NAAF), she has also overseen programs that encourage young Aboriginal people to reach their educational and career goals.

SOURCES

A Declaration of First Nations

This declaration is posted on the Assembly of First Nations' Web site.

We the Original Peoples of this land know the Creator put us here.

The Creator gave us laws that govern all our relationships to live in harmony with nature and mankind.

The Laws of the Creator defined our rights and responsibilities.

The Creator gave us our spiritual beliefs, our languages, our culture, and a place on Mother Earth which provided us with all our needs.

We have maintained our Freedom, our Languages, and our Traditions from time immemorial.

We continue to exercise the rights and fulfill the responsibilities and obligations given to us by the Creator for the land upon which we were placed.

The Creator has given us the right to govern ourselves and the right to self-determination.

The rights and responsibilities given to us by the Creator cannot be altered or taken away by any other Nation.

Source: www.afn.ca/article.asp?id=52.

FIGURE 9.1 Nunavut resident Jordin Tootoo (left) is the first Inuit athlete to play in the National Hockey League. The Nunavut territorial government features Jordin and four local teenagers on an inspirational poster encouraging young people to stay in school and set goals.

CivicStar

DR. LILLIAN EVA DYCK

She was born Lillian Quan to a Cree mother and a Chinese father in 1945. Living in a number of small towns in Saskatchewan and Alberta, she and her brother struggled for acceptance. In grade 9 she was placed in a class for slow learners, despite her high intelligence.

Lillian considered becoming a high school science teacher but eventually withdrew from teacher's college. She didn't enjoy speaking in public, and she realized she wanted to pursue a career as a scientist.

Inspired by her mother, Eva, Lillian obtained a master's degree and a doctorate from the University of Saskatchewan. She also overcame her fear of public speaking through constant practice. After becoming a professor of biological psychi-

atry, she went on to research treatment for conditions such as Parkinson's disease, schizophrenia, and Alzheimer's.

Until receiving her doctorate in 1981, Lillian kept her Aboriginal origins hidden. She has said, "The 1950s were a time when there was actually a hierarchy of racism, when being Chinese was difficult enough."

Today, however, she exults in her heritage: "I am my mother's daughter. Like her, I am part of the circle of women warriors, each of us in our own way fighting for a better world for our children and our children's children."

In 2005, Lillian Dyck was appointed to the Canadian Senate.

Your Play

1. Describe three obstacles in life that Lillian Dyck had to overcome.
2. Do you think it is ever justifiable to hide who you are? Why or why not?

PAUSE, REFLECT, APPLY

1. List three characteristics of Canadian citizenship.
2. How are the rights of Aboriginal peoples guaranteed?

3. What has the Assembly of First Nations identified as a top priority for Canada and its Aboriginal peoples? Why is this issue a priority?

▶ **KEY QUESTION**

Why is Canada a bilingual nation?

The Two Founding Peoples

The first Europeans to settle in Canada were the French, followed by the British. These two nations have contributed a great deal to the collective past of Canada, especially to its bilingual identity.

CITIZENSHIP AND FRENCH CANADIANS

▶ **DID YOU KNOW** ◀

In 1666, Jean Talon conducted the first census (official analysis of the population) in North America. He found 3,215 citizens in New France.

The first French settlement dates back to 1534, when explorer Jacques Cartier claimed areas around the St. Lawrence River. France established settlements in Acadia (now Nova Scotia and New Brunswick) and Quebec. In Quebec, individuals such as Jean Talon, a chief administrator, and Marguerite d'Youville, the founder of the Sisters of Charity, made important contributions to society.

The Origins of French-Language Rights

In 1759, New France was defeated by the British in the Battle of the Plains of Abraham. To maintain the loyalty of French-speaking colonials, the British granted Quebec language, religious, and legal rights.

When Canada was created in 1867, the *British North America Act*, its constitution, recognized French language rights in Parliament and in Quebec. In the 20th century, recognition of Canada's French–English linguistic heritage was extended with the issuing of

- dual-language postage stamps (1927)
- dual-language currency (1937)
- simultaneous translations of House of Commons debates (1959)
- dual-language labels for consumer products (1974).

Canada adopted bilingual policies under Prime Minister Lester Pearson in 1963. At the same time, groups in Quebec were working for separation from Canada. Two roads to independence emerged. The Front de Libération du Québec (FLQ) advocated terrorism. The Parti Québécois (PQ) used legal democratic methods.

In 1969, Prime Minister Pierre Trudeau oversaw passage of the ***Official Languages Act***. This Act proclaimed French and English Canada's two official languages—and made the federal public service and judicial systems bilingual.

FIGURE 9.2 This bill, issued in 1935, was one of the last single-language bills ever printed in Canada.

In the same year, New Brunswick, where one out of three persons is a francophone, became Canada's only officially bilingual province. In 1982, the *Canadian Charter of Rights and Freedoms* further guaranteed pre-existing language and education rights for official-language minorities. In Ontario, your community probably has a French-language school at both the elementary and secondary levels.

LITERACY COACH

Prior Knowledge/New Knowledge

You have probably picked up some knowledge of Quebec language laws by listening to the news or by hearing other people talk about bilingualism. Before reading the paragraphs below, make a table with two columns. Label the left column Prior Knowledge and the right column New Knowledge. In the left-hand column, write down what you currently know about language laws in Quebec (or the use of French in Quebec). In the right-hand column, summarize the new information you learned after reading these paragraphs.

Bill 101 and Quebec Language Rights

The province of Quebec took a different approach to language. In 1976, the Parti Québécois, led by founder René Lévesque, came to power. With a goal of making Quebec "as French as Ontario is English," the PQ passed Bill 101.

Bill 101 made French the official language of Quebec. The use of any other language in the workplace and on outdoor signs was strictly regulated. Today, only children with at least one parent educated in an English school in Quebec can be educated in English. Immigrants must send their children to French-language schools. Although the law may sound rigid, its intention is simply to protect a minority language— French—in an English-dominated country.

French Canadian Citizens

French Canadians have been an integral part of Canadian culture and society—including politics, art, education, sports, entertainment, and philosophy. Canada's first French-speaking prime minister was Wilfrid Laurier. He was succeeded by leaders such as Louis St. Laurent, Pierre Trudeau (architect of the *Canadian Charter of Rights and Freedoms*), and Jean Chrétien. Around the world, high-profile French Canadian performers such as the Cirque du Soleil and Céline Dion have thrilled millions of fans and stirred an interest in Canada.

CITIZENSHIP AND ENGLISH CANADIANS

The **United Empire Loyalists** were the first large-scale wave of English-speaking immigrants to arrive in Canada. They came to Nova Scotia and Upper Canada (Ontario) in the years following the American Revolution (1775–1783). The Loyalists, 40,000 strong, voted with their feet in rejecting revolution and **republicanism** (rejection of monarchy). These men and women formed the backbone of early English Canada. They believed in "peace, order, and good government"—the phrase that describes Canada's governing philosophy in the 1867 constitution.

Canada's Parliament, judicial system, and many street and place names are modelled after the English system. The May 24 holiday, for example, is a celebration of Queen Victoria's birthday. The English monarchy has been a part of Canada for much of its history. The monarchy still adorns Canadian money and is commemorated in the royal anthem, "God Save the Queen."

Canadians are also familiar with the Royal Canadian Mail, the Royal Canadian Mounted Police, the Royal Canadian Air Force, the Royal Canadian Mint, and royal commissions. Some movement away from the British influence has taken place, however. The Canadian flag appeared in 1965, Canada Post was created in 1969, and "O Canada" was proclaimed the national anthem in 1980.

FIGURE 9.3 Sending up Canada's traditions is part of the Canadian identity. (From left:) Jessica Holmes, Luba Goy, Don Ferguson, and Roger Abbott star in the CBC's weekly satirical program, *Royal Canadian Air Farce.*

Scottish Canadians

Tens of thousands of Scots (Scotland is also part of Great Britain) immigrated to Canada to escape hardship and unemployment at home. Some went on to take their place in Canadian history. Rebel leader William Lyon Mackenzie, clergyman John Strachan, inventors Sanford Fleming and Alexander Graham Bell, and prime ministers John A. Macdonald and Alexander Mackenzie were all Scottish immigrants to what is now Canada.

Irish Canadians

In the 1840s, the people of Ireland depended on the potato as their staple food. Faced with mass starvation as the potato crops failed, hundreds of thousands sailed for Canada on crowded "coffin ships," so called because many people died en route or shortly after arriving in Canada. Most of those who survived the Atlantic crossing settled in Ontario and Quebec.

PAUSE, REFLECT, APPLY

1. Create a timeline to outline the development of French language rights in Canada.
2. By the 1970s, Quebec's birth rate, traditionally the highest in Canada, had become the lowest. Using this information, explain what you think are some of the reasons for the passage of Bill 101 by the Parti Québécois government in 1977.
3. List six examples of the English presence in Canada.
4. Scottish Canadian writer Hugh MacLennan (1907–1990) observed that the four immigrant groups that helped found Canada—the French, Loyalists, Scots, and Irish—had all suffered defeats at home or in their adopted land. He wrote that this tradition of being on the "losing side" has had a psychological impact on the Canadian character: Canadians try not to offend, they are humble, they seek approval, they do what they are told. Do Canadians act like "losers"? Support or reject MacLennan's argument by using evidence from your experiences, this text, or both.

Canadian Immigration

In 2005, immigration accounted for more than 50 percent of Canada's population growth. Canada's immigrants continue to come mainly from Asia and the Middle East. One in six Canadians is a member of a visible minority.

▶ **KEY QUESTION**
Why has the concept of Canadian citizenship changed?

► **DID YOU KNOW** ◄
Three hundred seventy-five Sikh emigrants on board the *Komagata Maru* in May 1914 were barred from entry into Canada at Vancouver despite the fact that they all had valid British passports. The ship was sent back to India.

► **DID YOU KNOW** ◄
In 1939, 907 Jewish passengers who fled Nazi persecution on the ocean liner *St. Louis* were not granted promised entry at their destination of Cuba. Canada and the United States did not respond to their appeals for help. About half of the passengers died in the **Holocaust** after the ship returned to Europe.

HISTORY OF IMMIGRATION

Canada has welcomed immigrants for most of its history. At the beginning of the 20th century, it welcomed hundreds of thousands of Ukrainians, Scandinavians, Americans, and Eastern Europeans to help fill the vast prairie regions with people who would work the land. At this time, only white Europeans were considered desirable immigrants. Nonwhites were not actively recruited and were often turned away, unless there was a need for cheap labour.

Fifteen thousand Chinese men came to Canada in the 1880s to work on the Canadian Pacific Railway, but were denied citizenship. Other Asian immigrants had a difficult time entering the country because of regulations devised to keep numbers low.

- Only 400 Japanese immigrants per year were allowed until 1920.
- Chinese immigrants faced a "head tax" of $50 per person in 1885, an amount that was increased to $500 per person by 1904.
- Ships carrying passengers from India were discouraged by a regulation that required such travellers to arrive via a "continuous" or direct journey to Canada. No shipping company followed a direct route at that time.

Thousands of free black people were among the Loyalists who settled in Nova Scotia. Before the American Civil War (1861–1865), runaway slaves found refuge in Upper Canada. However, during the massive

FIGURE 9.4 *The Iron Road* is a contemporary Canadian opera that memorializes the work of thousands of Chinese Canadians on the Canadian Pacific Railway.

waves of immigration in the first half of the 20th century, people of colour were deliberately excluded. So too were many Jewish people, including those fleeing persecution in Europe in the 1930s.

Full citizenship was not granted to certain ethnic groups. In British Columbia, where most Asian Canadians lived, immigrants from China, Japan, and India did not win the right to vote until the late 1940s. Once groups were excluded from the voting list, they could also be excluded from certain professions, since the right to vote was a precondition for employment in areas such as law, medicine, and pharmacy.

Twenty-three thousand Japanese Canadians were placed in internment camps in the interior of British Columbia during World War II. They were accused of being "enemy aliens." After the war, almost 4,000 were forcibly repatriated to Japan. Of these, more than half were Canadian born and two-thirds were Canadian citizens.

> ▶ **DID YOU KNOW** ◀
> The father of hockey star Paul Kariya was born in a British Columbia internment camp for Japanese Canadians during World War II. Starting at age 6, scientist David Suzuki lived for three years in a similar internment camp.

THE CREATION OF CANADIAN CITIZENSHIP

In 1947, the Liberal government of Prime Minister Mackenzie King created the legal concept of Canadian citizenship. Until this point, Canadians had been defined as British subjects living in Canada or as immigrants. Immigrants could now qualify for full citizenship after they had resided in the country for five years.

SOURCES

Speech by Prime Minister W.L.M. King

The policy of the government is to foster the growth of the population of Canada by the encouragement of immigration. ...

[A]s respects immigration from Europe, the emphasis for the present should be on the admission of the relatives of persons who are already in Canada, and on assisting in the resettlement of displaced persons and **refugees**. ...

Selection officers will ... consider applicants for entry into Canada, examine them on a basis of suitability and physical fitness, and make arrangements for their orderly movement and placement. ... In taking these steps, the government is seeking to ensure that the displaced persons admitted to Canada are of a type likely to make good citizens. ...

[M]uch has been said about discrimination. I wish to make it quite clear that Canada is perfectly within her rights in selecting the persons whom we regard as desirable future citizens. It is not a "fundamental human right" of any alien to enter Canada. It is a privilege. It is a matter of domestic policy. ...

There will, I am sure, be general agreement with the view that the people of Canada do not wish, as a result of mass immigration, to make a fundamental alteration in the character of our population. Large-scale immigration from the orient [Asia] would change the fundamental composition of the Canadian population. ...

Source: House of Commons Debates, May 1, 1947, pp. 2644–2646; www.abheritage.ca/albertans/speeches/king_1.html.

	Period of Immigration									
	Before 1961		1961–1970		1971–1980		1981–1990		1991–2001*	
	Number	%	Number	%	Number	%	Number	%	Number	%
Total immigrants	894,465	100.0	745,565	100.0	936,275	100.0	1,041,495	100.0	1,830,680	100.0
United States	34,805	3.9	46,880	6.3	62,835	6.7	41,965	4.0	51,440	2.8
Europe	809,330	90.5	515,675	69.2	338,520	36.2	266,185	25.6	357,845	19.5
Asia	28,850	3.2	90,420	12.1	311,960	33.3	491,720	47.2	1,066,230	58.2
Africa	4,635	0.5	23,830	3.2	54,655	5.8	59,715	5.7	139,770	7.6
Caribbean, Central and South America	12,895	1.4	59,895	8.0	154,395	16.5	171,495	16.5	200,010	10.9
Oceania and other countries	3,950	0.4	8,865	1.2	13,910	1.5	10,415	1.0	15,385	0.8

* Includes data up to May 15, 2001

FIGURE 9.5 Place of birth by period of immigration, Canada, 2001. *Source: Statistics Canada, www12.statcan.ca/english/ census01/products/analytic/companion/etoimm/tables/canada/period.cfm.*

A COLOUR-BLIND POLICY

By the 1960s, some of the old prejudices that had shaped Canadian immigration and citizenship were fading. In 1962, Conservative Minister of Immigration Ellen Fairclough eliminated most of the entrance regulations that discriminated on the basis of race and country of origin. However, most immigrants to Canada continued to be Europeans.

In 1976, Canada created different admission categories for immigrants. It streamlined the process for sponsoring (supporting) family members and created a **points system** for independent applicants. This system awarded prospective applicants points for knowing English or French, having a certain level of education, and having certain job skills. A separate category was also created for refugees.

FIGURE 9.6 Students at a Winnipeg elementary school laugh as a Lion Dancer performs on Chinese New Year, February 8, 2005. The traditional Lion Dance is said to bring good fortune in the New Year.

Removing racial regulations and introducing the new points system led to unprecedented immigration from Africa, Asia, the Caribbean, and Latin America in the 1970s. The newcomers settled mainly in Vancouver, Toronto, and Montreal, making those cities vibrant centres of **multiculturalism**. By the end of the 20th century, Canada had become one of the largest refugee-receiving countries in the world, admitting thousands of refugees from Bosnia, Kosovo, Rwanda, and other places.

> ► **DID YOU KNOW** ◄
>
> Canada accepted 60,000 Vietnamese refugees in 1979–1980, in the aftermath of the Vietnam War (1965–1973). It also accepted approximately 30,000 American draft dodgers and army deserters as immigrants during the period of the Vietnam War.

► FACE OFF   Immigration: Open Borders or Lockdown?

Should Canada welcome as many immigrants as it does—about 200,000 annually? Many people say yes. Immigrants are eager to contribute to the well-being of the country. They often bring with them valuable skills in medicine, law, research, engineering, and the humanities. They enrich Canada culturally and economically.

Those who support immigration also applaud Canada's acceptance of refugees. Canada abides by the 1951 United Nations *Convention Relating to the Status of Refugees*, which states that nations have a duty to accept those from the world community who have a "well-founded fear of being persecuted for reasons of race, religion, nationality, membership of a particular social group or political opinion" (article 1A).

In 2005, immigration accounted for more than 50 percent of Canada's population growth. Because of a declining birth rate in many parts of Canada, immigrants are seen by many as contributing vitally to the country's labour, industrial, and consumer markets.

> Canada still needs the skills, talents and enthusiasm of newcomers to build our country, together with those who have come before them.
>
> — Government of Canada, "A Newcomer's Introduction to Canada," www.cic.gc.ca/english/newcomer/guide/section-07.html#6

Others argue that Canada should not accept so many immigrants when some Canadians are still without jobs. They say that even those immigrants with a professional background still have to retrain in Canada, a costly proposition. It is also expensive for Canada to fund all the support services associated with immigration, such as welfare payments and ESL (English as a second language) classes.

> An immigration tsunami is heading for North America.
>
> — Paul Fromm, white supremacist, speaking in Texas, USA, March 12, 2005

Another argument against widespread immigration is that it might also result in problems such as terrorism. This argument says that countries have a right and a duty to control their borders, and that dangerous people should be kept out. If that means accepting fewer immigrants, that is a reasonable compromise.

Your Play

1. In your opinion, is immigration good or bad for Canada? Explain why.
2. How would you go about evaluating the argument that the threat of terrorism means that fewer immigrants should be accepted into Canada? What information would you need?
3. Are there any measures that the Canadian government could undertake to increase the country's birth rate? Propose some, and explain how they might work.

> ► **DID YOU KNOW** ◄
>
> In 2003 Canadians adopted 2,181 children from abroad. Adoptions from China accounted for 51 percent of all international adoptions.

1. Explain three ways in which the entry of certain groups of immigrants to Canada was limited in the late 19th and early 20th centuries. How might these limitations have reflected the values of the times?

2. a) Summarize Prime Minister King's view of Canadian citizenship in the Sources feature on page 157.

   b) Do you agree or disagree with this view?

   c) In what ways is the policy a political mixture of generosity and racism?

3. Examine Figure 9.5 on page 158. What area of the world provided the largest number of immigrants to Canada in the period before 1961? In the period 1991–2001? What is the percentage in each case?

4. Describe Canada's current immigration policy.

5. Why has the concept of Canadian citizenship undergone changes since the beginning of the 20th century?

Citizenship and Multiculturalism

In 1971, Canada became the first country in the world to adopt multiculturalism as an official policy. Multiculturalism ensures that all citizens can keep their identity, heritage, and language once in Canada. Immigrants can take pride in their ancestry and also feel a sense of belonging. Through multiculturalism, programs and services are provided to many different groups that preserve heritage, and individuals are helped to participate fully in Canadian society.

CELEBRATING DIVERSITY

As citizens of the world, Canadians celebrate diversity in a number of ways. Some of these are described below.

Human Rights Day

On December 10, 1948, the United Nations General Assembly adopted the *Universal Declaration of Human Rights*. This declaration has become a standard for defending and promoting human rights. Every year on December 10, people around the world are reminded that "all human beings are born free and equal in dignity and rights" (article 1 of the Declaration). By marking this day, Canadians are also reminded of their guaranteed rights and freedoms, and of the way of life that Canadians value.

Black History Month

In 1995, Canada's Parliament recognized February as Black History Month. Today, approximately 2 percent of Canada's population identify themselves as black Canadians. Their contributions, past and present, are recognized and celebrated.

American immigrant and anti-slavery advocate Mary Ann Shadd was Canada's first female newspaper editor in the mid-1800s.

Baseball pitcher Ferguson Jenkins—the only Canadian in the Cooperstown, New York, Baseball Hall of Fame—is the descendant of pre–Civil War refugees who settled in the same Chatham, Ontario, area where Mary Ann Shadd lived.

FIGURE 9.7 Canadian gold medal wrestler Daniel Igali hits the road to build a school in his home village in Nigeria, accompanied by two Canadian teenagers.

Lincoln Alexander, who was born in Toronto to West Indian immigrants, became Canada's first black member of Parliament, cabinet minister, and lieutenant governor. He served as Ontario's lieutenant governor from 1985 to 1991.

At the 1996 Olympics, Donovan Bailey became "the world's fastest man" when he won the gold medal in the 100 metre race. Bailey, who came to Canada at age 13 from Jamaica, took up business and charity work at the end of his running career. He has been a spokesperson for Big Brothers Big Sisters of Canada.

Athletes Jarome Iginla, a hockey star, and Olympic wrestling champion Daniel Igali are proud of their Nigerian heritage. After his Olympic victory, Igali went on to raise $200,000 to replace the one-room school in his impoverished Nigerian hometown of Eniwari. The Canadian International Development Agency (CIDA) matched the funds. In 2005, Igali entered provincial politics as a Liberal candidate.

Asian Heritage Month

To acknowledge the rich history of Asian Canadians and their contributions to Canada, Parliament in 2001 designated May as Asian Heritage Month. Some famous Asian Canadians:

FIGURE 9.8 Award-winning Canadian film and television star Sandra Oh

- Adrienne Poy was born to Chinese parents in Hong Kong in 1939. At age three, she and her family came to Canada as refugees. After a long career as one of Canada's first female television broadcasters, Adrienne Poy Clarkson was appointed governor general of Canada.

- Ujjal Dosanjh, who arrived in Canada at age 21, was born in a small village in Punjab, India. In Canada, Dosanjh established himself as a civil rights activist and lawyer. He became Canada's first Indo-Canadian provincial premier (British Columbia, 2000) and first Indo-Canadian federal cabinet minister (minister of health, 2004).

- Canadian actor Sandra Oh, who appeared in the 2004 Academy Award–nominated film *Sideways*, was born in Ottawa to Korean immigrants.

- The grandparents of David Suzuki and Vicky Sunohara came from different parts of Japan to Canada early in the 20th century. Today, broadcaster and author Dr. David Suzuki is recognized as a world leader in the study of sustainable ecology; Vicky Sunohara has been a star player on Canada's women's hockey team.

☐ DISCUSSION POINT
According to the Ethnic Diversity Survey, released in September 2003, almost half of the black Canadians surveyed said they had experienced some form of discrimination or unfair treatment in the past five years. Why might a country that has tried to eliminate racism still experience it to this degree?

International Day for the Elimination of Racial Discrimination

The International Day for the Elimination of Racial Discrimination is observed on March 21. On that day, in 1960, South African police killed 69 men and women who were demonstrating against apartheid, the government policy that enforced discrimination against non-whites. Proclaiming the day in 1966, the United Nations called on the international community to increase its efforts to eliminate all forms of racial discrimination. Canada was one of the first countries to support the UN's proclamation.

CANADIANS REACHING OUT

Canadians have a tradition of reaching out to the global community that dates back more than 50 years. In 1952, soon-to-be Canadian Prime Minister Lester Pearson was president of the UN General Assembly. Four years later, as Canada's minister of external affairs, Pearson proposed the creation of the UN's first peacekeeping force. Since that time, many Canadians have reached out to the global community by pressing for human rights, working for peace, or assisting with aid and development.

Rosalie Silberman Abella

Before her birth, Rosalie Silberman's parents were imprisoned for four years in Nazi concentration camps. They had lost their two-year-old son and other relatives to the Holocaust. Rosalie was born in a displaced persons' camp in Germany and arrived in Canada as a Jewish refugee at age four. She became a lawyer and a strong spokesperson for human rights in Canada and around the world. She was a member of the Ontario Human Rights Commission (see Chapter 3) and the Ontario Court of Appeal. In 2004, Rosalie Silberman Abella was appointed one of nine justices to the Supreme Court of Canada.

Roméo Dallaire

Retired General Roméo Dallaire was born in Holland and arrived in Montreal at age one. He later joined the Canadian military and was active in many peacekeeping missions. Dallaire accepted the leadership of the United Nations mission in Rwanda in 1994. This mission was a turning point for him. Because of the ongoing **genocide**, combat soldiers as well as peacekeepers were needed, yet the UN would not supply them. Following this gruelling mission, Dallaire became a strong international spokesperson for equal treatment of all peoples.

You, too, can reach out by taking part in volunteer work that relates to the local or global community. Every act of positive involvement makes you a better citizen of Canada and the world. Consider the ideas presented in this chapter's Study Hall under the heading Active Citizenship.

PAUSE, REFLECT, APPLY

1. Describe the accomplishments of one representative for each of the following groups: black Canadians, Japanese Canadians, Korean Canadians, Chinese Canadians, Indo-Canadians, and Jewish Canadians.

2. a) In what sense does Canada contain "the globe within its borders"?
   b) How does Canada reach out to the globe?

REPLAY ■ ■ ■ ■ ■ ■ ■ ■ ■ ■

This chapter has informed you of these civics concepts:

1. Canada has three founding peoples—the Aboriginal peoples, the British, and the French.
2. The concept of Canadian citizenship has developed since Confederation.
3. In the past, full citizenship was denied to some groups because of their race, ethnic origin, or religion.
4. Canada's multicultural identity has been shaped through extensive immigration during the 20th century.
5. Multiculturalism ensures that all citizens can keep their identity, heritage, and language once in Canada.
6. Canadian citizenship is associated with certain fixed rights, but may be viewed differently by different groups of people.

CIVICS ▶ TOOLKIT

How Best to Present This? Writing a Formal Essay

Written assignments may include point-form notes, informal reports, research reports, or formal essays. This example guides you through the writing of a formal essay.

- Decide on an order for your material.
- If there is a thesis or argument in your essay, be certain to gather evidence for your arguments. One way to do this is to bundle your evidence by argument. You may wish to do some mind-mapping or preliminary note-taking in order to organize your material.
- Organize your ideas into paragraphs, with one major topic per paragraph. Your introductory paragraph should identify the importance of the topic and indicate what you will speak about in the body of the paper. You may find it best to write the introduction after you have written the paper.
- Write a topic sentence for each body paragraph. The topic sentence tells the reader what is contained in the paragraph. Remember that topic sentences with transitions may be used to link paragraphs.
- At the end of the essay, write a concluding paragraph in which you restate your thesis (using different wording) and summarize your arguments.
- Identify your sources by using the reference style preferred by your teacher.
- Write a first draft. Read it out loud to check for correct grammar and flow of ideas.
- Write your final draft.

Skill Practice

Write a five-paragraph essay on one of the following topics related to citizenship:

- Standing up to racism in Canada
- Canada: Nations within a nation?
- How has history shaped Canadian citizenship?

STUDY HALL

Informed Citizenship

1. a) Find out more about Canadian citizenship by inviting one or more of the following people to your class to speak about their views of citizenship:

    ■ representative of First Nations

    ■ World War II veteran

    ■ survivor of the Holocaust

    ■ representative from Greenpeace

    ■ immigration lawyer assisting refugees

    b) Once a selection has been finalized, develop questions to ask your visitor.

2. Read about the United Nations *Convention on the Rights of the Child* (1989) at www.emp.ca/civics. In a written report, argue whether or not Canada is meeting its obligations toward its non-adult citizens.

3. To review your knowledge of Canadian citizenship, take the test found at www.emp.ca/civics.

Purposeful Citizenship

4. In 2001, the Aboriginal Justice Implementation Commission recommended an **affirmative action** program that would allow Aboriginal people to be employed in the justice system at a rate equal to their representation in the Manitoba population (12 percent).

    a) Present reasons for this type of program.

    b) Explain how such a program might work.

    c) Find out what other groups in Canada have been targeted for affirmative action in the past. How did they benefit?

    d) In your opinion, is affirmative action a good way to achieve greater equality in Canadian citizenship? Explain.

Active Citizenship

5. Create a national day for some group that you think has not been given sufficient attention. Write a brief history of this group, outline its contributions to Canada, and suggest some events for the day. Present your idea to the class, using a combination of posters, speakers, displays, music, announcements, or videos.

6. In this chapter you read about many citizens who made contributions to the global community by undertaking specific projects. From a list of possible projects described at www.emp.ca/civics, select a project to work on. As a followup activity, write a brief report on how the project expanded your own view of global citizenship.

7. Exercise some aspect of citizenship by becoming involved in an activity such as one of the following:

    ■ Volunteer to teach ESL students.

    ■ Volunteer to work at a food bank.

    ■ Join a human rights and anti-discrimination organization such as Amnesty International.

    ■ Join an anti-poverty organization such as Oxfam or Habitat for Humanity International.

CHAPTER 10
Human Rights in the Global Village

Employees making shoes at a factory in Zhongshan, China.

What You Need to Know

- What problems were there in developing support for universal human rights?
- How did international law change to recognize human rights?
- What key precedent did the Nuremberg trials establish?
- How has Canada contributed to universal human rights?
- Why is the *Universal Declaration of Human Rights* important?
- How can using multimedia tools enhance your presentations?

Key Terms

Universal Declaration of Human Rights (UDHR)
Geneva Conventions
humanitarian
communism
fascism
genocide
Nuremberg trials
conventions
protocols
International Criminal Court (ICC)

Key Question

How and why did the world come to recognize the importance of universal human rights?

"We have a factory in China where we have 250 people. We own them; it's our factory. We pay them $40 per month and they work 28 days a month. They work from 7 a.m. to 11 p.m. [that's $.09 per hour]. They all eat together, 16 people to a room, stacked on four bunks to a corner. Generally, they're young girls from the hills."

—President of Ava-Line (a company that makes lapel pins), *Business News*, August 21, 1996, p. 98

What human rights are being violated in the quotation above? How could this company and others like it be held accountable?

How Did Universal Human Rights Gain Recognition?

Not until 1948 did nations of the world agree to a set of universal human rights. That agreement, the ***Universal Declaration of Human Rights*** **(UDHR)**, was passed by the United Nations (an international organization formed after World War II, in 1945). Why did it take so long to reach international agreement on rights that some democratic nations had guaranteed citizens hundreds of years earlier?

Citizens of most democratic countries have much the same rights (the right to a fair trial, the right to vote and hold office, the right to free speech, and so on). Originally, these rights were written into constitutions or charters such as the English *Bill of Rights* in 1688, the French *Declaration of the Rights of Man and of the Citizen* in 1789, and the US *Bill of Rights* in 1791. These documents became famous, inspiring newer democracies when they drew up their own constitutions.

INTERNATIONAL LAW AND HUMAN RIGHTS

Before 1948, nations had agreed to many human rights in principle, but the term "human rights" was not in use. In the early 19th century, for example, Britain led other countries in abolishing the slave trade.

The first of the four ***Geneva Conventions*** was signed in 1864 to protect the sick and wounded in wartime. This convention was inspired by Swiss **humanitarian** Henri Dunant, founder of the Red Cross. Dunant visited a battlefield in Italy, where he was stunned to see thousands of wounded soldiers left to die. He wrote a book that prompted his government to establish the Red Cross to help soldiers wounded in war. In response, the Swiss government held the first of a series of international conferences to establish rules for war.

The first *Geneva Convention* established that neutral groups such as the Red Cross could help wounded soldiers in a conflict zone without being attacked. Later conferences at Geneva and The Hague in the Netherlands established rules for how war would be conducted, how prisoners were to be treated, and which weapons were prohibited.

A body of international law was slowly being built, dealing mostly with human rights violations during war. It was law in that it was a moral code that most countries agreed to obey. Compliance was in a country's self-interest because such laws promised humane treatment for its own soldiers.

At the end of World War I, the Versailles Conference of 1919 in many ways put defeated Germany on trial. Germany, accused of waging an aggressive war, was forced to surrender territory and pay a fine to the victorious countries. The principle was that a country was a legal entity and therefore could be tried for waging a destructive war. However, the individual rulers and citizens of Germany were not held accountable.

Communism

Other political events in the 20th century also helped bring human rights issues to world attention. In the fall of 1917, a communist revolution overthrew the Russian monarchy. The goal of **communism** was to establish equality of income for all Russians. In a communist system, the state is governed by a single party with no opposition. The state owns all property, controls the economy, and to some extent controls the social and cultural life of citizens. When Vladimir Lenin (1870–1924) and, later, Joseph Stalin (1879–1953) led the Communist Party, they became dictators, using secret police and the military to crush all opposition.

Stalin was determined to industrialize the Soviet Union rapidly and increase production, raising the standard of living for all citizens. He planned to eliminate private ownership of farms by millions of Russian peasants by reorganizing them into huge, state-run collective farms. When the peasants resisted, Stalin sent in the Red Army to push them off their land. Millions of peasants were deported to Siberia and died of cold and hunger. The upheaval caused a catastrophic drop in food production, leading to widespread famine.

In 1935, Stalin decided to eliminate all possible political opposition by using informers, secret police, and torture. Thousands of Russians were falsely charged with treason and either shot or sent to labour camps in Siberia. Imagine the terror that Russians felt during those years, when a careless comment about the government or a lie told to authorities by an unfriendly neighbour could result in arrest.

Fascism

While these events were occurring in Russia, Italy and Germany came under the influence of two charismatic dictators—Benito Mussolini (1883–1945) and Adolf Hitler (1889–1945). Mussolini came to power first, in 1923. Leading a popular political movement called **fascism**, he overthrew Italy's struggling democratic government.

Fascism grew out of an anti-democratic set of beliefs. It played on fears of communism and glorified militarism and extreme nationalism. In a fascist system, property is privately owned but all industry and labour are controlled by a strong national government that suppresses all opposition.

Hitler adopted Mussolini's fascist ideas and added a violent anti-Semitism (hatred of Jews). Hitler came to power in Germany in 1933 (through a democratic election) during the economic hardship of the Great Depression. Using the Gestapo (secret police) against his opponents, he seized power and became dictator of Germany. The Nazis passed laws that stripped German Jews of their legal, economic, and human rights.

The Holocaust

Hitler moved from the persecution and stripping of German Jews and other "non-conformists" (communists, Roma (gypsies), and Jehovah's Witnesses, among others) of all rights to an attempt to exterminate all European Jews. He called this the "final solution." Nazi Germany pursued this policy with ruthless efficiency and a huge commitment of human and material resources.

What about ordinary people in Germany and other conquered countries who did nothing to stop their Jewish neighbours from being rounded up by the Gestapo? Were they accomplices in the wrongdoings? What, if anything, did they know about the death camps? What could they have done? Could soldiers and the guards in the camps claim to be "just following orders"? These questions and others were raised after the war and are still debated today.

> ### SOURCES
>
> *Article 3.* Only citizens of the Reich, as bearers of full political rights, can exercise the right of voting in political matters, and have the right to hold public office.
>
> *Article 4. (1)* A Jew cannot be a citizen of the Reich. He cannot exercise the right to vote; he cannot hold public office.
>
> — From the Nuremberg Laws, 1935

FIGURE 10.1 Nazis burn books considered "un-German" in Berlin's main square, 1933.

PAUSE, REFLECT, APPLY

1. Why do you think countries could more easily agree on human rights violations during wartime than in peacetime?

2. In what sense are the *Geneva Conventions* law?

3. What legal principle justified the penalties placed on Germany at the end of World War I?

How Can Universal Human Rights Be Enforced?

▶ **KEY QUESTION**
What vital principle of international law was established to advance human rights in response to the Holocaust?

Although there were some problems deciding which rights are universal, the greater challenge was enforcing those rights. There was no universal government with the power to enforce laws respecting human rights. For such a government to exist, national governments would have to surrender some of their own power to it. Most countries are reluctant to surrender any sovereignty, fearing it may limit their power to act independently.

THE RESPONSE OF WESTERN DEMOCRACIES

How did Western democracies respond to violations of human rights in Russia and Germany? The Western democracies were not well informed about the crimes committed by Stalin against the Russian people. The communist government was careful to shield visitors from the famine and deportations, although news of the purges and deaths from hunger did spread. But the condition of the Jews in Germany was known through news reports and through the protests of Jews who had managed to escape. In 1938, after Germany seized Austria, Austrian Jews came under attack and tried to flee to the United States, Britain, Canada, and other countries. American President Franklin Delano Roosevelt convened a conference at Evian in France in 1938 to address the Jewish refugee problem.

Thirty-two countries attended; Germany was not invited. During the nine-day conference, delegate after delegate expressed sympathy for Jewish refugees. Yet only one country, the Dominican Republic, offered to accept more Jewish immigrants.

SOURCES

Canadian Complicity

...Tim Reid's link to the Holocaust—although he has no recollection of it—dates back to 1939. He was just three years old.

His father, a newly minted Foreign Service officer, was second secretary at the Canadian Embassy in Washington. One of Escott Reid's jobs was to turn away Jews who wanted to bring their relatives into the United States through Canada.

The U.S. had a quota for accepting Jews but it was filled. Desperate to get their loved ones out of Germany as Adolf Hitler herded them into urban ghettoes, American Jews begged for Canada's help.

It tore Reid apart to say no. "Every time one of them comes in it leaves me shaken and ashamed of Canada," the young diplomat wrote. "It's like being a bystander at an especially cruel and long drawn-out murder. If I could find a loophole, I'd feel I'd justified my existence."

Reid did everything in his power to convince his superiors in Ottawa to relax their opposition to Jewish immigration. He made the case on humanitarian grounds, arguing that Canada could at least let in children. He tried economics, arguing that Canada needed the dollars that European Jews would bring to finance the war effort. ...

During the 12-year Nazi regime, Canada let in just 5,000 Jews, as Irving Abella and Harold Troper recount in their heart-rending book, *None Is Too Many*. (The U.S. admitted 200,000; Britain accepted 70,000; and Argentina took 50,000). ...

It doesn't seem possible to say "never again" without understanding the forces that allowed a nation such as Canada to slam the gates on refugees facing almost certain death.

And it doesn't seem fair to overlook the fact that a few principled public servants dared to speak out against their own government. ...

Source: Carol Goar, "The Man Who Said No to Evil," *The Toronto Star*, Friday, February 4, 2005, p. A20.

THE NUREMBERG TRIALS

When World War II ended in 1945, the invading Allied Armies were horrified to find concentration camps scattered all over Eastern and Central Europe and Germany. Newsreel cameras were sent into the camps, and the resulting pictures of the dead and starving prisoners were seen by millions of people. The sense of outrage was so great that the Allies decided to charge those most responsible for the **genocide** with war crimes at the **Nuremberg trials**.

There was a legal problem. International law had never held individuals responsible for international crimes if there was no domestic law forbidding the crime. In other words, Germans could not be charged as individuals because there was no German law forbidding them from starting World War II or carrying out the genocide.

The Nuremberg prosecutors put 22 German leaders on trial, including Hermann Göring, second in command to Hitler. They were charged as individuals for planning an aggressive war, and with the murder of

THE WEB ►►►

Link to a site called the Righteous Among the Nations at www.emp.ca/civics. This Israeli program honours individuals who risked their lives to save Jewish people from the camps.

► **DID YOU KNOW** ◄

Besides individuals, the Righteous Among the Nations site honours the country of Denmark. When the German army invaded, the Danish people smuggled almost all of 8,000 Danish Jews to safety by boat at night to Sweden.

millions of people. Some claimed neither a direct role in starting the war nor knowledge of the genocide. The defence argued that the court was making up law to hold its clients individually responsible for the acts of a country.

The Nuremberg judgment (11 German leaders were condemned to death) set a precedent in international law. It established for the first time that individuals could be held responsible for aggressive war and crimes carried out by a country in defiance of international laws.

PAUSE, REFLECT, APPLY

1. Explain the enforcement problem of universal human rights.
2. How did the Evian conference show the prejudices of Western democracies? How could it have encouraged the Nazis to go even further in their persecution of Jews?
3. Explain the legal problem that prosecutors faced at the Nuremberg trials. What precedent were the prosecutors determined to set?
4. Defence lawyers for the German leaders argued that the Nuremberg court decision simply expressed the vengeance of the victors (the Allies) upon the defeated (Germany). They argued that their clients could not be held individually responsible for the actions of a country. What do you think of this defence?

Canada and Human Rights

◼ KEY QUESTION
Has Canada actively furthered human rights?

Like other countries, Canada has struggled for recognition of human rights. In the past, slavery and child labour existed in Canada, and women and minorities were denied the right to vote. Over time and with continued pressure on governments from citizens, human rights improved dramatically.

Today, the Canadian government says human rights are central to Canada's relations with other countries. It says Canadians expect their government to be a leader in human rights for the following reasons:

- Canadians played a key role in founding the United Nations (UN). The UN was established to avert war, contribute to economic development in less developed countries, and promote human rights. Canada has supported UN peacekeeping operations with over 100,000 personnel over 45 years.
- Canada has signed every UN convention to strengthen human rights since 1948. Canadians expect their governments to honour and promote the human rights agreements Canada has signed.

- Many Canadians came from countries with poor human rights records. These citizens and others want Canada to pressure those countries to reform.
- It is in Canada's interest to promote human rights in other countries. Governments that respect the rights of citizens are less likely to erupt into civil conflicts, creating a flood of refugees requiring humanitarian assistance.

☐ **DISCUSSION POINT**
What does the record actually show about Canada and human rights since the Universal Declaration was signed in 1948?

JAPANESE CANADIANS AND WORLD WAR II

During World War II, 23,000 Japanese Canadians were uprooted from their homes, separated from their families, and interned in camps. Japanese Canadians on the West Coast were seen as a threat to Canada, which was at war with Germany, Italy, and Japan.

No Japanese Canadian was ever charged, let alone convicted, of being a spy or saboteur for Japan. Yet, Japanese Canadians lost their homes, businesses, automobiles, and fishing boats (which were sold at a fraction of their worth). The camps were lonely, isolated places, where many families spent up to four years. Released at the end of the war, Japanese Canadians had to rebuild their lives and businesses. Some were deported, and many left British Columbia to settle in Ontario.

After being lobbied for years, the Canadian government finally apologized to Japanese Canadians for this abuse of their human rights. In 1988, Prime Minister Brian Mulroney said, "We cannot change the past. But we must, as a nation, have the courage to face up to these historical facts."

NOTICE TO ALL JAPANESE PERSONS AND PERSONS OF JAPANESE RACIAL ORIGIN

TAKE NOTICE that under Orders Nos. 21, 22, 23 and 24 of the British Columbia Security Commission, the following areas were made prohibited areas to all persons of the Japanese race:—

LULU ISLAND (including Steveston)   SAPPERTON
SEA ISLAND   BURQUITLAM
EBURNE   PORT MOODY
MARPOLE   IOCO
DISTRICT OF QUEENSBOROUGH   PORT COQUITLAM
CITY OF NEW WESTMINSTER   MAILLARDVILLE
                                         FRASER MILLS

AND FURTHER TAKE NOTICE that any person of the Japanese race found within any of the said prohibited areas without a written permit from the British Columbia Security Commission or the Royal Canadian Mounted Police shall be liable to the penalties provided under Order in Council P.C. 1665.

AUSTIN C. TAYLOR,
Chairman,
British Columbia Security Commission

FIGURE 10.2 (Left:) An internment camp for Japanese Canadians, 1942. (Right:) This notice was distributed throughout British Columbia. Any Japanese Canadian found in a prohibited area would be jailed.

THE WEB ▶▶▶

Learn more about the
Canadian Race Relations
Foundation by linking
to its Web site at
www.emp.ca/civics

A $300 million compensation package included $21,000 for each of the 13,000 survivors, $12 million for a Japanese community fund, and $24 million to create a Canadian Race Relations Foundation, to ensure that such discrimination never happens again.

THE INTERNATIONAL CENTRE FOR HUMAN RIGHTS AND DEMOCRATIC DEVELOPMENT

In 1988, the Canadian government also established the International Centre for Human Rights and Democratic Development. Its purpose is to educate Canadians about human rights issues and to work with other countries to promote human rights. In 1993, it warned of the possibility of another human rights catastrophe in the small African country of Rwanda (see pages 176–178).

CivicStar

LLOYD AXWORTHY

Lloyd Axworthy was Canada's minister of foreign affairs from 1995 to 2000. He became known internationally for his leadership in the movement to ban landmines.

Millions of landmines remain buried in former war zones. In Afghanistan alone, 10 to 15 million mines continue to maim and kill civilians, especially children. Adults caught in the blast of an anti-personnel mine often survive with treatment, though they usually lose a limb. Children are smaller and are less likely to survive a blast.

Axworthy cooperated with other people, particularly US activist Jody Williams, in building a global network dedicated to banning landmines. In just over a year, Axworthy helped persuade 121 countries to sign an anti-landmine treaty in Ottawa in 1997. For this, he was nominated for the Nobel Peace Prize.

In 2004, Axworthy spoke out against the use of child soldiers by the Tamil Tigers in the civil war in Sri Lanka.

Your Play

1. Suggest reasons why some countries might be reluctant to sign the landmines treaty. Consider a) financial and b) military reasons.
2. Lloyd Axworthy lost the Nobel Prize to Jody Williams of the International Campaign to Ban Landmines (ICBL). Which do you think is a more powerful force in human rights campaigns: statesmen like Axworthy, or NGOs like the ICBL? Explain.

FIGURE 10.3 Landmine clearance in Afghanistan, 2001. It costs less than $3 to manufacture a mine but about $1,000 to remove it.

PAUSE, REFLECT, APPLY

1. What evidence is there that Canada is a firm supporter of the UN?
2. Why does Canada have an interest in promoting human rights in other countries?
3. a) Why did Canada take actions against Japanese Canadians during World War II?

b) How did those actions violate the human rights of Japanese Canadians?

4. How did the Canadian government compensate Japanese Canadians? In your opinion, was the compensation adequate? Explain.

The *Universal Declaration of Human Rights*

After the United Nations was formed in 1945, it set about to protect human rights. At that time, 51 countries were UN members. A Human Rights Commission was set up in 1946 with Eleanor Roosevelt, US ambassador to the UN, as chair. Roosevelt had long campaigned for human rights and was widely respected in the world community. John Humphrey, a Canadian professor of law from McGill University in Montreal, helped draft a declaration of human rights.

After two years, the commission produced the *Universal Declaration of Human Rights* (UDHR). In it, every human being was granted the right to life, liberty, security of person, and an adequate standard of living. The last article of the UDHR specifies that "standard of living" includes the right to adequate food, clothing, shelter, medical care, and social security.

The Declaration was finally put to a UN vote on December 10, 1948. There were no dissenting votes, although six communist countries abstained, along with Saudi Arabia and South Africa.

THE UDHR AND RECOGNITION OF HUMAN RIGHTS

Even though the UN had endorsed the UDHR as international law, it could not enforce the Declaration. Instead, the UDHR became a guideline that nations could follow or to which they could aspire. The *Canadian Charter of Rights and Freedoms*, for example, echoes ideas found in the Declaration. The UDHR also inspired other UN human rights agreements, called **conventions**:

> **KEY QUESTION**
> What impact has the UDHR had on human rights?

FIGURE 10.4 An Amnesty International march marking International Human Rights Day, December 10, 2002, in Belleville, Ontario. Such events raise public awareness of human rights violations by governments.

- The *Convention on Genocide* (1948) defined genocide as the attempt to destroy a national or racial group by any means. It obligated governments to recognize genocide as a crime against humanity.
- The *Convention on the Elimination of All Forms of Discrimination Against Women* (1979) urged nations to abolish all laws and customs that discriminated against women.
- The *Convention Against Torture* (1984) outlawed torture and defined what constitutes torture by a state against a citizen.
- The *Convention on the Rights of the Child* (1989) declared that children have rights to survival; to develop to the fullest; to protection from harmful influences, abuse, and exploitation; and to participate fully in family, cultural, and social life.

These conventions addressed emerging violations of human rights. For example, several countries use child soldiers in combat. This offence against children prompted additions, or **protocols**, to the original *Convention on the Rights of the Child*, pledging governments not to force children to bear arms.

The media's focus on these conventions and protocols brings human rights abuses to the world's attention. Informed citizens can and do pressure their own and other governments to take action against human rights abuses.

The Rwandan Genocide

Rwanda, a small central African country, is composed primarily of two peoples, the majority Hutu and the minority Tutsi. As a colony of Belgium (1919–1945), Rwanda and its people were brutally exploited. The Belgians favoured the Tutsi and gave them more power than the Hutu. This created tension between the two groups.

Belgium continued to support the Tutsi until the 1950s. Then, facing the end of colonial rule, pressure from the United Nations, and growing violence between the two groups, the colonial administrators began replacing Tutsi authorities with Hutu. With political and military help from the Belgians, the Hutu attacked Tutsi in positions of power. Many displaced Tutsi resettled elsewhere in Rwanda, but another 10,000 fled the country.

In 1961, some of these refugees began to attack Rwanda. After these attacks (10 over the next six years), Hutu officials led reprisal attacks on Tutsi inside Rwanda, accusing them of helping the invaders. During these years, some 20,000 Tutsi were killed and more than 300,000 were forced to flee abroad.

Following this legacy of colonialism and brutal killings, open conflict between the two groups erupted in the 1990s. In response, a UN peace-keeping force, under the command of Canadian General Roméo Dallaire, was sent to restore order in 1994. Dallaire and various human-itarian groups warned of a possible disaster. He asked the UN to send more troops and for permission to use force to protect civilians. When a plane carrying the Hutu president was shot down in April 1994, the Tutsi were blamed. Almost immediately, Hutu began to slaughter Tutsi and moderate Hutu with machetes. Moving from the towns into the countryside, men, women, and children were hacked to death by the hundreds of thousands.

Dallaire pleaded with UN headquarters in New York for help with-out success. No major power would get involved. Dallaire's small forces were forbidden to use their weapons even to save people. Then, Belgium pulled its peacekeepers out of Rwanda when 11 of its soldiers were killed. In July 1994, after the extremist Hutu government fell from power, many Tutsi sought revenge. By the time the slaughter ended, close to 1 million people, most of them Tutsi, had been killed in the worst genocide since the Holocaust.

The UN had failed to prevent another genocide.

LITERACY COACH

Find Out More

After you read a profile or a description of someone featured in this textbook, write down any questions you have about that person's life or work. Then, type the person's name into a search engine and click on the top three articles returned in the search. Try to find the answers to your questions in these articles. If you can't find the information you were looking for, refine your search by typing in more key words, such as "Roméo Dallaire" or "Belgian soldiers."

DID YOU KNOW

"In the 20th century, genocides and state mass murder have killed more people than have all wars."

— Web homepage banner for the Institute for the Study of Genocide (www.isg-iags.org)

Year	Region	Number of Deaths
1992–1999	Sierra Leone	*
1992–1995	Bosnia–Herzegovina	*
1994	Rwanda	1,000,000
1988	Iran (Kurds)	5,000
1975–1979	Cambodia (Pol Pot)	2,000,000
1975–1979	East Timor	*
1972	Burundi	*
1965–1966	Indonesia	*
1938–1945	Germany (the Holocaust)	6,000,000
1937–1938	Nanking	300,000
1932–1933	Ukraine (USSR forced famine)	5,000,000
1915–1919	Turkey (Armenians)	1,500,000

* Accurate statistics not available

FIGURE 10.5 Genocides in the 20th century

Following the genocide in Rwanda, the UN set up an international tribunal (special court) to try individuals accused of the killings. Similar tribunals tried those associated with conflicts in the former Yugoslavia (Bosnia–Herzegovina).

THE INTERNATIONAL CRIMINAL COURT

Human rights advocates had long tried to set up a permanent international court to prosecute individuals responsible for genocide, crimes against humanity, and war crimes. In July 2002, that goal was achieved with the establishment of the **International Criminal Court (ICC)** at The Hague in the Netherlands. The ICC works with national courts, acting only when countries are unable or unwilling to investigate or prosecute.

The court was ratified by 120 countries. Seven voted against it, including the United States, China, and Israel. These governments were reluctant to give power to an outside body that might, for political reasons, try to punish their soldiers and citizens.

A Canadian chaired the first working group that met in Rome to work out how such a court would be organized. Canada also helped finance poorer countries to send delegates to the Rome Conference. In 2003, in recognition of Canada's contribution, Canadian Philippe Kirsch was elected the first president of the ICC. Kirsch is also serving as one of 18 judges elected to the court from around the world.

THE WEB

Learn more about the ICC at www.emp.ca/civics

▶ FACE OFF   The International Criminal Court: Giant Step or Stumble?

In the promise of a universal criminal court lies the promise of universal justice.

— UN Secretary General Kofi Annan, "War Crimes After Nuremberg"; www.law.umkc.edu/faculty/projects/ftrials/ nuremberg/NurembergEpilogue.html

Supporters say that the International Criminal Court (ICC) is a great improvement over the tribunals set up to try war crimes. Tribunals set up to deal with Germany after World War II, and Rwanda and Yugoslavia in the 1990s, risked looking like victors trying the losers. Trying individuals charged with crimes against humanity in the countries where the crimes occurred might mean no justice at all. A permanent international court with recognized laws and procedures was seen as a better alternative.

The ICC tries individuals only if their country of origin refuses or is unable to prosecute. The prosecutor and the 18 judges are chosen by a majority of the countries supporting the ICC. Countries can still try their own citizens under their own laws. The ICC is intended to complement, not compete with, national laws and procedures.

> [The ICC] has the same flaw as all international institutions. In a world ruled by force, the rich and powerful do pretty much what they like. It is next to inconceivable that the ICC could try, even investigate, Western criminals.
>
> — Noam Chomsky, The ZNet Forum System, June 30, 2002; www.globalissues.org/ Geopolitics/icc/intro.asp

Critics say that an international court to promote human rights can be effective only if the United States and China recognize it. The US government, however, believes that its citizens have the right to be tried only by US law. In fact, the United States has tried its own citizens for war crimes (for example, those committed in Vietnam and Iraq). Is there any reason to believe that an American guilty of crimes against humanity would be more lightly treated in a US court than at the ICC?

> [I]t appears that many of the legal safeguards American citizens enjoy under the U.S. Constitution would be

FIGURE 10.6 Judge Sylvia Steiner of Brazil (far left) is sworn in with other judges (seated) during the first session of the International Criminal Court in The Hague on March 11, 2003. Judges were sworn in by Prince Zaid of Jordan (far right).

suspended if they were brought before the court. Endangered constitutional protections include the prohibition against double jeopardy [being tried twice for the same crime], the right to trial by an impartial jury, and the right of the accused to confront the witnesses against him.

> — "Reasonable Doubt: The Case Against the Proposed International Criminal Court," Cato Institute; www.cato.org/ pubs/pas/pa-311es.html

What Do You Think?

1. This comment was made about the Nuremberg trials of Nazi leaders: "The people sentenced there were some of the worst gangsters in human history, no doubt, but the operational definition of 'war crime' was 'war crime that they committed and we did not.'" Is this a valid criticism of war tribunals in general? Support your opinion with a reasoned argument.
2. How might the ICC get around the problem of public perception of war tribunals?
3. Do you think countries can handle their own human rights abuses without international institutions such as the ICC? Explain.
4. Who do you think should be tried by the ICC? Why?

PAUSE, REFLECT, APPLY

1. Why were conventions and protocols needed to support the rights listed in the UDHR?
2. Does signing a convention or protocol solve or prevent human rights abuses?
3. What factors explain (but do not excuse) the Rwandan genocide?
4. What is the purpose of the ICC?
5. Research the reasons behind the US and Chinese decisions not to participate in the ICC. What is your opinion of these countries' dissent?

REPLAY

This chapter has informed you of these civics concepts:

1. Recognition of universal human rights emerged from efforts to treat wounded soldiers humanely and to develop humane rules for war.
2. The abuses of fascism and communism helped bring human rights issues into focus after World War II.
3. The Nuremberg trials established the principle that individuals following state orders can be tried for crimes against humanity.
4. The *Universal Declaration of Human Rights* (UDHR, 1948) and related conventions and protocols have formed a universal code of human rights.
5. The UDHR is not enforceable, but it pressures countries to respect the principles underlying human rights.
6. The permanent International Criminal Court (ICC) tries individuals charged with war crimes and crimes against humanity.
7. Canada has been a leader in promoting human rights.

CIVICS ▶ TOOLKIT

How to Use Multimedia Technology

Multimedia presentations are more effective than simple oral presentations for three reasons:

1. Multimedia technology offers a better way to communicate any topic. Visuals, sound, and music stimulate the right side of the brain, the seat of our intuitive and emotional nature. Speech stimulates the left side, the seat of our logical and deductive nature.
2. Multimedia presentations improve the audience's perception of the presenter because the speaker appears better prepared and more professional. An appreciative audience is more likely to ask questions and participate in discussions.
3. Audience participation improves a speaker's confidence. An average speaker can look better with a good multimedia presentation than a good speaker relying on notes alone. For example, bulleted point-form notes on a screen provide both visual interest for the audience and cues to the presenter, who no longer needs to refer to paper notes.

The most common presentation software today includes three major functions:

1. a slide show system to display multimedia content
2. an editor that allows text and shapes to be manipulated
3. a graphics system for creating graphs and tables.

Visual material can be downloaded to the program from the Internet, a digital camera, or a scanner. Music and auditory effects can also be downloaded.

Preparing an effective multimedia presentation requires planning. Suppose your civics topic is "A Day in the Life of a Politician."

1. Decide what you are trying to communicate about your subject (a politician has many duties and busy days) just as you would in preparing an oral presentation. You could create a typical schedule on the computer (in point form) to

serve as cues for both you and the audience as you explain the politician's working day.
2. Prepare a storyboard outlining the content of each slide you plan to use. Consider the kinds of visuals that you wish to include as slides. Be sure to gather materials that are relevant to the subject and are not too distracting.
3. Gather visual materials (e.g., photos, graphics, video footage). Use the program to edit and modify the visuals to enhance their look and perspective. Try using different fonts, colour schemes, and transitions.
4. Consider adding special slides with topics for discussion and specific questions to the audience. Give these slides a common appearance to set them off from the rest of the slide show and encourage audience participation.
5. Use the program's clip art and design features to dress up your slides.
6. Consider printing a handout (including questions for discussion) for your audience.

Remember, the multimedia format is meant to liven up your ideas, not take over the presentation.

Get ready for presentation day by doing three things:

1. Rehearse your presentation.
2. Check the space where you will be presenting beforehand to locate air conditioning controls and electrical connections.
3. Make your speaking voice the most important sound in your presentation.

Skill Practice

1. What techniques do television news programs use to maintain viewer interest? Are any transferable to an individual multimedia presentation?
2. Prepare a mock storyboard for a topic in civics that interests you. Consider the visuals, auditory component, and music that would be most effective in supporting your topic.

STUDY HALL

Informed Citizenship

1. What human rights are seen as universal? Categorize them under basic, legal, political, economic, and gender rights.

2. Explain why wars are likely to produce human rights abuses.

3. What essential principle or precedent important to universal human rights was established at the Nuremberg trials?

4. State the major arguments that support the International Criminal Court. Why does the United States not support it? State your opinion on the US position.

5. What was the importance of the *Universal Declaration of Human Rights* (UDHR) to the recognition of human rights?

Purposeful Citizenship

6. How did the Nuremberg trials affect the extension of human rights and international law?

7. a) Take the side of the defence of the German leaders at the Nuremberg trials. How would you argue their case?

   b) Take the side of the prosecution of the German leaders. How would you argue its case?

8. Explain how the UDHR and the conventions that followed helped the cause of human rights.

9. After further research on a specific recipient of the "Righteous Among the Nations" honour (see page 171), assume the role of that person. Explain how you assisted Jewish citizens, reflecting on your actions and the reasons you took action.

10. Other genocides have occurred since World War II and the events in Rwanda. Do some research to discover details—key events, why they occurred, world reaction.

11. "Universal human rights can never have the force that domestic laws have because there is no international enforcement agency." Do you agree? Can laws and principles bring about good behaviour without an enforcement agency? Explain your views.

12. Conceive an international human rights enforcement agency. Who would be involved? What would the agency do?

Active Citizenship

13. Do some research to find out about the International Court of Justice (ICJ). How does it differ from the International Criminal Court (ICC)?

14. Amnesty International is an organization dedicated to human rights. Locate the group's Web site and report on its methods and results.

15. Prepare a multimedia presentation on one of the 20th century genocides listed in Figure 10.5 (page 178).

CHAPTER 11
Are We All Global Citizens?

This puzzle won second prize in the Canadian International Development Agency's Butterfly 208 contest (Group Visual Art and Multimedia category) in 2004. It's titled "Only the Educated Are Free." The butterfly represents the spirit of global cooperation. What do the other symbols and words say about global citizenship and responsibilities? (Learn more about the art at www.emp.ca/civics.)

What You Need to Know
- How are global issues and problems interrelated?
- What current events demonstrate that we cannot simply cut ourselves off from the rest of humanity?
- How have Canada and individual Canadians tried to improve the global situation?
- What actions can you take to be a responsible global citizen?
- How can self-assessment help you become a better global citizen?

Imagine a school where only Class A has books and a teacher. Any adults in other classes are there only to keep order. At lunch, Class A goes to the cafeteria. Once Class A is finished and leaves, small bowls of soup are set up for sale to the other students. Only a few can afford them, but there isn't enough soup to go around, anyway. Fights erupt in the non-A classrooms, and no one breaks them up. Bigger kids beat up smaller kids. After lunch, Class A uses two new washrooms. The other classes share two dirty washrooms that have no flush toilets or running water. One day, a few angry kids break into Class A. They are caught and forcibly expelled as troublemakers.

From your knowledge of current events, in what way does this fictional scenario parallel the world today?

Key Terms
non-governmental organizations (NGOs)
ambassadors
gross domestic product (GDP)
HIV/AIDS
sanctions
multilateralism
terrorism
weapons of mass destruction
global warming
Millennium Development Goals
sustainability

Key Question
What makes a "global citizen"?

What Is a Global Citizen?

There is no official certificate or ceremony to make one a global citizen. Global citizenship is a state of mind, an attitude.

To be a global citizen, you must

- appreciate that the peoples and countries of the world are all interconnected
- understand that poverty, pollution, epidemics, natural disasters, and terrorism require international cooperation
- be aware of, and care about, problems and people—locally and globally
- respect diversity and the human rights of all peoples
- view events from the perspective of other peoples and countries
- realize that Canada is not the centre of the universe
- take action to make the world a more just place.

The Structure of Canada's Foreign Policy

In Canada, the federal government is in charge of international relations. Foreign Affairs Canada, International Trade Canada, and the Department of National Defence are three major departments that deal with international responsibilities.

Canada also belongs to international organizations and agencies, such as the World Trade Organization, the Organization of American States, and the United Nations. **Non-governmental organizations** (**NGOs**) also play a vital role in Canada's global relations.

FOREIGN AFFAIRS AND INTERNATIONAL TRADE

Foreign Affairs Canada manages Canada's international relations and maintains embassies and consulates in 180 countries. **Ambassadors** (top diplomats who officially represent a country) and their aides act as Canada's eyes, ears, and voice. These people listen carefully and bring insights to Canada's international relations. Foreign Affairs also issues passports and assists Canadians travelling or living outside Canada.

Through trade, all countries can interact and develop economically. International Trade Canada sends representatives around the world to locate potential buyers for Canadian goods and services. It also negotiates trade agreements with other governments and with businesses.

THE CANADIAN INTERNATIONAL DEVELOPMENT AGENCY

The Canadian International Development Agency (CIDA) distributes approximately $3 billion a year in aid and loans. Funds are distributed through grants to projects in developing countries in Africa, Asia, the Middle East, and South and Central America. Funds for projects are granted either directly or through NGOs.

Since 1968, CIDA has funded projects in over 150 countries. Key development areas include

FIGURE 11.1 Stephan Hachemi sits outside Iran's embassy in Ottawa, July 2004, beside a portrait of his mother, Iranian-born Canadian photographer Zahra Kazemi. Kazemi died from a blow to the head while jailed in Iran for taking pictures of a student protest in June 2003. Hachemi wanted Canada to take the case to the International Court of Justice and criticized Foreign Affairs Canada for doing too little.

- basic human needs
- gender equality
- **infrastructure** (e.g., water supply, power, communication networks)
- business
- the environment.

THE WEB
For more on Zahra Kazemi, go to www.emp.ca/civics

WORLD POVERTY AND FOREIGN POLICY

In 2005, Canadian and UN studies reported that more than 1 billion people live in extreme poverty; 104 million children lack any kind of schooling; 1 billion people have no access to safe drinking water; and 2.4 billion people lack proper sanitation.

Global poverty does not just happen. The foreign and trade policies of wealthy, developed countries contribute to it. Those policies could be changed. For instance, the developed world could invest more in education and new industries in developing countries. We could reduce government **subsidies** (grants and money) that support our own industries, and adopt fairer trade policies with developing countries. We could forgive debts owed by developing countries.

THE WEB
Check out an application form for CIDA's Global Classroom Initiative through the link at www.emp.ca/civics

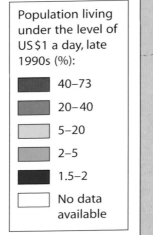

Population living under the level of US$1 a day, late 1990s (%):

- 40–73
- 20–40
- 5–20
- 2–5
- 1.5–2
- No data available

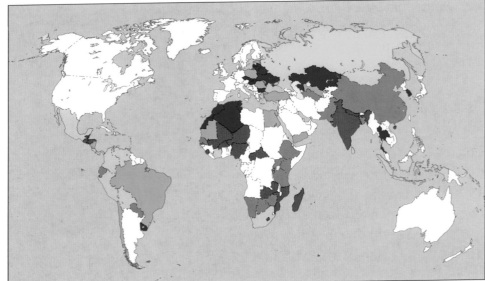

FIGURE 11.2 This map shows countries where many people live in extreme poverty—on less than US$1 a day. *Source: United Nations Environment Network and World Bank, 2000.*

Such policy changes would incur costs. For example, we might have to pay higher prices for clothing and foodstuffs imported from developing countries. Competition for jobs and industry between Canada and the developing world might also increase.

The 0.7 Percent Solution

In 1969, Prime Minister Lester Pearson led a panel of the world's wealthiest countries to set a goal for foreign aid to developing countries: 0.7 percent of **gross domestic product (GDP)**. (Gross domestic product is the value of all of the goods and services produced in a country in a year.) The UN adopted this "0.7 percent solution," and it has been reaffirmed as a goal by such celebrities as Bono of the rock band U2.

How Are We Doing?

In 2005, Canada pledged $2.87 billion to foreign aid and development—or approximately 0.3 percent of Canada's GDP. In the same year, the United States gave 0.13 percent. Of the world's wealthiest countries, only Norway (0.87 percent), Denmark (0.84 percent), Luxembourg (0.85 percent), Sweden (0.77 percent), and the Netherlands (0.74 percent) gave 0.7 percent or more of their GDP to foreign aid.

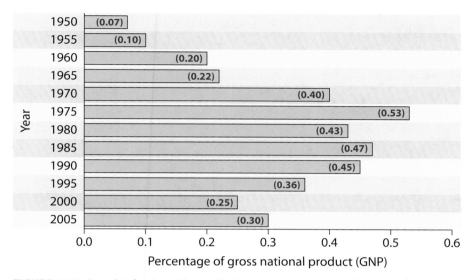

FIGURE 11.3 Canada's foreign aid contributions as a percentage of GNP (similar to GDP) since 1950. When was the level highest? What has been the trend in the last decade? *Source: Canadian International Development Agency, Statistical Report on Official Development Assistance, Fiscal Year 2003–2004.*

CANADA AND THE UNITED NATIONS

Canada was a founding member of the United Nations, which since 1945 has been a global forum for finding solutions to international problems (see Chapter 10).

The UN is not a government, even though it is structured like one. The UN's largest body is the General Assembly. Here, representatives of the 191 member countries debate issues and crises and vote on resolutions.

The most powerful UN body is the Security Council. It is composed of 15 countries and deals with issues of peace and security. China, France, Russia, the United Kingdom, and the United States are permanent members. The other 10 countries are elected for two-year terms. The Security Council's decisions are binding on UN members. It nominates the secretary general, who is then voted on by the General Assembly. The secretary general is the UN's chief executive and spokesperson.

A wide range of UN agencies deal with global concerns, such as human health and welfare, human rights, and social reforms. The UN also consults with business leaders and hundreds of NGOs to achieve progress in these areas.

PAUSE, REFLECT, APPLY

1. Identify the three federal departments or agencies that deal with international relations, and describe the role of each.
2. What do the following abbreviations stand for? Explain the meaning or function of each: UN, CIDA, NGO, and GDP.
3. What kinds of projects does CIDA fund?
4. What policies of developed countries can hurt developing nations?
5. Describe the concept of the "0.7 percent solution."
6. Which UN body resembles Canada's House of Commons?
7. Which UN body is the most powerful? Why?

▶ **KEY QUESTION**

How can ordinary people improve the world without relying on governments?

┌**THE WEB** ▶▶▶

Link to the Canadian Council for International Cooperation (CCIC), a coalition to end global poverty, which lists hundreds of NGOs and campaigns on global issues, at www.emp.ca/civics. Many organizations—such as Canadian Feed the Children, Operation Beaver, and Canada World Youth—have a youth focus.

NGOs and International Relations

Non-governmental organizations work to improve the world. They are not-for-profit and non-partisan and function independently of government. NGOs focus on longstanding global issues, such as poverty, hunger, disease, and educational needs. They also respond to sudden disasters, such as earthquakes, droughts, and political crises.

In Canada, CIDA fully or partially funds many NGOs. Each NGO must apply for sponsorship assistance, usually for a specific project. NGOs are also expected to raise funds through individual or business donations. CIDA inspects the work of the NGOs it funds, but it does not control staff or operations. Like service organizations, NGOs rely on volunteers.

NGOs operate on the belief that privately run projects administered by citizen volunteers are preferable to government-run projects. Why? For one thing, NGOs are free to criticize government policies. Also, volunteers who work for NGOs do so out of a deep sense of commitment, not because it is their job.

Thousands of NGOs operate in Canada in a wide variety of areas (Figure 11.4).

DOCTORS WITHOUT BORDERS

Médecins sans Frontières (MSF), or Doctors Without Borders, is a well-known and widely respected NGO. Founded in France in 1971, MSF became established in Canada in 1991. In 1999, MSF International won the Nobel Peace Prize.

When international crises occur, MSF sends people to evaluate medical needs. It then recruits medical and non-medical personnel. Resources and services include everything from sanitation, nutrition, water, and

Development	Environment	Humanitarian/Health	Human Rights
CCIC	Greenpeace Canada	Canadian Red Cross	Amnesty International
CUSO	Pollution Probe	Care Canada	Free the Children
Development and Peace	Sierra Club of Canada	Doctors Without Borders	Human Rights Watch
Oxfam Canada	David Suzuki Foundation	Foster Parents Plan	Physicians for Human Rights

FIGURE 11.4 A few well-known NGOs operating in Canada

vaccination, to medical assistance and food supplements for breast-feeding mothers.

Like many NGOs, MSF trains local people to run the projects that it initiates. Since 1991, the Canadian MSF has operated in more than 40 countries. Doctors and nurses who could be establishing well-paid careers sometimes volunteer years of their lives to this work.

DIFFERENT CRISES, DIFFERENT RESPONSES

On December 26, 2004, a massive earthquake under the Indian Ocean sent tsunamis (giant tidal waves) ripping through coastal areas in Asia. In Indonesia, Malaysia, Thailand, Sri Lanka, India, and Somalia, entire villages were swept away. More than 200,000 people were killed. Almost immediately, the news media broadcasted images of the devastation around the globe.

Canadians—including many students—responded with open hearts, and NGOs were flooded with contributions. At first, many people felt that the Canadian government responded too slowly. As public donations flowed in to NGOs, the federal government agreed to match public donations. Eventually, it pledged $425 million in tsunami assistance.

Some NGOs, such as MSF, received more funds than they needed for tsunami relief. MSF asked the public to donate to other, on-going crises that desperately needed action —such as **HIV/AIDS** in Africa and Asia. (HIV stands for *human immunodeficiency*

FIGURE 11.5 After the tsunami disaster, the Canadian military's Disaster Assistance Response Team (DART) was sent to Sri Lanka to repair infrastructure. There was controversy over the cost. The team included doctors, nurses, engineers, soldiers, and technicians.

virus, the retrovirus that attacks the body's immune system and that leads to acquired immune deficiency syndrome, or AIDS.)

The spread of HIV/AIDS in the developing world is a terrible crisis, one often overlooked by the wealthy countries of the developed world. One Canadian has been appointed by the UN to advocate for change.

CivicStar

STEPHEN LEWIS

Even as a toddler, Stephen Lewis had a social conscience. It's something that has shaped his life. Lewis was elected to the Ontario legislature in the 1960s at 25 years of age. By the mid-1970s, he was leader of the Ontario NDP. In 1984, he was appointed Canadian ambassador to the UN. From 1995 to 1999, Lewis served as deputy executive director of the United Nations Children's Fund (UNICEF).

In 2001, Lewis was appointed UN Special Envoy for HIV/AIDS in Africa. The posting has consumed him. No wonder. In 2005, the UN predicted that more than 80 million people in Africa would die of AIDS by 2025. If the international community does not do more, and soon, another 90 million Africans will become HIV positive in the same period.

In speeches around the world, Lewis describes a "litany of lunacy," from genocide and war crimes to epidemics and inhuman indifference. He condemns the growing gap between rich countries and poor.

Nowhere is the "lunacy" more heartbreaking than with HIV/AIDS in Africa. In sub-Saharan Africa alone, more than 25 million people are living with HIV/AIDS.

"Every day, there are more than 11,000 new infections in sub-Saharan Africa alone, half of them contracted by young people between the ages of 15 and 24," says Lewis. "Country after country faces monumental dilemmas: what to do about mother-to-child transmission; how to establish a network of testing and counselling; where to find the money to pay for treatment; how to fashion a campaign of prevention for adolescents; above all, how to absorb 10 million orphans into extended families when there are no extended families left?"

Lewis's passionate speeches have raised public and political awareness of the catastrophe in Africa. Governments have increased aid. Pharmaceutical companies have made HIV/AIDS drugs more accessible. But for Lewis, the pace is cruelly slow. In 2003 he started the Stephen Lewis Foundation to support people living with AIDS in Africa, particularly women and children.

Lewis works seven days a week, 17 to 19 hours a day. He has admitted that his commitment may have "an element of the irrational to it." But knowing what he knows, seeing what he has seen, what else can he do?

Your Play

1. How does Stephen Lewis demonstrate global citizenship in action?
2. Create a table or graph comparing the populations of Canada and Ontario with the numbers of people living, dying, and being infected with HIV/AIDS in Africa in 2004–2005. Include AIDS orphans.
3. Locate the Stephen Lewis Foundation's Web site, and report on three ideas for actions that you can take.

PAUSE, REFLECT, APPLY

1. How does CIDA work with NGOs?
2. Why do some people believe NGOs run projects more effectively than governments?
3. a) Why do you think Canadians reacted so generously to the 2004 tsunami disaster?
   b) Why do you think there was not a similar response to the HIV/AIDS crisis in Africa?
   c) Research and report on what Bob Geldof did in 2005 to raise public awareness of HIV/AIDS and other issues.
4. List three reasons why the AIDS epidemic is worse in impoverished nations than it is in developed countries.

A Good Citizen Intervenes

Canada's interventions in world conflicts have earned it respect. One method that Canada has used is to impose **sanctions** against countries that deny human rights to citizens or attack other countries. This means the Canadian government stops trading with such countries. Aid can also be stopped. In 1977, for example, Canada joined other nations in imposing trade sanctions against South Africa to protest apartheid, the government's policy of racial segregation. In some cases, the military may enforce sanctions. Sanctions pressure governments to respect human rights and international law.

Canada has also intervened through peacekeeping.

PEACEKEEPING: 50 YEARS AND CHANGING

A Canadian, Lester Pearson, proposed the creation of UN peacekeeping in 1956. Since then, Canadian forces have often been peacekeepers. This reflects Canada's commitment to **multilateralism**, an approach to peace and security that involves cooperation among many countries.

Traditionally, peacekeepers literally came between combatants to ease tensions. In the 1990s, peacekeeping began to evolve. Actions now include

- supervising elections
- delivering humanitarian supplies
- setting up local police forces
- mediating or arbitrating differences.

Canadian peacekeeping activities have created an image of Canada as a good global citizen. At times, Canadian soldiers have paid for this image with their lives.

> ▶ **KEY QUESTION**
> Has Canada been a poor, fair, good, or excellent global citizen in dealing with world conflicts?

FIGURE 11.6 (Left:) The UN's blue helmet and blue beret identify soldiers as peacekeepers and have become international symbols of Canadian pride. (Right:) An eagle feather adorns the beret of a Mi'kmaq peacekeeping veteran at Remembrance Day ceremonies in Halifax in 2002. What does the image say to you about commitments to global citizenship and peace in Canada?

PEACEKEEPING: AT THE BREAKING POINT?

Since the 1990s, increased conflicts have strained the ability of the UN and the world's countries to work together for peace. From 1991 to 1999, ethnic clashes erupted in the Balkans, in south-central Europe. UN missions struggled to bring peace to Bosnia and Serbia, where Serbs and Bosnians (who are largely Muslim) were pitted against Croats (who are predominantly Christian). In Kosovo, Albanian rebels fought the Serb government. In the end, hundreds of thousands were killed, including civilians and soldiers.

In 1994, genocide engulfed Rwanda as UN peacekeepers, under Canadian General Roméo Dallaire, looked on helplessly (see Chapter 10). In his book, *Shake Hands with the Devil* (2003), Dallaire described the horror he felt when the international community could not agree to act: "We watched as the devil took control of paradise on earth and fed on the blood of the people we were supposed to protect."

Death in Darfur

In 2003, catastrophe gripped Darfur, in western Sudan, the largest country in Africa. After decades of civil war, Sudan's Arab-dominated government and militias fought local rebels. They killed perhaps tens of thousands of Darfur's black population. Homes and farms were burned and destroyed. More than 1 million people became refugees.

The UN called Darfur the "worst humanitarian crisis facing the world." The UN and NGOs found evidence of genocide and of Sudanese government complicity in killings of civilians. Although hundreds of thousands were at risk, not all countries agreed that this was a "genocide"—and so the UN could not impose sanctions. Critics said the UN had learned nothing from Rwanda.

Is There a Better Way?

The UN cannot enforce its rules and resolutions without members' support. Currently, the UN can intervene in a country's business (or territory) without its consent only if that country threatens the peace and security of other countries or there is proof of genocide.

In 2004, Prime Minister Paul Martin reminded the UN of its responsibility to protect civilians in cases like Darfur. Martin told the General Assembly: "We should have the legal right to intervene in a country on the grounds of humanitarian emergency alone when the government of that country is unwilling or unable to protect their people from extreme harm as a result of internal war or repression."

At the 2004 World Economic Forum in Switzerland, Martin also warned that "the concept of intervention could be misused." One controversial example he cited was the invasion of Iraq.

"What is required," said Martin, "is an open discussion about the need for intervention in situations that offend the most basic precepts of our common humanity."

PAUSE, REFLECT, APPLY

1. What is multilateralism?
2. What actions can UN peacekeeping troops take in a conflict?
3. Locate Bosnia–Herzegovina, Serbia–Montenegro, Rwanda, and Sudan on a map. What similarities were there in the conflicts in all three areas?
4. Under what circumstances does Prime Minister Martin want the UN to be able to intervene in a country?
5. Should any other country, or the UN, have the right to tell Canada how to treat its own citizens? Discuss, and write a supported-opinion paragraph.

The Changing Face of Global Conflict: Terrorism after 9/11

Terrorism is not new. Unlawful and extreme violence has been used for centuries to achieve political or ideological goals. The 20th century was full of bloody instances of terrorism—for example, by the Irish Republican Army (United Kingdom), the Tamil Tigers (Sri Lanka), and the FLQ (Quebec).

In this century, terrorism has redefined international relations. "Nine-eleven" has become part of everyday speech. It refers to the terrorist attacks on the United States on September 11, 2001. Three thousand civilians died in those attacks, and their deaths have changed how the United States and the world approach global peace and security.

> **KEY QUESTION**
> How have Canada and the United States differed in their responses to terrorism? Why?

FIGURE 11.7 A relative floats candles of remembrance for victims of Air India flight 182 on June 23, 2005. Twenty years before, the airplane—en route to London from Vancouver, Toronto, and Montreal—was shattered by a terrorist bomb and plunged into the sea near Ireland. All 329 people on board—mostly Canadians—perished. In 2005, two men were tried for the worst mass killing in Canadian history and found not guilty. Many people demanded a public inquiry into the Crown's handling of the case. Do you agree? Why or why not?

Terrorists see themselves as patriots, freedom fighters, and idealists. Victims see them as fanatics who use kidnappings, assassinations, suicide bombings, beheadings, hijackings, and even killings of schoolchildren to achieve their goals. Usually, terrorists operate outside government, but are sometimes secretly sponsored by states.

Terrorists' goals may include

- overthrowing a government
- achieving political independence
- expelling oppressive businesses
- pursuing religious goals.

MODERN RESPONSES TO TERRORISM

Modern terrorists use technology to coordinate attacks and cross borders. The threat of terrorism has required governments to cooperate to identify and combat terrorist groups.

After 9/11, the United States passed the *USA PATRIOT Act*. In November 2001, Canada passed the *Anti-terrorism Act*, amending the *Criminal Code*. Both acts increase the powers of police and security agencies to collect and keep information on suspected terrorists. People can be stopped, searched, and questioned at border crossings and held for questioning for long periods of time.

Many critics argue that such laws weaken democratic rights and freedoms, and that members of identifiable groups—such as Muslims—have been targeted. Others say the changes are necessary to fight terrorism.

CANADA'S DILEMMA: GOOD GLOBAL CITIZEN OR LOYAL NEIGHBOUR?

The 9/11 attacks were carried out by al-Qaida, an Islamist terrorist organization led by Osama Bin Laden. Based in Afghanistan, al-Qaida was sheltered by the extremist Taliban government. After 9/11, the Taliban rejected UN and US requests to hand over al-Qaida's leaders for trial.

In October 2001, the United States led a UN-endorsed multilateral invasion of Afghanistan. Troops came from the United States, Canada, Britain, Australia, Germany, and other countries and quickly overthrew the Taliban government. Many members of al-Qaida were killed or captured; others, including Bin Laden, escaped.

An international effort operating with the UN is trying to rebuild Afghanistan's economy and establish democratic institutions.

US-Led Invasion of Iraq

After Afghanistan, the United States accused Iraqi dictator Saddam Hussein of supporting terrorists. It also accused Iraq of hiding **weapons of mass destruction** (WMDS)—nuclear, biological, and chemical weapons designed to kill large numbers of people. The United States lobbied the UN to support an invasion of Iraq. Instead, the UN sent in weapons inspectors. After months of inspections, no WMDs were found.

The UN opposed an invasion of Iraq. Prime Minister Jean Chrétien was equally clear: Canada would not take part. Regardless, the United States led an invasion into Iraq in March 2003, with Britain as its chief ally. Hussein was quickly overthrown.

No WMDs were ever found in Iraq, and Hussein was never linked to al-Qaida. Canada–US relations became strained because Canada had made a decision that did not support its neighbour to the south.

SOURCES

"The important thing is that always Canada should work closely with its closest allies, particularly its military allies. ... That's where our bread is buttered."

— Stephen Harper, leader of the Canadian Alliance (which merged with the Progressive Conservative Party in 2003), September 17, 2002

"The Canadian position is that on matters of peace and security, the international community must speak and act through the UN Security Council. ... We believe in multilateralism very strongly."

— Prime Minister Jean Chrétien, January 15, 2003, on not joining the US invasion of Iraq

PAUSE, REFLECT, APPLY

1. In what ways is a terrorist similar to and different from a traditional soldier?
2. Why would a terrorist feel justified in killing?
3. What laws were passed in the United States and Canada to deal with the threat of terrorism?
4. What are the benefits and sacrifices for Canadians under the *Anti-terrorism Act*?
5. What were the main reasons that Canada and the UN a) supported the United States in Afghanistan and b) did not support the United States in Iraq?
6. Refer to the Sources feature on page 195. Compare Stephen Harper's and Jean Chrétien's positions on the US invasion of Iraq.

Environmental Interdependence

▶ **KEY QUESTION**

How can the way people separate their garbage or drive to work make them responsible global citizens?

▶ **DID YOU KNOW** ◀

Canadians generate 4.42 t of CO₂ per capita each year. Only Americans produce more, at 5.48 t. The figure for India is 0.29 t. What might account for these differences?

┌ **THE WEB** ▶▶▶

Check out ways you can lower emissions through the One-Tonne Challenge at www.emp.ca/civics

One of today's most controversial issues is **global warming**. The UN predicts that the Earth's temperature will rise 5 °C over the next 100 years. The result will be floods, storms, heat waves, droughts, and the melting of the polar icecaps. Entire ecosystems will be upset. Environmental damage respects no borders.

Most scientists believe that global warming is caused by greenhouse gas (GHG) emissions, which trap the sun's heat in the atmosphere. Carbon dioxide (CO_2) is considered one of the most damaging GHGs. It is produced when fossil fuels—such as gas, coal, and oil—are burned.

In 1997, 160 countries signed the *Kyoto Protocol* to combat global warming. The goal is to cut back GHG emissions overall by 5 percent by 2012. Canada promised a 6 percent reduction.

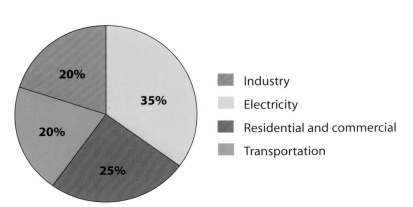

FIGURE 11.8 Carbon emissions from fossil fuel burning by sector, 2002. *Source: John Browne, "Beyond Kyoto,"* Foreign Affairs, *July 1, 2004.*

FIGURE 11.9 Carbon dioxide emissions by the top 10 emitting countries, 2002. *Source: Earth Policy Institute.*

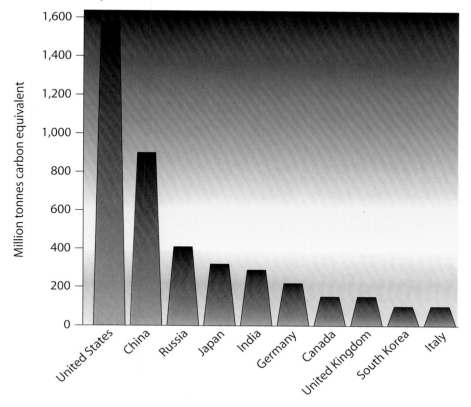

SOURCES

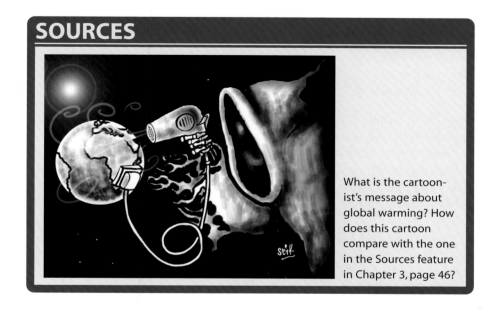

What is the cartoonist's message about global warming? How does this cartoon compare with the one in the Sources feature in Chapter 3, page 46?

FACE OFF   The *Kyoto Protocol*: Is It Worth the Price?

Supporters say the *Kyoto Protocol* is an essential example of international cooperation. Others have called it a colossal waste. Main arguments go something like this:

No

Kyoto's goals are costly and unreachable. To reduce emissions, industries will have to cut energy use and production. In 2002, Lorne Taylor, Alberta's environment minister, warned that doing so would eliminate 450,000 jobs. It would also wipe out $8 billion a year from Alberta's oil-producing economy. Taylor questioned Kyoto's science:

> I think that's a bunch of what I would call hokey science. The South Saskatchewan River was dry in 1862. Are you going to tell me that that was caused by global warming?
>
> — Source: www.cbc.ca/fifth/kyoto/debate.html

The Canadian Manufacturers and Exporters organization said consumers would have to "drive less, drive smaller cars, take public transit, and pay up to 100 percent more for electricity." Pierre Alvarez, president of the Canadian Association of Petroleum Producers, asked:

> What are those folks in Toronto prepared to do? Are they prepared to use less electricity? Drive less? Change their work patterns and their commuting patterns? I've not seen evidence of that.
>
> — Source: www.cbc.ca/fifth/kyoto/debate.html

The biggest "no" came in 2001, when US President George W. Bush rejected Kyoto. He said it would interfere with US sovereignty and hurt American businesses. Canadian manufacturers warned that they would now have to compete with US businesses, which did not face the burden of Kyoto.

Yes

Kyoto supporters argue that the majority of scientists agree with the science behind Kyoto. If ignored, global warming will be as destructive as nuclear war. In 1999, federal environment minister David Anderson issued his own warning:

> Even if countries meet their Kyoto targets, we may only succeed in slowing the rate of climate change. In other words, ... [Kyoto targets] clearly are only the beginning of what is necessary to combat climate change. It's time we woke up to that reality.
>
> — Source: www.ec.gc.ca/minister/speeches/ kyoto_s_e.htm

Environmentalist Ralph Torrie, of the David Suzuki Foundation, agreed that it will cost Canadians money to reach Kyoto goals. People will have to retrofit homes and buy energy-saving appliances. But long-term benefits will outweigh the costs. Businesses and consumers will save on energy, not to mention reducing costs associated with environmental disasters.

Wind, solar, and hydro power are more environmentally friendly and more efficient than oil, coal, and gas. Besides, supplies of oil, coal, and gas are not renewable.

A 2005 survey of senior Canadian businesspeople showed that 57 percent believed emission levels could be cut with little economic damage. Other polls show that 60 percent of Canadians are willing to combat global warming, even if it costs them money.

What Do You Think?

1. In an election, one party promises to meet Kyoto goals. Another promises to pull out of the agreement. Make a list of points for each side. Add a third list of questions that you still want answered to improve your understanding of this issue.

2. Go to the Web site of Environment Canada (www.ec.gc.ca) and report on Canada's most recent actions on Kyoto. Look for answers to your questions from activity 1.

Hope through Global Citizenship

At the turn of the century, all UN members formally authorized the Millennium Declaration. In a commitment to global renewal, all countries agreed to work to achieve the following **Millennium Development Goals** by the year 2015:

1. Eradicate extreme poverty and hunger.
2. Achieve universal primary education.
3. Promote gender equality and empower women.
4. Reduce child mortality.
5. Improve maternal health.
6. Combat HIV/AIDS, malaria, and other diseases.
7. Ensure environmental **sustainability** (meeting the needs of the present without compromising the ability of future generations to meet their own needs).
8. Develop global partnerships so that countries trade fairly.

MEASURING PROGRESS

In March 2005, UN Secretary General Kofi Annan presented a five-year report on the Millennium Declaration to the General Assembly. Annan called for major UN reforms—and action:

> I am profoundly convinced that the threats which face us are of equal concern to all. I believe that development, security and human rights go hand in hand. In a world of interconnected threats and opportunities, it is in each country's self-interest that all of these challenges are addressed effectively.
>
> We all know what the problems are, and we all know what we have promised to achieve. What is needed now is not more declarations or promises, but action to fulfill the promises already made.

CivicStar

RYAN HRELJAC

In 1998, six-year-old Ryan Hreljac learned that thousands of children die each year because they lack safe drinking water. Disturbed by this information, he began doing extra chores to raise $70 for a village well in Africa. Ryan's determination attracted media attention, and soon donations were coming in from across Canada. Then, CIDA gave a matching grant to the well project. Within two and a half years, Ryan travelled to Angolo Public School in Uganda, where the well was located. Five thousand local children lined up to cheer the Canadian boy who had done chores to help them have safe water.

By 2005, Ryan's Well Foundation was working with CIDA and had raised over half a million dollars.

It had projects in five African countries. Today, Ryan Hreljac travels internationally to promote the cause of the 1.1 billion people worldwide who need safe water. "I want all of Africa to have clean drinking water," says Hreljac. "I think I'll get there when I'm 50."

Your Play

1. a) Describe the impact of the news media on Ryan Hreljac's work.
   b) Why do you think the media paid so much attention?
2. a) What Millennium Development Goal(s) could you address? Explain why, based on the criteria of the goal's importance and your ability.
   b) Which goals will be the most difficult to meet? Why?

The Global Citizen Takes Time to Know

"Knowledge is power. Information is liberating. Education is the premise of progress, in every society, in every family."

—UN Secretary General Kofi Annan, June 22, 1997, Toronto, addressing the GlobalKnowledge 97 Conference

This has been called the Information Age. The ever-expanding Internet links citizens around the globe, offering riches of information. No single source can provide all that you can and should know about world events. However, there are good starting places. You will find Web sites for the following at www.emp.ca/civics:

- Foreign Affairs Canada and CIDA offer good resources. See also the UN's CyberSchoolBus, designed for students and teachers.
- Background information and breaking news on national and global issues are available at the Canadian Broadcasting

Corporation. The CBC News Indepth main page lists hundreds of topics alphabetically, as does CBC Archives.

■ Different countries view global events differently. The Internet Public Library lists hundreds of the world's newspapers and magazines.

PAUSE, REFLECT, APPLY

1. Why are the UN's development goals called "millennium" goals?
2. Explain the meaning of "gender equality" in education.
3. Explain why universal education is seen as a critical need by the UN.
4. At what ages is a child most vulnerable? Why?
5. What types of information can be found at the CyberSchoolBus? (Hint: Take a look.)
6. What two goals would you add to the Millennium Development Goals? Justify your choices.

REPLAY ■ ■ ■ ■ ■ ■ ■ ■ ■

This chapter has informed you of these civics concepts:

1. A global citizen investigates and analyzes global issues from multiple perspectives, respects the diversity and equality of humankind, and acts responsibly to improve the world.
2. All countries are interconnected; Canada cannot isolate itself.
3. Canada's commitment to multilateralism is expressed through diplomacy, trade, aid, and participation in UN peacekeeping missions and agreements.
4. A few developed nations, such as Canada, have most of the world's wealth.
5. Canada is committed to the Millennium Development Goals to reduce global poverty and inequality.

CIVICS ▣ TOOLKIT — How to Assess Yourself and Your Work

The purpose of self-assessment is self-improvement. There are steps that can be followed in any self-assessment. This is true whether the task is academic, such as writing a report, or behavioural, such as becoming a global citizen.

1. Examine where you are now.
   - How successful has your work been to date; what areas need improvement?
2. Understand terms and concepts.
   - For a report, what is the best structure or format? Ensure the accuracy of your information.
   - For being a global citizen, examine information and concepts in this chapter and other resources.
3. Identify your criteria. Be specific.
   - On what basis will you assess your report? (Examples: accuracy, clarity, grammar, bibliography, unity, coherence.)
   - What are the characteristics of a global citizen? Review the information and definitions in this chapter.
4. Find models or standards.
   - Your teacher will have a variety of models (exemplars) of good report writing.
   - Consider the actions and attitudes of people in this chapter. Research other people whom you admire.
5. Set goals. Plan the steps you will undertake. Be realistic.
   - You cannot research and write about everything. Decide in advance what points you want to make, what examples you are going to use, and how long the report will be.
   - Do not immediately set up unrealistic expectations. Identify what you actually can do.
6. Define your "levels of achievement." What is the difference between excellent, good, fair, and poor?
   - Base these levels on your criteria.
   - Know how your results can be proven and measured. How will you know how well you have achieved each goal?
7. Review and revise. Do you have:
   - correct information?
   - clear criteria?
   - reasonable standards?
   - examples or models?
   - a way to measure your success?

Skill Practice

1. a) Write a 150-word report on the topic, "Am I a Global Citizen?" Assess yourself using the steps above.
   b) Assess the quality of your report.
2. Share your report with a peer or peers. How do your assessments compare?
3. Have your teacher look at your assessment. Compare his or her comments with your own.

STUDY HALL

Informed Citizenship

1. What are the characteristics of a global citizen?

2. List three ways in which humanitarianism is practised through CIDA and NGOs.

3. Did multilateralism affect Canada's actions in conflicts in the Balkans, Rwanda, Afghanistan, and Iraq? Justify your answer.

4. What makes terrorism more difficult to fight than traditional warfare?

5. How does the *Kyoto Protocol* attempt to reduce global warming?

6. What objectives are the Millennium Development Goals meant to achieve?

Purposeful Citizenship

7. a) Calculate your spending in one month, including charitable donations, money that you earn and save, and money that your family spends for your food, clothing, travel, shelter, and so on. Determine whether your donations equal or surpass 0.7 percent of your total spending.

   b) If they do not, what would you have to give up to reach 0.7 percent?

8. Using the UN CyberSchoolBus Web site or another reliable, up-to-date source, find Canada's per capita GDP (the GDP divided by total population). Compare it to the per capita GDPs of the United States, Japan, four western European and four African countries, and two countries from each of Central America and East Asia. Create a graphic poster or chart to show the gaps between countries. Why is it important for global citizens to know these statistics?

9. Analyze the types of humanitarian assistance that Canada has contributed globally. What sacrifices might Canadians have to make to help less economically developed countries?

10. Identify a person who is an example of a global citizen. Justify your choice using the criteria in this chapter. A starting list: Muhammad Azam Dogar; Cardinal Paul-Émile Léger; Nelson Mandela; Wangari Maathai; Mother Teresa; David Suzuki.

Active Citizenship

11. Prepare a piece of artwork or a presentation that illustrates your perspective on global interconnectedness. Focus on one area, or several. You may wish to search the Internet for examples. CIDA and the UN CyberSchoolBus, for example, run contests on global cooperation and youth involvement. Your goal: to convince yourself and others to take action.

12. Obtain information on the federal government's One-Tonne Challenge.

    - Prepare a report describing the One-Tonne Challenge and how it connects to global warming and the *Kyoto Protocol*.

    - Prepare a plan of action for yourself, your family, class, or school to meet the One-Tonne Challenge.

13. Write a one-minute radio or television advertisement urging people to donate to an NGO that inspires you. Be sure to connect your NGO's work to the Millennium Development Goals. Use an NGO from this book, or check out the CCIC Web site for a list of suggested organizations.

CULMINATING ACTIVITY
Active Citizenship: A Critical Thinking Approach

Go back to Chapter 1 and Rousseau's belief in the "social contract" and the common good (page 8). A culminating activity is a way for you to review and use what you have already learned. In this activity, you will apply your new knowledge and thinking skills by taking action for the common good: you will fulfill your democratic responsibility. You will contribute to or participate in a civic action project.

For your assessment, keep a portfolio of all of the lists, charts, and notes you make throughout this activity. Be sure to update your portfolio regularly.

STAGE 1: Review what you have learned.

STEP 1-1 Make a list of the skills you have learned in the Civics Toolkit features in each chapter of this book, and record the page numbers for each feature. Know when to use the Toolkit skills.

STEP 1-2 Draft a short list of "ordinary citizens" from the individuals profiled in the CivicStar features in each chapter. Identify one person who stands out as an example for you. Why do you think this particular individual is special?

STEP 1-3 Review the Pause, Reflect, Apply and Study Hall questions you answered during the course. As a class and working from your notes, make a list of ways in which citizens can take action to influence government policy or effect change in their community or in the world. (See Chapters 4, 8, 11.)

STAGE 2: Prepare to select a project.

STEP 2-1 Identify an issue that is important to you. Consider the following resources to help you identify an issue:

- Publications (e.g., *Take More Action* by Mark and Craig Kielburger, Toronto: Gage Learning, 2004; available in most schools)

- The Internet (e.g., check out volunteer activities at www.emp.ca/civics and link to a Seven-Step Guide to getting organized for action)
- Your community (e.g., invite representatives from service clubs [see Chapter 8], social agencies, the police, political parties to speak at your school)
- Your school (e.g., brainstorm local or school issues in class or with your principal)

Consider the following issues:

- School issues (e.g., smoking, bullying, littering, organizing a charity event, organizing forums on important social issues)
- Community issues (e.g., street safety/jaywalking, assisting youth or seniors, informing students about gang activity)
- National or international issues (e.g., disaster relief, collecting library materials for isolated communities, raising funds for or distributing information about HIV/AIDS, digging a well)

STEP 2-2 Identify a civic activity that you will contribute to or participate in. Look for activities that you (or your group) can accomplish in a few weeks.

Consider the following activities:

- Fundraising for a local, national, or international group (e.g., Red Cross, food banks)
- Fundraising for a specific project (e.g., Ryan's Well, building a school in the developing world)
- Raising awareness (e.g., letter-writing or poster campaigns, speaker forums)
- Social service (e.g., helping out at a seniors' home, targeting an area for litter or graffiti cleanup)
- Participation (e.g., in cultural or political celebrations or activities; see Chapter 8 for examples)

STAGE 3: Prepare a project proposal.*

STEP 3-1 Research your project. To learn more about it (the issue and the civic action you will take), answer the following questions:

- What is the issue or problem that you are addressing?
- How did this issue or problem come about?
- Who are the stakeholders, and what are their interests?
- Where is your focus (e.g., school, community, international site)?
- When is this project to be done? (I.e., is this a long-term issue or something you can complete?)
- Why does this issue or problem need to be addressed?
- What civic action has so far been taken by citizens to address the issue or problem?
- What civic activities have worked and what activities have failed? (Civics Toolkits, Chapters 1, 2, 3, 6)

Remember to take on a manageable, small-scale task.

Use the skills from the Civics Toolkits in planning your project. Organize your project research and plan for civic action using lists, charts, and graphs. (Civics Toolkits, Chapters 2, 6, 7)

STEP 3-2 Define project success. How will you know if you have succeeded? Develop a list of your own criteria with which to evaluate your work. Ask yourself:

- What are my indicators of success? Be realistic, specific, and concrete. You do not have to change the world (but you might change it for one person!).
- Have I considered different perspectives in judging my success? Review the issue of homeless people (Face Off, Chapter 4, page 66) for clues to what to look for. (Civics Toolkits, Chapters 4, 11)

Meet with your teacher to assess how your project proposal is shaping up (both your understanding of the issue and your plan for civic action).

STEP 3-3 Submit a project proposal to justify your project selection and plan of action (or a reflection to explain the reasons that your project is important). Include the actions you will take; what you will

achieve; and how much time you will spend. (Civics Toolkits, Chapters 8, 9, 10)

If you are working as part of a group, identify what each group member will do, and get teacher approval for your evaluation plan. (Civics Toolkit, Chapter 11)

STAGE 4: Do it.

Approach the issue with caring. Be prepared to persevere. Keep an open mind (i.e., consider new ideas and perspectives).

Throughout your project, follow these general guidelines:

- Stay focused on the manageable task.
- Plan thoroughly.
- Keep records.
- List clear, measurable goals.
- Make the issue your own (i.e., make it personal).
- Be original.

STAGE 5: Evaluate your success.

Do not leave the evaluation stage to the last minute. Ask your teacher to assess how well you are doing throughout this activity, and review your own criteria for success (Step 3-2).

STEP 5-1 Create a written article, speech, video, or multimedia presentation to communicate your achievements. (Civics Toolkits, Chapters 8, 9, 10)

STEP 5-2 With your teacher, evaluate your civic action project based on one or more of the following criteria, depending on the time available:

- Organization and planning
- Tracking your actions through a portfolio
- Participation in or contribution to a civic action
- Achieving a goal based on selected criteria
- Communication of your findings (oral, visual, or written)
- Knowledge, perspective, understanding gained (a reflection).

---

* These considerations for analyzing an issue are adapted from Roland Case et al., *Active Citizenship: Student Action Projects* (Richmond, BC: The Critical Thinking Consortium, 2004).

GLOSSARY

Aboriginal justice: a justice system managed by Aboriginal people within Canada's criminal justice system that respects and employs Aboriginal traditions (e.g., see "healing circle" and "sentencing circle")

activist: one who actively campaigns for or against a policy or social reforms

adversarial system: a system in which two or more sides have opposing interests and argue different positions

affirmative action: a policy designed to increase the participation of groups that have suffered discrimination

ambassador: the highest-ranking diplomat appointed by a government to be its country's official representative in a foreign country

amendments: changes to an existing law or to legislation in the process of being made into law

arbitrate: to decide or settle a dispute

authoritarian: a form of decision making or a government system in which one person or a small group holds all power (see also "dictatorship")

authority: the right to give orders or make decisions

backbenchers: elected members of a parliament or legislature who are not government ministers or spokespersons for the opposition party; the "front bench" is where cabinet ministers and the opposition's "shadow cabinet" sit

bail: money or other security given to the court in exchange for an arrested person's temporary release from jail and to ensure his or her later appearance in court

band councils: government bodies elected by Aboriginal peoples to look after certain local matters

basic needs and wants: things that are required for survival, such as food, shelter, and water, as well as more complex desires, such as recognition or a sense of belonging

beliefs: what one accepts as true

bias: a distorted or prejudiced view not based on fairness and accuracy

bill: a written proposal for a law that is presented to a legislature or parliament for approval

burden of proof: the duty to prove a disputed fact or facts

bylaws: laws passed by local governments

cabinet: advisers selected by the prime minister or premier to head ministries or departments and run the executive branch of government

cabinet solidarity: the rule that cabinet members must publicly agree with government policy or resign

censor: to edit, ban, suppress, or prevent public display or expression

censure: criticize

centrist: one whose political beliefs lie between left and right on the political spectrum

charge to the jury: the judge's review of the facts of a case on trial and instructions concerning the law that applies

charismatic: an ability to attract and influence people by the force of one's personality

chief electoral officer: the officer appointed by the Canadian House of Commons to head Elections Canada and conduct elections

citizenship: membership in a political community, such as a country, including rights, duties, and responsibilities

civics: the study of the rights and duties of citizenship

civil disobedience: non-violent refusal to obey laws in order to publicize an issue or political viewpoint and force reforms

civil society: the broad web of voluntary organizations, movements, and associations outside government and business that take action on important public issues in a democracy

coercion: the use of force or threats to ensure orderly behaviour; sometimes known as "government by force"

collective: characteristic of a group that acts together

collective bargaining: a negotiation process in which representatives of employees bargain with employers to reach an agreement on wages, hours, workplace safety, job security, and other working conditions

commissioner: the representative of Canada's monarch in each of the three territorial governments

common good: that which benefits all (or most) people in a community or society

communism: a left-wing political system that eliminates private ownership in favour of public ownership of all property, and uses central planning to achieve economic equality among citizens. Russia was under **communist** control until 1989; by the beginning of the 21st century, communist dictatorships held power only in China, Cuba, Laos, North Korea, and Vietnam

compromise: to settle differences by finding an acceptable middle ground in which all sides give up something to get something

confidence: majority support by elected representatives for the governing party in the legislature on important legislation (see also "non-confidence")

conscience: one's inner sense of morality, or right and wrong

consensus: a group decision reached through discussion to which all members agree

conservative: politically, a person who tends to oppose change and favours tradition and less government involvement in people's lives

constituency: the body of voters represented by an elected legislator or official

constituents: the residents (voters and non-voters) in a riding, whose interests are looked after by the elected representative

constitution: the fundamental laws that establish the structure and processes of government and the rights of the people governed

conventions: formal agreements between two or more countries

councillors: elected representatives in municipal government; a councillor may be elected citywide or may represent specific geographical areas, known as wards

Crown: in Canada, the lawyer(s) representing the state in a criminal case, also known as the prosecution; "Crown" refers to the head of state, i.e., the monarch of Canada

damages: a legal term that refers to money paid to compensate for injury or loss

declaratory order: a decision in a civil case in which the court outlines the rights and responsibilities of the disputing parties

defendant: the person charged in a criminal case or being sued in a civil case

democratic: a form of decision making in which all group members have a vote

democratic rights: the rights to vote and hold public office as well as the requirement for periodic elections and annual sittings of legislative bodies, as outlined in sections 3, 4, and 5 of the *Canadian Charter of Rights and Freedoms*

deterrence: a means to discourage the repetition of undesirable behaviour

developed countries: countries that are technologically advanced and wealthy

developing countries: countries with low average income and little technology

dictatorship: a form of government in which one person or group of people has absolute, unlimited power

direct action: a form of political activity that seeks to achieve a goal by the most immediate means, including civil disobedience and actions that may be violent and illegal (e.g., protests, strikes, sit-ins, road blockades)

direct democracy: government in which all citizens directly participate in decision making without representatives

disability rights: rights that ensure that people living with physical or mental disabilities have access to a full range of

services, as outlined in section 15 of the *Canadian Charter of Rights and Freedoms*

discrimination: unfair treatment that is based on prejudice rather than respect for equality and individual worth

dissent: to disagree, oppose, or dispute openly

diversity: differences and variety

equality rights: rights that protect people from discrimination and ensure equal access to opportunity, as outlined in section 15 of the *Canadian Charter of Rights and Freedoms*

ethnic groups: cultural groups of people who share common customs and values based on language, religion, or homeland

executive: the branch of a government or organization that makes decisions and enforces rules

fascism: a right-wing political system that permits private ownership of property within an authoritarian national government. Italy under Benito Mussolini (1883–1945) and Germany under Adolf Hitler (1889–1945) had fascist governments that used a strong military to maintain control over civil society and the economy

figurehead: a head or chief in name only, often for ceremonial reasons; the real power is held elsewhere

First Nations: the indigenous (native, or original) nations, or peoples, of Canada, often referred to as "Indians" by Europeans; does not include the Inuit or the Métis people

first past the post (FPTP): an electoral system in which the candidate with the most votes wins, even if he or she receives less than 50 percent of total votes; sometimes called "simple majority"

franchise: the right to vote

freedoms: rights that do not impose a duty on the government. For example, citizens can exercise freedom of religion or expression without a duty on the part of the government

Geneva Conventions: internationally recognized rules of conduct during war that protect military personnel, prisoners of war, and civilians

genocide: the systematic and deliberate attempt to kill all members of an ethnic, racial, or other cultural group

global warming: the progressive, gradual increase in the average temperature of the Earth's surface

government: a system by which a group of people makes the laws that are enforced to guide the affairs of a community, such as a country, province, or municipality

governor general: the appointed representative of Canada's monarch as the official head of state in the Canadian federal system of government

grassroots: political action taken by ordinary people and organizations at the local level

gross domestic product (GDP): the value of all goods and services produced in a country in a given year

healing circle: a traditional approach in Aboriginal justice in which the offender admits guilt to the victim(s) and tries to reconcile with the victim(s) and the community. The circle is a central concept in Aboriginal belief systems, representing the "circle of life" into which all things are born (see also "sentencing circle")

hearsay: information that a witness has heard at second hand rather than personally

HIV/AIDS: HIV stands for human immunodeficiency virus, the retrovirus that attacks the immune system, leaving the body unable to fight off infections and cancers and leading to AIDS (acquired immune deficiency syndrome)

Holocaust: Nazi Germany's systematic extermination of 6 million European Jews (1941–1945)

House of Commons: the structure in Ottawa where the elected members of Canada's federal government meet to discuss and pass laws; sometimes called the "Lower House"

humanitarian: the belief that everyone deserves to be treated with respect and dignity and that the well-being of all humankind is a necessary and worthy goal

inadmissible: evidence that cannot be heard or presented during a legal trial

incarceration: imprisonment or confinement in a prison or similar institution

independent: an elected representative who is not a member of a political party

indictable offence: a serious or severe offence under Canada's *Criminal Code*

influence: a form of power; the ability to persuade people

infrastructure: the basic network of public services and installations that are needed for a society to function (e.g., radio, roads, railways, water, sewage, electrical power, hospitals, schools)

injunction: a court command to do or not do something (e.g., a broadcaster may be forbidden to publish details of testimony in a trial for a period of time)

interest groups: organizations of people who share social, political, and other goals and act together to influence governments; may be local, national, or international in scope

International Criminal Court (ICC): the world's first permanent international criminal court, which was established by the United Nations in 2002 to prosecute individuals accused of war crimes and crimes against humanity

Inuit: the Aboriginal people who live in the Arctic regions of North America, once called "Eskimos"; singular, "Inuk"

Iroquois Confederacy: a political alliance of five tribes (later, six) that occupied what is now Eastern Canada before contact with Europeans

judicial: the branch of government that deals with the administration of justice and the interpretation of laws

laws: the principles and regulations that govern a community and that are enforced by political authority and court decisions

left-wing: the left, or liberal, side of the political spectrum (see "liberal")

legislative: the branch of government that makes laws

levy: a fee

liberal: politically, a person who tends to favour social reform and more government involvement

lieutenant governor: the representative of the Canadian monarch in the provincial system of government

lobby groups: see "interest groups"

majority government: a government formed by a political party that wins more than half the seats in a parliament or legislature

margin of error: an indication of how much a poll's findings may differ from the results if all people were surveyed rather than a limited number, or "sample," of people. The smaller the sample polled, the greater the margin of error. For example, if a poll shows that 70 percent of people support an issue, with a margin of error of plus or minus 3 percent, that means the actual number of supporters could range from 67 percent to 73 percent.

mayor: the head of a municipal government in a town or city

mediate: to help parties involved in a conflict negotiate a mutually agreeable solution; the mediator must be a "third party," i.e., not involved in the dispute

members of Parliament: the elected representatives of the people, who sit in the federal House of Commons

Métis: a people of mixed Aboriginal and European origin (e.g., Scottish, French, Ojibwa, and Cree)

Millennium Development Goals: a set of eight goals agreed to by all UN member countries in 2000 (the beginning of a new millennium), to be achieved by 2015. Issues include world poverty and hunger, education, women's equality, child deaths, the health of mothers and their babies, disease, environment, and trade

minority government: a government that is elected with fewer than half the seats in the legislative body

mobility rights: the right to move around freely

multiculturalism: a government policy that guarantees all citizens their identity, heritage, and language

multilateralism: an approach to international relations in which nations consult and cooperate to address world problems; the opposite of "unilateralism," in which a country acts only in its own self-interest regardless of the opinions or support of other countries

negotiate: to try to reach agreement through discussion

non-confidence: in a parliament, a motion by the opposition party to try to force the government to resign over important legislation. If more than half the members present do not support the legislation, the government is defeated and an election will usually be called

non-governmental organizations (NGOs): not-for-profit voluntary organizations that work to improve life and social conditions around the world (e.g., Oxfam, Greenpeace, Doctors Without Borders); although they may receive some funding from government, NGOs are independent of government control

non-partisan: not attached to any political party

Nuremberg trials: international trials held in the German city of Nuremberg (1945–1949) to try Nazis who oversaw the Holocaust for war crimes. The trials influenced the creation of international criminal law and a movement for the establishment of an international criminal court

Official Languages Act: the federal law that made French and English Canada's two official languages and made the federal public service and judicial systems bilingual

Official Opposition: the party with the second-largest number of seats in the legislative body

ombudsman: an appointed, impartial, and independent official who investigates complaints. The ombudsman is intended to give those with less power some protection and a voice in dealing with large organizations such as government, business, and educational systems

open custody: a form of supervised detention, often in a group home, that is less restrictive than secure custody

petitions: formal requests signed by members of the public and presented to legislators or other authorities in support of persons or ideas

plaintiff: the person, or party, who sues in a civil case

platform: a formal, written statement outlining the policies of a political party

pluralistic society: a society composed of people with different beliefs, cultures, and ethnic and racial backgrounds and in which these differences are formally recognized and mutually respected

points system: the Canadian system that awards immigration applicants points for knowing English or French and having certain job skills; to be successful, an applicant must be awarded a certain minimum of points. The points system was designed to be free of racial prejudice, or "colour blind"

policy: a plan of action by a political party or government to achieve certain goals

polises: the Greek communities known as "city-states" in which democracy emerged (800–400 BCE)

political parties: organized groups of people with common values and goals who compete to get candidates elected and to form the government

political patronage: the granting of political favours by the governing political party

political spectrum: a line showing the range of political beliefs from liberalism (left) to conservatism (right)

politics: a human activity in which opposing individuals or groups mobilize support to obtain power to govern

poll: a) a survey of public opinion; b) the place where one goes to vote on election day

portfolios: departments that cabinet members supervise (e.g., finance, justice, health, defence)

power: the ability of an individual or group to get what it wants

pressure groups: see "interest groups"

privacy rights: rights that limit the ability of others to enter citizens' private spaces, seize property, or collect personal information

proportional representation (PR): an electoral system in which the number of seats each political party wins is in proportion to its share of the total vote

prosecution: the lawyer(s) working for the state, or Crown, to prove the guilt of the defendant in a criminal case

protection: shielding the public from dangerous people; one goal of sentencing. Often this is done through imprisonment, or segregation of offenders from the community

protocols: formal agreements between two or more countries; codes of correct conduct

punishment: as a goal of sentencing, the practice of imposing penalties on a convicted offender, most often through fines or imprisonment

Question Period: the 45-minute period put aside during daily sessions of the legislature when the opposition parties can question the government; also known as "Oral Questions"

random sample: the method by which people questioned in a poll (the "sample") are selected to ensure that everyone in the population has an equal opportunity of being interviewed

reasonable limits: limitations of rights and freedoms to which a "reasonable person" would agree, as stated in section 1 of the *Canadian Charter of Rights and Freedoms*

recall election: a vote by which electors can remove (recall) an elected official before his or her term is completed

reeve: the head of a rural municipal government

referendum: a direct yes–no vote of the electorate on a particular issue, policy, or law

refugees: people who leave their native country because of a well-founded fear of persecution for reasons of race, religion, nationality, political opinion, or membership in a particular social group

rehabilitation: as a sentencing goal, treatment and training to help convicted offenders acquire the skills to rejoin society as healthy, law-abiding, productive members

remedy: the compensation that a plaintiff expects to receive in a civil case

representative democracy: a democracy in which citizens periodically elect others to represent them in government

republic: a form of government in which the head of state is elected rather than hereditary; often, the head of state in a republic is a president

republicanism: a political philosophy that the head of state must be elected by the people, not a hereditary monarch

resolution: a decision or position on an issue taken by a group

responsibilities: things for which one is accountable

restorative justice: a method of criminal justice that uses Aboriginal sentencing circles or healing circles to bring offenders and victims together to restore losses suffered by victims and the community as a whole

ridings: geographical areas, each of which elects a representative to a federal or provincial legislature; also known as "constituencies"

rights: claims to which all people are entitled by moral or ethical principles or by legal guarantees

right-wing: the right, or conservative, side of the political spectrum

royal assent: approval by the monarch or the monarch's representative (governor general or lieutenant governor) that turns a bill passed by a legislature into law

rule of law: the fundamental constitutional principle that no government or person is above the law and that society is governed by laws that apply fairly to all; sometimes referred to as "law and order"

sanctions: military or economic measures by which one or more countries try to force another country to respect international law or human rights (e.g., by stopping trade or aid)

secession: official withdrawal from an association, organization, or political union

secure custody: imprisonment for young offenders convicted of serious offences, with guards, usually in a youth detention centre. In contrast, open custody is for less serious offences

self-government: a group or nation's power to administer its own government

Senate: in Canada, the legislative branch of the federal government that is composed of senators, who are not elected but appointed by prime ministers; sometimes called the "Upper House"

sentencing circle: a custom in Aboriginal justice in which the offender comes before a "circle" of the victim(s) and community to take responsibility for the harm he or she has caused. Through consensus, the circle decides on a sentence (punishment), which can include banishment, treatment, and community service

sexual harassment: unwelcome conduct, of a sexual nature, directed toward a person

society: a group of interacting people who share a community

sovereignty: freedom from any higher or external control; independence to pass laws

sovereignty-association: independence with close economic ties to Canada

Speaker of the House: an elected representative who is selected to act as a referee to enforce the rules of parliamentary conduct and debate

stakeholder: a person or group that will be affected by a decision and that has something to gain or lose from it

standing committee: a small group of elected representatives from all parties that is selected to examine all bills relating to a certain area of policy (e.g., finance, foreign affairs, health)

strike: in labour issues, a cessation of work by employees to pressure the employer to bargain in good faith or to meet employees' demands (e.g., better compensation, fewer work hours)

subjects: people who are under the control of a government and owe it complete obedience

subsidies: government grants or money to help support industries that are seen to benefit society

sue: to take legal action against a person, usually under civil law

summary offence: a minor criminal offence, in contrast to an "indictable offence" (see above)

sustainability: having the ability to use or harvest a resource without completely depleting or destroying it

terrorism: the unlawful use or threatened use of extreme violence by individuals and groups to create widespread fear to achieve political goals

trade unions: workers' organizations that seek to improve wages and working conditions through collective bargaining with employers

United Empire Loyalists: the approximately 40,000 English-speaking people who immigrated to what is now Canada because they were "loyal" to the British Empire during the American Revolution (1775–1783)

United Nations Human Development Index (HDI): a measure of countries' quality of life through such factors as income, literacy, education, and life expectancy

Universal Declaration of Human Rights (UDHR): the international document adopted by the United Nations in 1948 that proclaims basic human rights for all people. Even though it cannot be enforced, the UDHR firmly establishes the principle of human rights and has inspired other human rights agreements

values: qualities that one considers important

veto: the ability or right to block or reject a proposal

victims' rights: the rights of people affected by criminal acts

wards: geographical areas in municipal government, each of which elects a representative or councillor

warrant: a legal document issued by a court or judge that authorizes police to perform certain acts (e.g., arrest a person, search a house)

weapons of mass destruction: nuclear, biological, and chemical weapons designed to kill large numbers of people and cause widespread destruction

young offenders: in Canada, people between the ages of 12 and 17 who commit a criminal offence

Youth Criminal Justice Act: federal legislation passed in 2002 under which youths aged 12 to 17 are prosecuted in Canada's criminal justice system

youth wings: groups within political parties in which young members, including those under the voting age, can be active in forming policy and supporting party candidates

INDEX

CREDITS

Page 1 Clockwise: Fred Chartrand/CP Photo Archive, © Hulton-Deutsch Collection/CORBIS, Reuters/Landov; Page 2: Jean-Marc Bouju/CP Photo Archive; Page 4: Reuters/Landov; Page 5: Reprinted with permission from The Globe and Mail; Page 6: © Bettmann/CORBIS; Page 13: Jonathan Hayward/CP Photo Archive; Page 17: © Bettmann/CORBIS; Page 18: Tom Hanson/CP Photo Archive; Page 22: © Royalty-Free/CORBIS; Page 29 Left to right: Colonel The Honourable Lincoln M. Alexander, PC, QC. Photo Courtesy of the Senate of Canada, Frank Gunn/CP Photo Archive; Page 30: Denis Dubois/CP Photo Archive; Page 33: With the permission of the House of Commons Collection, Ottawa; Page 34 Top to bottom: Fred Chartrand/CP Photo Archive, With the permission of the House of Commons Collection, Ottawa; Page 37: Fred Chartrand/CP Photo Archive; Page 42: © Hulton-Deutsch Collection/CORBIS; Page 44: © Jose Luis Pelaez, Inc./CORBIS; Page 45: John Rennison/CP Photo Archive; Page 46: www.CartoonStock.com; Page 47: Paul Chiasson/CP Photo Archive; Page 48: Scott Hanson/CORBIS; Page 49: CP Photo Archive; Page 51: Courtesy of Justine Blainey; Page 52 Top to bottom: Molly Riley/Reuters/Landov, Heller Syndication; Page 55: Ian Hodgson/Reuters/Landov; Page 59: Reprinted with permission—TorStar Syndication Services; Page 59: Shaun Best/Reuters/Landov; Page 65: U.S. Missile Defense Agency, Department of Defense; Page 66: Dave Abel, Sun Media Corp; Page 67: Tom Hanson/CP Photo Archive; Page 68: Courtesy of Annie Kidder; Page 73: © Bettmann/CORBIS. Page 77 Clockwise: Toby Melville/Reuters/Landov, Ruth Bonneville/CP Photo Archive, Fred Chartrand/CP Photo Archive; Page 78: Erik De Castro/Reuters/Landov; Page 80: Ryan Remiorz/CP Photo Archive; Page 86: Artizans.com; Page 88: Courtesy of Free the Children; Page 95: © Images.com; Page 97: © Hulton-Deutsch/CORBIS; Page 100: Phil Carpenter/CP Photo Archive; Page 103: © Royalty-Free/CORBIS; Page 105: Dave Chidley/CP Photo Archive; Page 106: Aaron Harris/CP Photo Archive; Page 107: Fred Chartrand/CP Photo Archive; Page 111: © Jeffrey Coolidge/CORBIS; Page 113: Jeff McIntosh/CP Photo Archive; Page 116: J.P. Moczulski/CP Photo Archive; Page 118 Left to right: © Michael Prince/CORBIS, © Mauro Panci/CORBIS; Page 122: Richard Lam/CP Photo Archive; Page 123: © Roy Morsch/CP Photo Archive; Page 125: Ruth Bonneville/CP Photo Archive; Page 129: © 2 FACE/CORBIS; Page 131: Paul Chiasson/CP Photo Archive; Page 133: Fred Chartrand/CP Photo Archive; Page 136: Toby Melville/Reuters/Landov; Page 137: Ernest Doroszuk/CP Photo Archive; Page 139 Clockwise: Courtesy of Canadian Civil Liberties, Courtesy of the Ontario Coalition Against Poverty, Courtesy of Leaders Today, Courtesy of Free the Children, © Rotary International/Used with permission, Courtesy of Habitat for Humanity, Courtesy of Centre for Social Justice; Page 141: Larry MacDougal/CP Photo Archive; Page 144: Paul Chiasson/CP Photo Archive. Page 147 Clockwise: Darko Zeljkovic/CP Photo Archive, Photo courtesy of Lalita Krishna, Andrew Vaughn/CP Photo Archive; Page 148: © Steve Prezant/CORBIS; Page 151 Top to bottom: John Russell/CP Photo Archive, Courtesy of the Senate of Canada; Page 153: National Currency Collection, Currency Museum, Bank of Canada; Page 154: Copyright 2005, CBC. All Rights Reserved; Page 156: Zhu Ga Zeng & The Iron Road Chorus. Photo by Cylla von Tiedeman. Courtesy of Tapestry New Opera Works; Page 158: Ruth Bonneville/CP Photo Archive; Page 161 Top to bottom: Photo courtesy of Lalita Krishna, © Chris Farina/CORBIS; Page 166: © Michael S. Yamashita/CORBIS; Page 169: © Austrian Archives/CORBIS; Page 173 Left to right: Vancouver Public Library, 1397, Vancouver Public Library, 12851; Page 175 Left to right: Tom Hanson/CP Photo Archive, Amir Shah/CP Photo Archive; Page 176: Darko Zeljkovic/CP Photo Archive; Page 179: Dusan Vranic/CP Photo Archive; Page 183: Courtesy of the Butterfly 208 contest (www.bp208.ca) for the Canadian International Development Agency (CIDA); Page 185: Jim Young/Reuters/Landov; Page 189: Reuters/Landov; Page 190: Photo by WFP/Brenda Barton, 2003; Page 192 Left to right: © Leif Skoogfors/CORBIS, Andrew Vaughan/CP Photo Archive; Page 194: CP Photo Archive; Page 197: www.CartoonStock.com; Page 200: Courtesy of Ryan's Well Foundation.